WRITERS' RIGHTS

Writers' Rights

Freelance Journalism in a Digital Age

NICOLE S. COHEN

McGill-Queen's University Press
Montreal & Kingston • London • Chicago

ISBN 978-0-7735-4796-4 (cloth)
ISBN 978-0-7735-9976-5 (ePDF)
ISBN 978-0-7735-9977-2 (ePUB)

Legal deposit fourth quarter 2016
Bibliothèque nationale du Québec

Printed in Canada on acid-free paper that is 100% ancient forest free (100% post-consumer recycled), processed chlorine free

This book has been published with the help of a grant from the Canadian Federation for the Humanities and Social Sciences, through the Awards to Scholarly Publications Program, using funds provided by the Social Sciences and Humanities Research Council of Canada.

McGill-Queen's University Press acknowledges the support of the Canada Council for the Arts for our publishing program. We also acknowledge the financial support of the Government of Canada through the Canada Book Fund for our publishing activities.

Library and Archives Canada Cataloguing in Publication

Cohen, Nicole S., 1980–, author
    Writers' rights : freelance journalism in a digital age
/ Nicole S. Cohen.

Includes bibliographical references and index.
Issued in print and electronic formats.
ISBN 978-0-7735-4796-4 (hardback). – ISBN 978-0-7735-9976-5 (ePDF). –
ISBN 978-0-7735-9977-2 (ePUB)

    1. Journalists – Legal status, laws, etc. 2. Self-employed – Legal status, laws, etc. 3. Freelance journalism. 4. Online journalism. 5. Freelance journalism – Economic aspects. 6. Online journalism – Economic aspects. 7. Digital media. I. Title.

PN4731.C63 2016   070   C2016-903239-6
                                       C2016-903240-X

This book was set by True to Type in 11/13.5 Sabon

For Matt and Marlo

Contents

Acknowledgments

Thank you to all of the freelancers, activists, and organizers who were so generous with their time and encouragement for this project, especially Karen Wirsig and datejie green. Portions of select chapters appeared in *Just Labour*, *tripleC*, *South Atlantic Quarterly*, and the *Communication Review*, and I appreciate valuable feedback from the journals' editors and reviewers. I am grateful to the Social Sciences and Humanities Research Council and the Connaught New Researcher Award at the University of Toronto for research funding. Patricia Mazepa, Leah Vosko, and Stephanie Ross made vital contributions to the formation and completion of this project, and lent ongoing mentorship, support, and enthusiasm. Enda Brophy, Vincent Mosco, Catherine McKercher, Nick Dyer-Witheford, Matt Stahl, Alan Galey, Tanner Mirrlees, Leslie Shade, Brett Caraway, Anthony Wensley, and all of my inspiring colleagues at the Institute of Communication, Culture, Information and Technology at the University of Toronto Mississauga provided crucial support and encouragement along the way. Philip Cercone, Carolyn Yates, and everyone at McGill-Queen's University Press helped me bring this book into the world, as did two anonymous reviewers and their insights. Yasmin Jajarmi provided meticulous and diligent research assistance. Thank you to Greig de Peuter for unparalleled generosity and collaboration and for incisive comments on the manuscript (all errors and omissions remain my own), and to Mark, Caryl, Andrea, and Darrin Cohen for indefatigable support – in every sense of the word. And extra special thank yous to Matt Carrington, whose love and friendship sustained me through this project and beyond.

WRITERS' RIGHTS

Freedom's Double Edge:
Freelance Journalism and Precarity

On a grey April evening in 2007, in a drab second-floor union office on Toronto's Queen Street East, seventeen people gather to discuss the nascent Canadian Freelance Union (CFU). As a new local of the Communications, Energy, and Paperworkers Union of Canada (CEP), the CFU will be the first trade union in Canada established to represent freelance journalists and writers (the CEP has since merged with the Canadian Auto Workers to form mega-union Unifor). The freelancers seated around a table listen as an organizer explains that the CEP views its survival as dependent upon organizing media workers outside of the union. It has offered funding and freelancers must decide what kind of organization they want to create. The organizer understands some freelancers' reluctance to call their new organization a union, as most regard themselves as individuals running small businesses – not the type of people who join unions. He asks them to consider what a union could accomplish that individuals have yet been unable to do.

The freelancers in the room are skeptical but intrigued. Most know little about unions; their experience with the CEP is limited to its efforts to prevent newspaper work from being contracted out, restricting freelance work at certain media outlets. They are wary of paying dues and of joining a bureaucratic organization. They want to know how, exactly, a union for freelancers would work. Yet they all face challenges that compelled them to attend this meeting and to consider a union's potential: freelancers' pay rates are at a historic low, writers feel undervalued, and publishers' contracts demand unprecedented copyrights to writers' works without adequate compensation. Individually, freelancers have only been able to work more to try increase their earnings or do less low-paying journalism and more higher-paying corporate or commercial work. The time has come to consider acting together.

Two and a half years later, eight kilometres west on Queen Street, a different group mingles in a hip boutique hotel bar. Around two-dozen freelance journalists and writers gather to launch a partnership between the Canadian Writers Group, a literary agency for freelancers, and the Canadian Media Guild (CMG), the 6,000-member local of the Communication Workers of America-Canada. They sip drinks as Derek Finkle, the Canadian Writers Group's founder, and Lise Lareau, then-president of the CMG, describe the partnership – the first of its kind. After participating in a multior-ganization boycott of a magazine publisher's restrictive contract in 2009, Finkle sought a more effective way to increase writers' rates and secure improved contracts. And so he founded an agency, following a literary agency model, and plans to represent one hundred freelancers. The alliance with the CMG extends a second tier of membership to any freelancer willing to pay $150 in union dues. In return, members can access the CMG's group benefit plans and advocacy efforts, and Canadian Writers Group writers receive individual contract negotiations and promotions. The freelancers in the bar, many of whom Finkle represents, are excited. They speak of the benefits of having an agent to do the unpleasant work of negotiating fees and contracts with editors. Finkle believes there is a limited talent pool for "in-demand" freelancers in Canada, and that only he has the personal relationships with publishers needed to convince them to improve the terms under which those writers work. He is confident that his model will change freelancers' fortunes.

These two events represent two different approaches to the collective organization and representation of freelance writers in Canada. Freelancers' different responses – skepticism and uncertainty in the union office, excitement at the hotel bar – signify a long history of remaining outside of organized media labour, yet reflect growing dissatisfaction with contemporary conditions of freelance journalism. That writers are gathering in formal settings to discuss working conditions and new ways to collectively address work-related challenges is significant. That has not happened since 1976, when a dozen Toronto-based freelancers met at a writer's home to discuss forming an organization to improve their lot. At the time, pay rates and copyright were low on the agenda. Mostly, freelancers wanted to be treated with respect. They wanted writing to be considered real work and they sought to standardize practices and formalize freelance writing in Canada, primarily for magazines (PWAC 1976b). The fledgling group became the Periodical Writers Association of Canada, which in 2005 changed its name to the Professional Writers Association of Canada (PWAC). Since its inception, PWAC has given freelancers access to professional development, training, and networking opportunities, and has advocated for improving writers' pay and for government funding for the magazine industry.

But things have changed since 1976. Media industries in Canada are larger, more profitable, and highly concentrated. Magazines and newspapers are integrated into the largest networked media conglomerates in the country (Winseck 2010). The spread of profitable and growing digital-first media outlets means there is more work for freelancers, but that work pays very little and writing exclusively for online outlets is often difficult to sustain. Despite the thousands of journalists laid off in Canada between 2008 and 2015, overall the media labour force has expanded. More people than ever work as freelancers, by choice or not. Neoliberal globalization has propelled the spread of precarious employment. Corporations have harnessed digital technologies to transform journalism and business practices, and new digital publishing models are emerging faster than their implications for journalists and journalism can be fully understood. With limited critical analysis, commentators and pundits have embraced the notion that "everybody's going freelance" (Baer 2013), deploying terms such as "independent worker," "microentrepreneur," and "free agent" to describe a new, liberated workforce, often conflating the vastly different experiences of, for example, temporary workers, consultants, and freelance cultural workers.

More critical accounts show that working as a writer and as a journalist is more difficult than ever. The Writers' Union of Canada (2015) reports that writers today must do more work to earn less: earnings are down 27 per cent from 1998; the average writing income of the 947 writers surveyed is $12,879. Studies of journalists show declining working conditions and pay, pressure to multitask without meaningful skills development, work speed up, stressful workloads, declining autonomy, and a lack of confidence about the future of journalism (Spilsbury 2013; Willnat and Weaver 2014; Siegelbaum and Thomas 2015). Statistics Canada (2014) reports that journalistic employment in Canada is expected to "decrease significantly" in the coming years, and will be marked by fewer job opportunities and greater competition. American freelancers find that it has become too expensive to produce investigative journalism and difficult to obtain press passes from credentialing organizations (Project Word 2015; Hermes et al. 2014). Mid-career journalists write discouraging newspaper columns to aspiring journalists that generally amount to "good luck with that" (Silcoff 2015; Salmon 2015). "The difference from when I started freelancing twenty-five years ago," Finkle tells me during an interview in 2015, "[is that] things tended to be longer, they had longer gestation periods, they paid more, they were more complicated. Now there [are] very few people who do anything that's over 2,500 words. So nobody can make a living as a feature writer." Finkle says that writers can hustle by "setting up a half-dozen small things a week," but "it's a churn. It's really hard, it's tedious, and I think the shorter stuff isn't as gratifying. Which is frankly why a lot of writers get into writing. They want the gratification much more than they want money ... That to me is as big a problem as anything monetary." Under such conditions, freelancers are ready to explore new ways to address how their work has changed.

This book is a study of the working conditions of freelance journalists, the political economic and cultural context in which they work, and their efforts to collectively address the challenges they face. I focus primarily on the experience of freelancers in English-speaking Canada, where I conducted empirical research, but I also draw on published accounts of freelancers and freelancers' organizations outside of Canada, especially the United States and England. I seek answers to a perplexing question: in a digital age, when more media forms and outlets exist than ever before and when all require written material, why is it so difficult for freelancers to earn a living? Popular discourse attributes challenges to the economic recession that plunged the journalism industry into "crisis" (a term often evoked but not necessarily justified) and the rapid advancement of digital technologies. Another common refrain is that freelance journalism is inherently low-paid, insecure work: *that's the way it has always been, that's the way it will always be.* A deeper study of freelancers' experiences shows, however, that working conditions are shaped by the organization of media production under contemporary capitalism. For many, freelancing as a form of work is a strategy to resist salaried labour – an effort to gain some control over the terms of commodification of their labour power and autonomy over their craft. Yet under contemporary conditions of media production, freelancing is at the same time a strategy for media firms to intensify the exploitation of freelancers' labour power, primarily through exploiting unpaid labour time and copyrights to writers' works. This double-edged nature of freelance work generates contradictory experiences among freelancers, such as high degrees of satisfaction and control over their immediate labour process, yet precarious material conditions and declining control over their time and other aspects of their work. Although freelancing holds great potential for worker autonomy, in its current form, capitalist production processes place intensifying pressures on workers: longer hours, lower pay, less control, heightened insecurity, deepened market pressure, and rationalization of the creative process. Freelance work arrangements provide capital with a convenient way to offload risk and responsibility onto individual workers. Although relations of exploitation can be difficult to detect in media and cultural work – which are widely understood to be creative, fulfilling, and autonomous – they remain at the core of the freelance labour process, driving changes in the industry and shaping workers' experiences.

My arguments are rooted in the assumption that journalism is a form of communication essential for meaningful participation in democratic life. Although today most journalism is produced as a commodity for private profit, in its ideal form it contributes to public discourse and debate, enables citizens to hold those in power to account, and provides space for debate about how to organize political, economic, and social life. Because powerful corporate and political interests influence so much of journalism today, freelancers are in a strategic position to produce independent, autonomous material free from corporate and government control. Freelancing can give journalists the time and space necessary to produce the investigative, critical, or exploratory work that working in understaffed, time-strapped newsrooms often cannot. And so, the increasing challenges freelancers face in doing their work is of concern for a just and democratic media system.

Because freelance writing has become so precarious, fewer people are able to afford to pursue journalism as a career, and the perspectives and voices in media are increasingly homogeneous, reflecting the interests of those already in power. In particular, women, people of colour, aboriginal people, and working-class people are underrepresented in media industries as journalists, editors, executives, and managers, as well as sources and subjects (Women's Media Center 2014; Gill 2014b; Macharia 2015). Rosalind Gill (2014b, 15) argues that sexism, racism, and other forms of oppression and marginalization have become "unspeakable inequalities" in media and cultural work because of "an investment in preserving the myth of egalitarianism and meritocracy" in these industries. Such silence belies the fact, demonstrated by ongoing empirical research and first-person media accounts, that deep divisions continue to mark media, culture, and creative industries (Oakley 2013; Ehrenreich 2015; Bennett 2015). Indeed, 93 per cent of the 206 Canadian freelancers I surveyed for this book identify as white, making clear that social location plays a critical factor in shaping who is able to engage in media or cultural work, particularly in precarious times. Ensuring that journalism is accessible and sustainable to workers regardless of gender, race, or class background is critical, as those who produce journalism have great influence over what types of stories are told and from what perspectives. Our media system remains dominated by white men who can afford to pursue careers in an insecure industry that requires most to perform extended bouts of unpaid work, usually in expensive cities where media companies are located. Andrea Bennett (2015), a freelance journalist and magazine editor who stocks shelves in a bookstore to make ends meet, writes about the need for greater discussion about the intersection of gender, race, and class in journalism: "We need to start speaking openly about these kinds of issues for two reasons: one, so that we can deepen our conversation about diversity, understanding that it's not and will never be enough to add one person or two people or five people to our mastheads or panel discussions – rather, we have to change the structure of our organizations and our conversations so that they suit a much broader range of people."

To address issues of sexism, racism, and classism in media, and to challenge the spread of precarious work that makes journalism so inaccessible to so many, we must develop strategies and responses to the intersecting challenges of transformations in digital technologies, the expansion of media industries and outlets, media workers' declining power, and the persistent, vital need for journalism. One strategy I examine is the potential for self-employed journalists to organize collectively to protect not only their labour rights, but also their craft. As conditions worsen, resistance to publishers' practices is taking root. Freelancers globally are engaged in several initiatives to resist and negotiate unequal power relations with publishers and media corporations, including unionization, professional associations, campaigns, and speaking out online and off.

Academic debates about freelance media and cultural work position freelance cultural workers on two extremes of the labour force: at one end, empowered, entrepreneurial members of the creative class who enjoy autonomy and control over their craft, and at the other, members of the precariat, a growing global class of overeducated, underemployed workers who face declining material conditions and economic uncertainty (Standing 2011). To traverse these two extremes, I argue that freelance media workers should be understood through the multiple contradictions that construct their lived work experiences, most of which flow from the form of employment under which freelancers labour in contemporary capitalism.

PORTFOLIO CAREERS OR PRECARIOUS EMPLOYMENT?

Freelance journalists are self-employed workers who sell pieces of writing or contract their services to several media outlets without being employed by a single firm. In legal terms, freelancers contract for services with publishers, which means they are not hired, but only paid for work performed (Canada Revenue Agency 2015). Freelancers are "solo self-employed" or "own-account" self-employed workers: independent contractors who do not have employees but who may have "ongoing relationships with a number of clients in the same sector, and who make a living bidding sequentially on various types of work" (Vosko 2005, 144). This arrangement situates freelancers outside of traditional labour law and denies them the social benefits that are usually accessed through an employment relationship (Dullroy 2013).

Freelancing, which appears as a taken-for-granted form of employment in scholarship on media and cultural labour, engenders tensions and contradictions that shape how this work is experienced. A core source of tension is that freelancers' self-employed status positions them as entrepreneurs, eclipsing their status as workers. Entrepreneurship is an "ideal type" of self-employment that enables individuals to control their labour process; grants independence, autonomy, and ownership of the means of production; and signals a more privileged position than that of other waged workers in the labour market (Cranford et al. 2005, 6–7). Such an ideal type of self-employment, however, is vastly different from the actual experiences of most self-employed workers. The ideal-type definition of self-employment equates self-employment with entrepreneurship, and so positions self-employed workers as small business owners, whereas most are more likely to occupy a position of disguised or misclassified dependent employment (ibid.). And so, freelance status is a site of contestation in media and cultural work: individuals seek work outside of a standard employment relationship to gain control over the labour process, yet at the same time, freelance status enables capital to increase the extraction of surplus value from workers.

Freelancers' experiences make clear that control is also a contested concept in labour-capital relations. Under contemporary capitalism, self-employed freelancers appear to have escaped employers' control because most do not work on employers' premises, can write for multiple publishers, and control their immediate labour process. However, the spread of precarious employment and the normalization of freelance work has enabled publishers to extend greater control over freelancers as a class of workers as work becomes increasingly insecure and low paid. Precarious employment keeps freelancers dependent on the terms that publishers offer, as most individual writers have little power to negotiate.

Another idealized vision of freelancers sees them enjoying "portfolio" or "boundaryless" careers, working for multiple employers on a project basis, often simultaneously (Platman 2004; Deuze 2007). The term boundaryless career developed to describe contemporary work styles severed from traditional employment relationships, including flexible work for a variety of employers sustained through personal connections and a primary commitment to individual rather than company success (Arthur and Rousseau 1996). Such work styles have become hegemonically constructed as markers of cultural work that grant workers the flexibility and autonomy that they desire and that creative production requires. The terms, however, tend to obscure more than they reveal. Portfolio work arrangements are not a choice for many, particularly for freelancers, as the work of writing is increasingly only available on a freelance or contract basis. To become cultural workers, people are compelled to adopt a strategy of working on multiple projects at once to ensure continuous income. What might appear to be supreme flexibility and constant variety is also a coping strategy for the realities of short-term projects, low wages, and no guarantee of future work (Menger 1999; Oakley 2014).

The underside of a portfolio career is precarious employment, or "employment with uncertainty, insecurity, and a lack of control" (Lewchuk et al. 2015, 14). More precisely, precarious employment is defined as "work for remuneration characterized by uncertainty, low income, and limited social benefits and statutory entitlements" (Vosko 2010, 2). While this definition applies to the experiences of freelance journalists (and indeed to many cultural workers), precariousness is shaped by a number of intersecting factors that can mitigate the severity of precarious employment, including employment status, form of employment, social context, social location, and dimensions of labour market insecurity (ibid.). Workers' experiences with precarious employment depend on their ability to access continuous employment, the degree of regulatory protection (from the state or a union, for example), whether they can exercise control over the labour process, as well as their overall wage level (ibid.). A conceptualization of freelancers as precariously employed requires recognition of what Cynthia Cranford and Leah Vosko (2006) call a "continuum" of precarious employment, where different workers experience (and are able to accept) different degrees of precariousness, including the quality of and rewards from work and chances of economic success and security.

For freelance writers, precarious employment is tempered by a range of social conditions, including economic class (whether a person can afford to pursue a freelance career in the first place), social or cultural status, the potential to earn high pay from some types of writing (usually corporate reports, advertising, or other nonjournalistic work), and the ability to access other supporting employment. Despite its precarious character, freelance writing remains a desirable and competitive occupation, and breaking in demands years of hard work. Although many writers feel their occupation is not taken seriously, it is still relatively high-status work that accrues varying degrees of social capital, especially to those with high profiles, despite often being low paid. Such features are important for understanding the variations between freelancers' experiences and the element of choice that, although limited, remains present.

A broader concept framing freelancers' experiences is precarity. The concept was developed in the context of social movements in Italy and France in the 1990s and 2000s and is becoming an increasingly common way to describe "the insecurity, discontinuity and randomness that now hangs over all work" (Gorz 2010, 24). Precarity speaks to the "financial, social, and existential insecurity" that has resulted from the shift to the post-Fordism period and the spreading flexibility and unevenness of work (de Peuter 2014, 266). The concept applies broadly to forms of employment (freelance, temporary, casual, illegal) and to the way that work increasingly "coloni[zes] more of life" (Neilson and Coté 2014, 3). While workers in low-income jobs are more likely to experience precarious employment, precarity is not determined by income alone (Lewchuk et al. 2014, 52). The concept reflects changing labour markets and the spread of temporary, part-time, casual, contract-based employment and related insecurity (52). Precarity, for most, is marked by less access to work-related training, social isolation, income instability, scheduling uncertainty, no access to health benefits, no payment for missing work, and less ability to speak out about work-related problems (12). Workers in precarious employment are more likely to volunteer "as a way to network or to advance their job opportunities" than to participate in communities (12), demonstrating the way precarity blurs the boundaries between work and the rest of life.

Scholars and activists, importantly, emphasize that precarity and precarious employment are not new phenomena. Rather, they have historically marked the lives of those long excluded from the standard employment relationship, including women, racialized workers, those without citizenship, and other marginalized workers (Vosko 2010; Neilson and Rossiter 2005). As a generalized condition, however, precarity is spreading into the lives of a growing number of workers in more occupations, sectors, and social locations, including media and cultural industries (Standing 2011; Lewchuk et al. 2015). Low-income precarious employment has "been growing twice as fast as non-precarious employment since 2001, and as a share of all employment in Canada, self-employment now accounts for one in ten workers" (Lewchuk et al. 2015, 19). Although many freelancers I surveyed earn relatively good incomes and report being satisfied with their work, my findings reflect generalized experiences of precarity: intermittent and insecure work; uncertainty about the future; a lack of access to social benefits and protections; and fluctuating incomes and levels of work. The United Kingdom's National Union of Journalists links workers' precarious employment status to mental health issues, and attributes experiences such as depression and isolation to media industries' reliance on freelancers, "for whom publishers offer no long-term commitment, career progression, or employment rights" (Christie 2004, 6). The characterization of work in media and cultural industries as boundaryless is often a gloss on the precarity that structures workers' lives.

MEDIA FLUX AND LABOUR FLEXIBILIZATION

A cheeky but concise description of Canada's journalism landscape puts it this way: "Broadcasters are shrinking, beloved magazines are closing down, and job security LOL" (Iddamsetty 2014). Others use the word "crisis," often in discussions of media industries. Conditions of journalism, however, are better characterized through less charged terms such as change, uncertainty, and flux, as media industries remain profitable and powerful amid ongoing transformations (Gasher 2007, cited in Compton 2010, 596). As one journalist puts it: "I'm not certain how much I agree that the press is in 'decline,' as opposed to perpetually beset by forces that can foster bad practices" (Cunningham 2015). Such bad practices are difficult to see at first glance. The volume of journalism circulating through digital networks and the diversity of opinion and perspective that one can find if looking leads one journalist to state: "I think this is probably the greatest era for journalism that the world has ever seen" (Salmon 2015). But what is good for journalism as an industry and for its consumers is not necessarily good for journalists. Media companies are dealing with change and uncertainty by putting pressure on labour costs, cutting as much as possible, and, as far as work is concerned, fostering the aforementioned bad practices. Over the past forty years, conditions of neoliberal globalization have compelled media industries to restructure to adapt to a more flexible, technology-enabled regime of accumulation. Strategies such as mergers, corporate and technological convergence, and consolidation have led to highly concentrated yet diversified media companies (Winseck 2010). Such strategies are designed to increase economic power and maintain profits amid technological change (McKercher 2002). The development of the Internet and use of digital technologies have changed the way consumers access media content (digitally, for free) as well as how companies produce it. In the case of newspapers and magazines, declining advertising revenues push corporations to seek ways to monetize – to use an industry term – content online and to produce more media with fewer employees and for lower costs (Project for Excellence in Journalism 2008; Compton and Benedetti 2010). Across the media industries, emphasis has shifted to niche publishing and programming, to more commercially oriented media, to interactivity and capitalizing on audience participation, and to the accumulation of copyrights as a way to expand profits indefinitely (Deuze and Steward 2011; Hesmondhalgh 2007).

Such conditions have brought about drastic changes in the work of journalism globally. Once an occupation regulated by union contracts and traditional journalistic practices, contemporary journalism is marked by flexibility at its core (Gall 2000; Marjoribanks 2003; Deuze 2007; Singer 2011, 103). Today's journalists must be multi-skilled and adept at a range of technologies and different media formats, and must take on extra work such as blogging, updating social media, filing for print and digital media, recording audio and video, and doing all of this at increased speed (Willnat and Weaver 2014; Anderson, Bell, and Shirky 2012). Whereas journalists used to work within bounded time and space – to deadlines set by the needs of printing plants and distribution schedules and under the spatial constraints of the printed page – the Internet, social media, and a breakneck twenty-four/seven news cycle means continuous deadlines and content that has no spatial boundaries (Singer 2011, 108). Under these conditions, researchers are concerned that journalism is being transformed from skilled, detailed work to "simple" labour that uses limited resources to produce and that anyone can perform, contributing to the craft's rationalization and media workers' declining power (Deuze and Fortunati 2011, 112). Shrinking workforces at traditional media organizations across North America have accompanied the growing flexibility of journalistic labour. The work of producing media has been outsourced to freelancers, to consumers, and to content-production companies (Project for Excellence in Journalism 2008; Deuze and Steward 2011, 3; Kperogi 2011).

Changes in media industries, particularly the shift to digital-based journalism, are well researched. Less examined are the implications for the growing numbers of freelancers. Some academic research and industry reports have tracked the experiences of Canadian freelance journalists over the past decade, raising issues of precarity and declining conditions (PWAC 2006; Scott 2009; Impresa Communications 2011; McKercher 2009, 2014; Gollmitzer 2014). Beyond Canada, other scholarly research primarily focuses on who freelancers are, what they do, and what they earn (Hannis 2008; Massey and Elmore 2011), or traces individual experiences with freelance work (Osnowitz 2010). Apart from showing that freelancers are predominantly women, the only consistent finding among studies is that there is inconsistency among freelancers, what they earn, their work experiences, whether or not they chose to become freelancers, and their job satisfaction. Brian Massey and Cindy Elmore (2011) argue that women freelance journalists report high job satisfaction, including satisfaction with their work hours, payment levels, and ability to balance household and paid labour, and Maria Edstrom and Martina Ladendorf (2012, 718) find that Swedish freelance journalists "seem to be more content with life than other journalists." Kathleen Ryan (2009) finds similar attitudes among television freelancers in the United States, but notes that many American freelance television news workers have access to union protections (650), which mitigates experiences of precarity. Ryan also notes the limitation of job satisfaction as a lens through which to study freelance work. This research, although generally positive in its assessment of freelancing as a form of work, tempers the unbridled optimism that courses through some academic and popular media accounts, which position freelance life as marked by utter freedom (Munk 2000; Pink 2000; Florida 2002). Indeed, among journalists, freelancers have long been romanticized and mythologized as "heroic figures" (Baines and Robson 2001, 353; Aldridge 1998). A starting point for interrogating freelance work is to consider freelancers' assessments of their work

in the context of uncertainty in all media work, and to take seriously freelancers' enjoyment of their work, even when they speak negatively about their working conditions.

Critical scholars have interrogated freelancers' working conditions, attending to the power relations that structure freelance work
and situating freelancing amid the growing precarization of employment. Research shows that freelancers are financially insecure
and low paid, and that their autonomy is negotiated – in other
words, that they're "powerless" (Ekinsmyth 2002, 1999; Gynnild
2005; Das 2007; Krasovec and Zagar 2009). Catherine McKercher
(2014) argues that freelance writing is highly gendered and is rapidly
becoming the only form of work available to journalists in Canada.
International studies show that freelance work is spreading through
media workforces and entails intermittent work and pay, low pay,
no job security, a lack of benefits and other social protections, and
little bargaining power or ability to protect oneself from publishers' pressures (Nies and Pedersini 2003; PWAC 2006; Walters, Warren, and Dobbie 2006).

A survey of British freelance journalists examines the mental and
physical health risks of freelancing, including isolation, depression,
drug and alcohol abuse, low self-esteem, and overwork (Christie
2004). More than half of the freelancers surveyed by the National
Union of Journalists report that they "sometimes" or "often" experienced depression. And although the survey did not ask freelancers
about income directly, more than half of all respondents report having "some" or "a lot of" worries about money (9, 8). Project Word's
(2015, 4) survey of freelance investigative journalists in the United
States found that 92 per cent of 137 respondents "reported experiencing 'anxiety on a daily/monthly basis regarding finances.'" In addition to freelancers' lack of social protections, most cannot access
help collecting late or unpaid wages (PWAC 2006). A 2010 report
commissioned by the Freelancers Union in New York City revealed
that self-employed workers in the United States (including but not
exclusively writers) were owed between US$474 and US$956 billion
in unpaid wages (Rodgers 2010, 1).

Freelancers also lack protections necessary to do their work: 45
per cent of imprisoned journalists worldwide are freelancers, who
cannot access the institutional, legal, and financial supports that
protect staff journalists (Committee to Protect Journalists 2011). Un-

like staff reporters, freelancers are not covered under media organizations' libel insurance, and self-purchased libel insurance can cost thousands of dollars a year. As news outlets around the world cut their foreign correspondence and war reporting budgets, the dangerous work of reporting on global conflict is outsourced to freelancers, who are in extremely precarious positions. "News outlets want stories from dangerous places without paying to staff them," notes freelancer Allison Shelley (2014). Freelancers who enter conflict zones are individually responsible for the protections staff journalists would receive: travel expenses, security guards, medical coverage, first-aid training, safe housing, payment for fixers and translators, logistical help, evacuation protocols, legal protections, and "editors who will tell you not to take foolish chances, and notify your family if something bad happens" (Keller 2013; Shelley 2014). As ex-war reporter Tom Peter (2014) explains: "Over the course of my career as a journalist I've survived an airstrike, been abducted at gunpoint, stepped through brain matter in the aftermath of bombings, and had many other close calls. And yet when people ask me about the stress of covering wars, more often than not what comes to mind is the two and a half years I spent working in Afghanistan when I paid about $30,000 out of pocket to cover basic work expenses that were never reimbursed." Beyond being too costly for many to pursue, the perilous position of freelance conflict reporters has reached a state of urgency as dozens have been kidnapped or killed while working in conflict zones.

Accounts of freelancers in a range of media and cultural industries demonstrate that freelance status, although sought by many, is a strategic business practice used to increase productivity and lower labour costs, offloading the risks of producing journalism from corporations onto individual workers. Participation in journalism's new ecosystem carries with it the expectation that individuals should pursue exciting, fulfilling, autonomous work that contributes to the public interest while shouldering all of the accompanying financial and social risk. Such a shift has implications for individual journalists and for journalism itself. The increasing encroachment of corporatization, commercialism, and commodification into news media leads to a paucity of investigative journalism, increasing "churnalism" – the repurposing of press releases without verification or original reporting (Davies 2008) – celebrity gossip, and clickbait. The values journalists have long upheld as core to their profession – a public service ethos and commitment to documenting facts as best they can – have always been constrained in the production process, but are being intensely undermined by media capitalists' ruthless profit-seeking. Studying the labour conditions workers face at the heart of these practices gives us insight into the contemporary media system and emphasizes the need to consider workers' role in processes of democratizing media and journalism.

INTERROGATING FREELANCE LABOUR

Definitions and terminology are contentious in studies of work and labour in the communication and cultural industries, as researchers in this field come from a range of academic disciplines (including, for example, media and communication studies, sociology, economic geography, and management) and write from a variety of theoretical perspectives. I review some of these theoretical perspectives in chapter 1, but at this stage must clarify my use of terminology. I refer to journalists as media workers and as cultural workers. By cultural workers, I mean people who work in cultural industries or those industries that generate and circulate commodities that "have an influence on our understanding of the world" and "produce social meaning" (Hesmondhalgh 2007, 3, 12). Mark Banks (2007, 2) defines cultural industries as "those involved in the production of 'aesthetic' or 'symbolic' goods and services; that is, commodities whose core value is derived from their function as carriers of meaning in the form of images, symbols, signs and sounds." Precisely which sectors count as cultural industries varies. Statistics Canada (2012), for example, includes a range of occupations (from librarians and curators to writers, artists, and technical occupations in film and broadcasting), but classifies magazines, books, and newspapers as part of the cultural industries. This perspective, while still somewhat broad, is useful because it views the character of cultural work through an understanding of the specificities of the industries in which it is performed, rather than through the content of the work. There is something distinctive about cultural goods and their consumption that can explain why cultural production is organized in particular ways (Miège 1989; Garnham 1997; Hesmondhalgh 2007, 101). This avoids attributing cultural workers' experiences to individual character traits, which is part of the argument I develop in chapter 1. The term "creative labour," for example, draws attention to qualities specific to a person (Smith and McKinlay 2009c, 3), whereas I argue that the organization of cultural production has a structural effect on workers' experiences, and that freelance writers' labour experiences flow directly from the logics of the industry in which they work. (In some instances I use the term "media work" instead of cultural work when I discuss the specificities of journalism as a particular form of cultural production.) Finally, the term "culture" references art and creative practice, and freelance writers tend to engage in more creative forms of media production compared to the writing of news, for example, which is typically produced in standardized formats by reporters in newsrooms. Traditionally, freelancing has enabled journalists to produce longer, more experimental, literary, or creative types of writing, so any description of their work must capture this creative aspect, even if it is increasingly more of a goal than a reality for most.[1]

The freelancers I discuss are primarily journalists who contribute nonfiction, fact-based writing to newspapers, magazines, and online journalistic outlets. However, because it is so difficult to earn a living solely from freelance journalism, many have expanded the types of work they perform to include a range of industries and formats, including corporate, commercial, government, nonprofit, and other media work. For this reason, I use the terms freelance writer and freelance journalist interchangeably – while "writer" generally describes most of the work the freelancers I discuss do, "journalist" roots my concerns in a debate about journalism as a particular form of (potentially democratic) communication.

Freelancers are difficult to study. They are difficult to locate and to count, and their experiences and interpretations of work experiences vary greatly. For a broad understanding of these experiences, I conducted an online survey of 206 self-identified freelance writers from across Canada in 2010 (unless otherwise noted, all quotations come from this survey). Because it is difficult to determine how many freelancers exist and who they are, it is difficult to know how representative a sample my survey provides and to gauge the extent to which my results can be generalized. Therefore, I do not treat the survey findings as definitive, but rather as raising questions for consideration and pointing to areas for inquiry. I analyzed survey responses in relation to interdisciplinary literature from communication, cultural, and labour studies; critical sociology; journalism; and journalism history. I draw on reports and studies from governments, industry, Statistics Canada, and international writers' and journalists' organizations, as well as archival research. I also participated in an email list for Toronto-area freelance writers and editors, to which I belonged before I began this research and of which I remain a member. As a former freelance journalist, I was aware of many of the issues I write about in the following chapters before I began my research. Indeed, it was questions about my own inability to earn a living as a freelancer that sparked my interest in this research. My participation on this email list contributed to background research that helped frame my inquiry, and can be described as an active form of virtual participant observation, which Angela McRobbie (2000, 260) argues is the closest one can get to observing a mobile, dispersed workforce.

Finally, I draw on semi-structured interviews with staff and organizers of several organizations, including the Professional Writers Association of Canada, the CFU, the Canadian Writers Group, the CMG and its freelance branch, the former CEP, the Freelancers Union, the National Writers Union, and the National Union of Journalists' freelance branch in London, England. Several of the people I interviewed are quoted anonymously.

In chapter 1, I introduce a critical political economy framework for understanding freelance media work and positioning freelance labour as a site of contestation over work time, quality, autonomy, and control. I argue that although freelance journalists enjoy a degree of autonomy in their work due largely to the fact that they retain control over their immediate labour process, exploitation remains at the core of freelance work under contemporary capitalism, exerting pressure on freelancers' material conditions and the articles they produce through the exploitation of unpaid labour time and of copyrights to writers' works. I outline the contradictions that emerge from freelancers' positions as self-employed workers imbued with a sense of entrepreneurship, self-sufficiency, and pleasure in their work, but also as precariously employed workers experiencing declining overall control in their occupation.

Proceeding from this theoretical frame, in chapter 2, I trace the historical development of freelance writing as an occupation, which was tied to the transformation and capitalization of magazine and newspaper publishing. As capitalism developed and penetrated literary and media production, writers were proletarianized, or brought under the system of waged labour. This process reached its apogee in the newsrooms of eighteenth- and nineteenth-century newspapers, where the process of writing became routinized and rationalized and working conditions declined. This history suggests that freelance work has long been a way for writers to gain control over their work, even as it has developed into a key corporate strategy for lowering production and labour costs.

I draw this history into the contemporary era in chapter 3, where I attend to the conditions of freelance work by understanding the nature of exploitation in freelance work arrangements. I trace the process and practices that have led to freelancers' declining working conditions, which indicate a tension between writers who seek freelance status as a form of freedom and capital's heightened ability to accelerate exploitation of labour power from workers outside the bounds of an employment relationship. In chapter 4, I continue to interrogate the structure and organization of freelance journalism as a form of self-employment, and its consequences, particularly the contradictory experiences self-employment generates. To survive and thrive as a freelancer often means embracing the very characteristics that undermine freelancers' working conditions: insecurity, entrepreneurialism, perpetual hustle, and a deeply individualistic outlook.

In chapter 5, I shift focus to understand how journalists are faring in digital journalism. Drawing on freelancers' own published accounts of their work experiences, I outline the pressures they face to work for free or for extremely low pay; how emergent, advertising-based digital journalism practices reduce journalism to "content"; and how, online, freelancers are on the forefront of the broad devaluing of journalistic labour and of journalism itself. I also begin to trace freelancers' tools for contesting and resisting nonpayment and other pressures.

Finally, I examine freelancers' efforts to collectively organize. In chapter 6, I outline the formation of freelancers' collective organizations, the myriad challenges facing freelance labour organizing, the potential of emergent alt-labour organizations and policy proposals, and a broad envisioning of social protections. I demonstrate that many freelancers are keen to collectively organize in some form and, in chapter 7, I examine four examples of their contemporary organization in Canada: a professional association, a literary agency, and two unions. While the pace of organizing is slow, especially in light of the rapid change in media industries, emergent organizations have great promise to offer individual freelancers new ways to participate in labour organizations.

As I conclude, the costs of not acting are high. Journalism faces what Wayne Lewchuk et al. (2015) call a "precarity penalty": the more precarious work in journalism becomes, the less accessible it will be to women, people of colour, working-class people, racialized immigrants, young workers, aboriginal people, and other marginalized people. This means the media industries will become even more homogeneous and the lack of diverse portrayals of gender, race, and class experiences in mainstream media will deepen. A linked aspect of journalism's precarity penalty is the type of media it is possible to produce under today's labour conditions. The current organization of freelance work inserts individuals into fiercely competitive and unequal social relations and infuses their work and their lives with insecurity. This, in turn, pressures workers to produce particular kinds of works: not just those that can be sold, but those that can be produced quickly, making the small fees paid per word, per article, or per hour worth a freelancer's time. Thus, collective organization in media industries is not just about protecting individual workers, but also about ongoing efforts to democratize journalism, make it inclusive, and protect it as a form of public-minded communication.

Many say that journalists must find their place in the system, adapt to new conditions, and engage in the practices needed to negotiate new media economies: flexibility, entrepreneurialism, and self-sufficiency. For others, adapting is not enough – workers must unite to transform the system. In this spirit, I aim to disrupt the sense of inevitability that pervades discussions about the state of freelance journalism in Canada to demonstrate that freelancers' conditions are deeply linked to specific and historical practices undertaken by capitalist media organizations. *Writers' Rights* contextualizes the freelance struggles bubbling up as we barrel toward journalism's digital future, and identifies points of contention and movements toward change. While individual freelancers have long coped with changes as best they can, proving to be adept at negotiating precarity, many are working together to improve their conditions and protect their craft. For them, the fight for the future of freelancing has just begun.

1

A Site of Struggle:
Theorizing Freelance Media Work

Freelance media workers' experiences with precarity are often attributed to technology or current economic conditions, or rationalized as features always inherent to cultural work in unpredictable industries. Freelancers justify the precarious nature of their work as the inevitable cost of pursuing their passion: "Most of us juggle two-and-a-half jobs, knowing the only thing worse would be a single stultifying career," write the young editors of the *New Inquiry* in the magazine's precarity-themed issue (2012, 3). Yet the challenges most freelancers face trying to earn a living stem from their positions as self-employed workers who labour under highly individualized conditions for powerful publishers in a context fuelled by ongoing transformations in capitalism and media industries. A critical political economy approach can challenge assumptions about media and cultural work and foreground the processes, practices, and social relations that structure the conditions of freelance work, which are often obscured by its individualized nature.

Critical political economy – or, more specifically, Marxist dialectical political economy – disrupts common-sense ways of viewing social and economic systems as fixed and unchangeable and regards them instead as "relational and always in process or flux" (Clement and Vosko 2003b, xiii). As a framework for analysis, critical political economy retains tensions and contradictions in explanations of media work and the conditions of cultural production, conceiving of media and culture as sites of political and social struggle (Artz 2006; Kumar 2007). Yet critical political economy is underused in scholarly research on media and cultural labour. While not dismissed outright, it is not often foregrounded as an approach, leaving room for focused attention to the power relations that flow from the specifically capitalist way of organizing media and cultural production. Critical political economy that draws on Marx and attends to labour-capital relations in cultural production contributes to a fuller account of the structural processes that shape freelance journalists' work and charts paths toward addressing challenges and inequalities.

Although labour was once considered a blind spot of communication studies (Mosco and McKercher 2006), researchers increasingly attend to issues of work and labour in media, cultural, and communication industries (see, for example, Banks, Taylor, and Gill 2013).[1] An attempt to summarize and condense this research in a few pages would do a disservice to the rich and varied body of scholarship that illuminates the complexities of cultural labour in contemporary capitalism. While I draw on the work of many of these researchers – especially that of critical cultural studies scholars and sociologists, who provide a nuanced understanding of cultural labour that foregrounds worker agency – in this chapter I argue for the usefulness of political economy, particularly Marx's fundamental concepts such as exploitation and the labour process.

Organizing my discussion around key questions that persist in research on cultural work, I draw on labour process theory to argue that although freelance journalists enjoy varying degrees of autonomy in their work, exploitation remains at the core of freelance labour, exerting pressure on freelancers' work and material conditions through the exploitation of unpaid labour time and of copyright to writers' works. Such conditions make it difficult for freelancers to earn a living and participate meaningfully in journalism's shifting landscape. Thus, while freelancing as a form of work appeals to journalists who seek an alternative to an employment relationship or control over their work, it is at the same time an ideal arrangement for capital to offload the risks and costs of media and cultural production. This double-edged nature of freelancing, with appeal for workers and capital alike, can account not only for the spread of freelance work throughout labour markets, but also for the heightened stakes around freelancing's future as it becomes a site of struggle over work time, quality of work, autonomy, and control. In this chapter, I address the tensions at the centre of this struggle.

Contradictions riddle freelance work. For one, freelance journalism is for most a precarious form of work, yet many freelancers also report high job satisfaction (see also Arvidsson, Malossi, and Naro 2010). This contradiction is linked to the way that self-employed media and cultural workers are positioned in contemporary capitalism: as entrepreneurs or "culturepreneur[s]" (Oakley 2014, 156), a position considered an "ideal" and idealized type of self-employment, characterized by independence, autonomy, and control (Fudge, Tucker, and Vosko 2002, 5). In contemporary scholarly and popular discourse on journalism, entrepreneurialism is touted as a strategic fix for a flailing industry. Individual journalists are encouraged to become entrepreneurs, and entrepreneurship is conflated with freelancing, mischaracterizing most freelancers' realities (Cohen 2015a). Although freelance journalism is a very old occupation, it has gained renewed currency as a viable and desirable career option, particularly as media industries shed jobs yet require increasing flows of content for expanding digital platforms. The valorization of freelancing as a form of journalistic work has been amplified under neoliberalism; the growing flexibility of work; and the simultaneous expansion of digital technologies, media, and cultural industries. Discourses of the creative class, the knowledge economy, and technologically enabled flexible work promote visions of freelancing as liberating and of freelancers as agile, empowered free agents (Florida 2002; Gregg 2008).

While freelance journalists are positioned as entrepreneurs, and indeed must be enterprising to succeed, they are generally not entrepreneurs. Individual freelancers do not accumulate capital. They may own the tools required for producing articles, but they do not own the means of production necessary to bring their works to market and be meaningfully compensated. And, while individual freelancers control their immediate labour process, they do not control the broader conditions in which they work, individually or collectively. Freelancers do not have the power and economic status that accrues to entrepreneurs. As Judy Fudge, Eric Tucker, and Leah Vosko (2002, 7, citing Linder 1992) argue, most self-employed workers "should not be conceived of as a class separate from employers and employees, but rather should be conceptualized as a hybrid class more closely resembling wage workers than entrepreneurs." Yet because they are self-employed, most freelancers do not consider themselves to be workers. Most think of themselves as small businesses or as enterprises of one. From this standpoint, their experiences of declining material conditions are filtered through a lens of self-empowerment and self-responsibility. Freelancers describe their constant need to seek out and secure work as motivated by passion and a drive to tell stories, reflecting the "do what you love" mantra that so thoroughly soaks contemporary discourses of work in the creative economy (Tokumitsu 2014). While they may love their work, most freelancers are – equally if not more so – motivated by the fundamental need to earn a living. Freelancers' self-directed work and the fact that their names are typically attached to the writing they produce generate feelings of control and intense self-reliance. They view their experiences as dependent on individual decisions and actions, not as linked to structural logics of capitalism.

Many accept precarious conditions as the new reality to which journalists in a volatile industry must adapt. Critical political economy disrupts assumptions about freelancing to attend to the manifold processes that shape journalistic work, and advances a deeper understanding of the nature of media work and how it has changed amid shifting patterns of capital accumulation and technological change. Drawing attention to relations of exploitation that structure freelance work repositions freelancing as contested, as a site of struggle. Such a dynamic lens is critical for improving freelancers' working conditions and for the possibility of transforming contemporary conditions of media production.

NEW WORKERS FOR A NEW WORLD?

The organization of work has been greatly transformed since the 1970s, when the Fordist system of accumulation and regulation based on standardized mass production and consumption and a Taylorist division of labour began to break down, making way for what many identify as a period of post-Fordism, or a flexible regime of accumulation (Amin 1994, 9–10; Harvey 1990).[2] Post-Fordism is broadly characterized by economic globalization and a shift to lean, flexible modes of production enabled by developments in information and communication technologies. These processes are fuelled by neoliberal ideology, which promotes free markets, individual freedom, privatization, a contracting state, and declining social protections, most recently under the banner of austerity (Harvey 2005). Under such conditions, labour markets have been deregulated and made flexible, and deindustrialization in advanced capitalist states has led to growth in the service industries, widespread precarious employment, and declining union membership. Significant to the transition to a flexible regime of accumulation has been the decline of the standard employment relationship, a gendered model of employment based on a male citizen worker who works full time, continuously, for a single employer, on the employer's premises and who receives employment-based benefits (Vosko 2010, 1). Although the standard employment relationship dominated for a short period in history, and although many workers have historically been excluded from the relationship and its benefits – primarily women, non-citizens, racialized workers, and youth (Das Gupta 2006) – it served as a normative model of employment and regulation under the Fordist period, its logic the bedrock for social and labour policy. The standard employment relationship's replacement with more precarious forms of employment, such as temporary, part-time, freelance, contract, and fixed-term employment, signals new expectations for and experiences of work (Vosko 2006b).

Accompanying shifts in the organization of production and work arrangements over the past decades have been explanations of the nature of these changes and the changing character of work. Many theorists, focused on technological developments and their implications, forecasted utter transformation, propelled by the growth of knowledge, creativity, and technology, and resulting in shifting class relations and social relationships. Visions of a new type of worker for a new type of world have generally celebrated the decline of the Fordist worker, who, according to Henry Ford (cited in Barbrook 2006, 64), "want[ed] a job in which he does not ... have to think," and welcomed the arrival of the thinking, feeling, creative worker. Characterizations of new forms of work have ranged from Daniel Bell's (1976) post-industrial society, where workers are skilled, fulfilled, and well compensated, to Manuel Castells's (2000) network society, where flexible, empowered informational workers labour in globally networked enterprises free from bureaucracy and hierarchy, to Richard Florida's (2002) creative economy, where the creative class leads the charge to fulfilling, meritocratic working lives. The spread of flexible and non-standard work arrangements, growth in self-employment, and the technological capacity to work remotely have encouraged researchers and commentators to declare that contemporary working conditions

signal a radical break with the past. Many welcome the change, herald-
ing the self-reliant, risk-taking character of contemporary work, con-
juring visions of entrepreneurs and "free agents" deftly navigating
boundaryless careers in a gig economy (Leadbeater 1999; Pink 2001;
Florida 2002). Such visions bid farewell to the rigidities of the "old"
economy, including workplaces themselves, and welcome a new era of
limitless possibilities for fulfilling work and financial success, especially in emergent creative industries (McRobbie 2002a).

Autonomist Marxists offer more cautionary accounts of the shift
to post-Fordist capitalism, and note that work is being transformed
in contemporary capitalism, particularly as digital technologies
evolve, but that this transformation has been detrimental for workers. Whereas creative-class advocates view the commodification of
creativity as signalling "the end of soul-destroying waged employment," autonomist theorists view the shift to post-Fordism as an effort to incorporate workers' very souls into capitalist production
(Brouillette 2014, 40; Berardi 2009). Faced with growing militancy
and worker demands for less alienating work in the 1970s, capital
underwent a "postmodernization, or informationalization of production," embracing technology and capturing workers' desires for
more autonomous and creative forms of work (Boltanski and Chiapello 2007; Hardt and Negri 2000, 280). This process imbued work
with a greater sense of autonomy, increased workers' participation in
decision-making, and made Fordist production more flexible. Yet
the postmodernization of work deeply incorporated workers' personalities into production as it shifted emphasis from the production of material commodities to the creation of text, images, and
symbols in the form of media and communication, at least in Western capitalist economies (Hardt and Negri 2000; Lazzarato 2004;
Boltanski and Chiapello 2007). Contemporary capitalist production
relies heavily on communication and information, and draws on
workers' communicative, cognitive, intellectual, and affective capacities in more intensified ways (Lazzarato 1996; Dyer-Witheford and
de Peuter 2009). Rather than liberating the creative class, then, post-
Fordist work is intensified and ever-present, extending beyond working hours and the workplace, leaving "no time free of work"
(Chukhrov 2011).

Today, many forms of work draw on immaterial labour, or labour
that produces an "immaterial good, such as a service, a cultural prod-

uct, knowledge, or communication" (Hardt and Negri 2000, 290). Immaterial labour describes the products workers create (media and communication, for example), as well as two different aspects of labour: the creation of "informational content" of the commodity through changes in workers' labour processes in manufacturing, where computers and other modes of communication are used; and the production of the "cultural content" of the commodity through activities not normally considered work. This includes "defining and fixing cultural and artistic standards, fashion, tastes, consumer norms and ... public opinion" (Lazzarato 1996, 132). Although contemporary capitalist production requires a range of workers doing a range of work – what Nick Dyer-Witheford (2001) categorizes as immaterial, material, and immiserated labour – growing numbers of sectors, occupations, and commodities involve some aspect of immaterial labour.

Immaterial labour remains a contested term, yet the concept draws attention to the subjective component of producing informational and communication commodities, which is a critical aspect of cultural work. For example, critical cultural labour theorists note that the "lure of self-realization" in cultural labour "brings about an over-identification of the self with work" (Hesmondhalgh and Baker 2011, 141). As Dyer-Witheford and Greig de Peuter (2009, 4) write, "Immaterial labour is less about the production of things and more about the production of subjectivity, or better, about the way the production of subjectivity and things are in contemporary capitalism deeply intertwined." The production of immaterial aspects of commodities requires increasing inputs of workers' cognitive skills, emotions, and personalities, which are often captured and redirected through the melding of work and leisure time, blurring in what autonomists call "the social factory" (Dyer-Witheford 1999, 67). The social factory refers to the way "the time of production continues well beyond the formal working day, the space of production reaches beyond the discrete workplace, and the relations of production extend beyond the specific employment relation" (Weeks 2011, 142). In the social factory, sociality is "put to work" for capital as we pour increasing time, energy, and personal identification into labour (Lazzarato 1996, 145). Contemporary characteristics of work have always been present, yet are amplified under current political economic conditions.

Efforts to understand work today are most productive in a historical context that considers how conditions of contemporary media and cultural work are not without precedent. Since the 1970s, feminist scholars and activists have interrogated the value for capital of social reproduction and the unpaid domestic work that women disproportionately perform outside of paid work time, what is now described as affective labour, "a form of labour that is neither accountable nor measured and yet is what makes us reproduce the labour power and allows for material production to take place" (Del Re 2005, 54, cited in Weeks 2011, 244n9). C. Wright Mills (1956, 65) foresaw the rise of what we now consider to be knowledge work, or immaterial labour: "Fewer individuals manipulate *things*," he wrote in 1956, "more handle people and symbols." Mills observed an escalating need for workers to sell their personalities along with their time and energy, essential traits of affective labour today: "Intimate traits are of commercial relevance" (xvii). These conditions are "made more obvious," writes Weeks (2011, 142), in conditions of neoliberal capitalism, which requires flexible, multitasking entrepreneurial workers who expect little from their employers or the state.

Rather than an utter break with the past, then, today's work and working conditions should be understood through the lens of continuity through change (Vosko 2000; Harvey 1990; Hesmondhalgh 2007). Although work today may appear radically different from that which came before, capitalist production remains fundamentally organized around the extraction of surplus value from workers, and capitalist social relations continue to deeply structure social life. Class antagonisms, inequality, hierarchies, control, and exploitation have not disappeared from work, but have been reconfigured and intensified under neoliberalism. One aspect of this process has been the feminization of employment, under which forms of employment that have historically been associated with women's work have become more prevalent among a range of workers, most notably those who previously had access to a standard employment relationship (Vosko 2010). Work overall is becoming more precarious, or marked by a lack of "standard forms of labour security" and "characterized by heightened labour insecurity" (Vosko, MacDonald, and Campbell 2009b, 2). From this perspective, growing evidence of boundaryless careers, which cultural workers are often said to enjoy, should be viewed not as liberation from the strictures of outdated modes of employment, but rather as "the normalization of precariousness" (Pupo and Thomas 2010, xiii).

Cultural workers have long negotiated such tenuous conditions. As William Baumol and William Bowen observed in 1966, the artist "is not quite as poor as might have been imagined, but he is likely to be harried by constant economic pressures and by the need for incessant work, often in occupations far removed from his profession, in order to eke out a living for himself and his family" (99). This condition, captured by the term precarity, has deepened with the expansion of the cultural industries, which have become more intensely market oriented and remain alluring sites of work for growing numbers of people. Old forms of work exist alongside new, and the logic of capitalist production puts pressure on all work, extending into new areas and types of work as they emerge (Huws 2003). Forms of insecurity that have always existed under capitalism are spreading into and among new occupations and strata of workers, particularly those who previously enjoyed employment security (Standing 2011; Huws 2014). Journalists are no exception. As Gillian Ursell (2002, 35) notes, "Journalists have been information networkers since their emergence with the Gutenberg printing press ... they cannot therefore readily be construed as a new breed." Still, it is critical to consider what *is* new in journalists' and media workers' experiences, as technological change disrupts established media industry practices and business models, challenging the ways corporations and, in turn, freelance writers have traditionally earned money.

SETTING CULTURAL WORKERS APART

Cultural workers have long been positioned as unique, and scholarly debates on cultural work often turn on the question of its specificities (Stahl 2013b). Economists and management theorists in particular posit that the skills required to perform cultural work are inherent to particular individuals and that cultural workers care about the objects they produce in a way that other workers do not. Cultural workers are understood to be driven primarily by "a desire to create" or to produce "art for art's sake": personal investment and a sheer love of their work motivates cultural workers to produce more creative products than they would if they only valued earning money (Caves 2000, 3, 4; Neilson and Rossiter 2005, 10). As Fritz Machlup observed in 1962, artists' low incomes can be attributed to "the psychic income" received from producing works, which is "so large that [the artist] continues to supply his services at earnings rates far below what persons of similar qualifications could obtain in other occupations" (244). Such an approach focuses on individual motivations and ignores the power relations always present in work under capitalism. Consider, for example, Florida's (2012, 25) claim that workers now own the means of production because creativity resides in their heads, falsely positioning cultural workers as outside of capitalist and market forces. Although a writer can create a book from the ideas in her head, the capacity to publish, print, distribute, promote, and sell it, and to meaningfully compensate the writer, remains primarily with companies (Towse 2003, 69; D'Agostino 2010, 236). As technologies change and media industries transform, the work of writing is becoming more sharply oriented toward exploitation, appropriation, and competition. Just being creative is not enough to earn a living. Cultural, media, or knowledge workers may have skills that give them advantages, yet most "do not necessarily have any real control *over the use* of those ... skills within production" (Wright 1978, 198).

The impulse to set creative workers apart flows from ongoing associations between cultural production and art, traditional perspectives on which romanticize the artist as an innovative genius uniquely endowed with extraordinary and innate creativity and talent (Ryan 1992, 41; Bain 2005). Artistic work – and, by historical association, media and cultural work – is positioned as special and glamorous, a discourse reinforced by popular culture representations of such work as inherently rewarding and enjoyable, a counter to dullness and routine work (McRobbie 2002b, 517). Just as notions of mental and manual labour have been conceptually separated (Schiller 1996), a disconnect persists between ideas of artistic production and of labour as toil or dutiful work, dating from Renaissance culture's expectations of artists to isolate themselves in order to produce brilliant works (Bain 2005, 28). However, as Marx's philosophy reminds us, human labour cannot be separated into "creative and non-creative absolutes" (Smith and McKinlay 2009c, 5). By definition, all human labour draws on creative capacities for purposeful activity (Sayers 2005). In his often-cited comparison between "the worst architect" and "the best of bees," Marx ([1867] 1990, 284) notes that the difference between these beings is that a human can envision producing something before she produces it, indicating that the capacity for mental work is integral to human nature. The division of labour that enables some workers to conceive of ideas and others to create the resulting objects is not a natural division based on individual workers' innate qualities, but rather stems from the historical organization of capitalism (Braverman 1974, 114). Analysis of cultural work must retain awareness of the processes that create these separations and of the practices that divide workers and enable or constrain their capacities.

Setting media and cultural work apart has several consequences. Most significantly, such an approach removes cultural work from an understanding of the labour-capital relationship and resulting antagonisms. A Marxist political economy approach maintains connections to the broader social totality by viewing cultural workers as part of a larger class of workers who must sell their labour power to survive and who therefore are compelled to enter into a specific set of social and power relations. As Marx ([1867] 1990) outlines in *Capital*, the wage labourer with nothing to sell but her labour power enters into a "free" relationship of exploitation with an employer, who must set the worker to work to realize the value of labour power. Under the capitalist's control, the worker toils for a long stretch of the day. After earning more than what is necessary to reproduce her labour power, she generates surplus value, or profit, for capital. In the process, she becomes part of a generalized class of labourers. Although work in the offices and studios of the creative economy may appear to be different from Marx's account of factory work, underlying processes persist.

Important differences between workers exist, but are not absolute. Whereas capital seeks to establish a hierarchy between mental and manual labour, Marx emphasizes the process "by which capital develops a socially unified labour capacity in which particular roles represent only 'a limb of the total labourer,'" while all work under capitalism is submitted to generalized exploitation (Wayne 2003, 15, citing Mandel 1972, 195). This understanding of cultural work retains a notion of labour-capital antagonisms and of class struggle, and draws on Marx's relational conception of the connections between all workers under capitalism, conceived through the lens of class as a social relationship. Mike Wayne (2003, 7) acknowledges the "wider social conditions of creative and intellectual labour as a collective relationship occupying a contradictory position between capital and the 'traditional' working class." He draws on Erik Olin Wright's (1978, 192) theorization of the class character of intellectuals – defined as "a category of people ... whose activity is primarily that of elaborating and disseminating ideas" – in advanced capitalist societies. Wright argues that because intellectual workers neither control the labour of others nor maintain "real control over much of their own labour process" (206), they "typically occupy a contradictory class location between the working class and the petty bourgeoisie at the economic level, but between the working class and the bourgeoisie at the ideological level" (204). By this account, media and cultural workers occupy a contradictory class location because they are integrated into capitalism yet differentiated from the working class by "cultural privileges, relative workplace independence and (usually) by remuneration levels." Still, they are workers: their "status as labour reasserts itself whenever they are subjected to similar processes of exploitation and proletarianisation as the working class below them" (Wayne 2003, 23). The class character of freelance journalists is difficult to recognize because of their contradictory class location and self-employed status, which casts freelancers as entrepreneurs, eclipsing their positions as workers. Writers have historically been considered "economically classless," neither professionals nor workers (West 1988, 7). However, precarious employment and changing publishing practices have reasserted freelance writers' status as workers and have led to renewed efforts to confront challenges collectively. An understanding of freelancers as workers is key to this analysis and to motivating action for change.

Cultural workers' experiences are shaped by the specific histories and political economic contexts in which they work. A Marxist conception of class avoids positioning cultural workers as exceptional and refuses the tendency to understand their actions as motivated by individual traits and passion for their work alone. Susan Christopherson (2009, 74) argues that cultural workers are not driven solely by "personal, internal motives," but rather are "influenced by the political and economic context within which they work," including a capitalist economy, regulatory frameworks, state and employer policies, the organization of industries, wages, and access to union protections. Cultural workers make this point clear in their writings about their labour. As novelist Camilla Gibb (2014) writes, "Of course, there is reward in art for art's sake, but few can sustain morale, motivation or mortgage on an income of private aesthetic fulfillment." While the specificities of cultural work – how the work is performed, what sector workers operate in, and what products are created, for example – are important,[3] these specificities are situated within broader social relations and dynamics of capitalist cultural production. Research on cultural work should "integrate the analysis of enduring features, particularly high levels of risk and uncertainty, with the political and economic context that constructs the level and distribution of risk" (Christopherson 2009, 74). For one, many of the challenges freelancers face are linked to their self-employed status. Project-based, freelance, and other precarious forms of employment lead to long hours and overwork, intermittent and low pay, financial insecurity, and the individualized lens through which freelancers view their experiences. Freelance journalists' precarious working conditions have less to do with qualities inherent to individuals and more to do with structures of exploitation in the production of media under capitalism.

Despite the critical orientation of cultural studies of cultural labour, a political economic approach is often dismissed, usually on charges that Marx was not concerned with workers' subjectivities and, therefore, agency.[4] The most prevalent critique is of Marx's (1978b) theory of alienation, which argues that under capitalism workers are separated from control of the labour process, from the products they create, from other workers, and from their own human essence. Under capitalism, work is experienced as an alien power, "not voluntary, but coerced" (74). Mark Banks (2007, 11) rightly warns against a vision of cultural workers as "condemned to serve as alienated labour ... assumed to be devoid of active subjectivity and suppressed 'from above' by managers and owners." Cultural work is more often described as the antithesis of alienation: as social and collaborative work that grants workers relative autonomy in the labour process and provides opportunities for self-expression, fulfillment, and engaging in total human activity.[5] Cultural workers feel great attachment to the products they create, particularly when these products outwardly bear their names, such as a book or a piece of writing. As Ursula Huws (2014, 110–11) writes, cultural workers "not only care about the monetary reward but also about the work's content ... which, even after it has been sold, may still be experienced as in some sense 'owned' – something of which it is possible to be proud."

In an effort to preserve workers' agency, cultural studies scholars trace how cultural workers' subjectivities are produced through work, examine the meaning that they get from and give to their work, and outline how changing labour conditions mediate these experiences (Mayer, Banks, and Caldwell 2009). Such studies argue that conceptions of cultural work cannot be subsumed under a blanket theory of alienated labour because workers draw pleasure, meaning, and creative fulfillment from their work. However, discounting alienation discounts political economy as a whole, which is often interpreted as being static and reductive. While subjectivity is very important for the study of cultural work, political economy approaches can retain an understanding of worker agency.

As I outline in the proceeding chapters, freelance journalists' self-employed status generates particular subject positions and occupational identities that shape their attitudes toward work, its challenges, and resistance. But to understand why work is experienced in particular ways requires broadening a focus from individual experiences to consider cultural workers as part of a class of workers struggling over the terms of the commodification and exploitation of their labour power. As David Harvey (2006, 113) argues, it is difficult to understand conditions of work primarily through workers' subjective experiences of labour. It is first critical to understand the objective conditions of labour, or "what it is that workers are being forced to cope *with* and to defend *against*; to come to terms with the manifest forces that impinge upon them at every turn." This approach stems from Marx's (1978b, 595) claim that people "make their own history, but they do not make it just as they please; they do not make it under circumstances chosen themselves, but under circumstances directly found, given and transmitted from the past." The critical political economic framework I draw on understands media workers as active subjects who negotiate fluctuating process of production amid contested power relations. While a variety of interdisciplinary approaches are necessary for thinking through the complexities of cultural work, which can be simultaneously precarious and satisfying, risky and rewarding, Marx and his foundational understanding of labour remain vital.

A CRITICAL POLITICAL ECONOMY
OF FREELANCE MEDIA WORK

A Marxist political economy of media and cultural work is concerned with understanding the labour-capital relation, the tensions and contradictions that structure this relationship, struggles over control and exploitation, and questions of power and resistance. This approach flows from an understanding that cultural work occurs within a particular historical context: capitalist commodity production, under which those who do not own the means of production must sell their labour power to earn a living, thus engaging in a consensual relationship of exploitation of surplus value. This frame understands Marx as a dialectical thinker concerned with "processes, flows, fluxes, and relations" rather than an analyst of structures and things (Harvey 1996, 49). Marx sought to uncover the processes that constitute and sustain capitalism and to account for "unfolding and dynamic relations between elements within a capitalist system" (Harvey 2010, 11–12; 1996, 50). Marx's concepts capture the dynamic relations and contradictions propelling the change and instability inherent in the process of capital accumulation (Harvey 1996, 54), and which play out in media and cultural industries. Whereas many analyses of cultural work tend to be static (Christopherson 2009, 73), a Marxist political economy approach speaks to the historical developments of cultural industries, which did not emerge fully formed but rather are the result of contestation over how to produce culture and how to organize work. A historical, process-oriented perspective enables us to see how taken-for-granted characteristics of cultural work – its volatile, project-based nature – are often the result of transformations in media and cultural industries that have occurred alongside shifting dynamics of capitalism.

Marx's concept of exploitation is key to analysis of cultural work yet is most often absent (Gill 2014a).[6] Exploitation occurs when one group of people, workers, produces a surplus that is controlled by another, capitalists (Himmelwit 1983a, 157). Under capitalism, exploitation occurs through the extraction of surplus value, which Marx viewed as arising from the division of the working day into two parts: during the first part, the worker spends socially necessary labour time producing the equivalent of her wage; during the second, she spends surplus labour time producing profit for the capitalist (Himmelwit 1983b, 474).[7] Exploitation and the generation of surplus value drive capital accumulation and class conflict. As Himmelwit writes, "The history of capitalist production can be seen as the history of struggle over attempts by capital to increase, and attempts by the working class to resist increases in, the rate of surplus value" (474).

Exploitation is a dynamic concept. It links antagonism and resistance: those who exploit workers also depend on them to realize surplus value, which gives workers power, an "inherent capacity to resist" (Wright 1997, 35). The concept of exploitation includes worker resistance and a desire for autonomous forms of work. Autonomist Marxism's theorization of capital as acting and reacting to worker resistance provides a frame for this approach (Cleaver 2000). Under this view, capitalist cultural production is not a top-down process of domination, but dynamic and constitutive, reacting to workers' agency and, often, militancy. However, as Marx explains in *Capital*, "Capitalism is characterized by fetishisms that obscure, for both capitalist and worker alike, the origin of surplus value in exploitation" (Harvey 2006, 113). As Michael Burawoy (1979, 28) writes, "The process of production appears to workers as a labour process, that is, as the production of things – use value – rather than the production of exchange value." This is especially relevant to freelancers, whose focus on producing a piece of work (an article, for example) outside of an employment relationship further obscures how surplus value is generated for a publisher. Many factors contribute to the inability to recognize labour-capital relations, including ideologies of enterprise and creativity; overidentification with the work itself; the empowering act of choosing to pursue cultural work; and the personal relations that muddy distinctions between friendship and economic transactions (Lorey 2009; Neff, Wissinger, and Zukin 2005; Ekinsmyth 2002). Critically, freelancers' self-employed status casts them as entrepreneurs rather than workers, which generates feelings of autonomy and self-satisfaction, making relations of exploitation difficult to identify. This experience is common across cultural industries, where relations of exploitation are so difficult to detect that it often seems as if cultural work is not really work at all (Beck 2003a, 3; Stahl 2013a). A return to Marx uncovers the capitalist antagonisms and social relations that pulse through freelance cultural work.

THE LABOUR PROCESS AND CULTURAL WORK

Marxist investigations of labour traditionally draw on labour process theory, which would seem to have limited value for understanding media and cultural work. Broadly, the labour process refers to "social relations in the workplace" (Peck 1996, 23). Marx ([1867] 1990, 290) defines the labour process as "purposeful activity aimed at the production of use-values," consisting of the activity of work, the object worked on, and the instruments used for labour (284).[8] This is a description of the labour process independent of a particular social formation (283). Marxists are concerned with the labour process under capitalism, which is designed to appropriate and expand surplus value, and the social relations people enter into when working under these specific historical conditions.

Labour process research developed from Harry Braverman's (1974) critique of the organization of work under capitalism. In the early 1970s, as post-industrialists were marvelling at the liberatory potential of information-related technologies, Braverman found that modern work required increased training, skill, and use of technology, yet produced greater dissatisfaction among industrial and office workers (3–4). Braverman argues that the application of technology in the capitalist labour process leads to the degradation of work and of workers' skills, and that technological transformations and new forms of work retain patterns historically familiar to capitalist accumulation. Under capitalism, the labour process is transformed from activity that creates something useful into a process explicitly designed to expand capital (52–3).

Structural logics of competition and accumulation push capitalists to constantly revolutionize the production process to increase productivity and lower labour costs. This impels capitalists to obtain control over the labour process. As Marx ([1867] 1990, 436–7) writes, "Capital ... has an immanent drive, and a constant tendency, towards increasing the productivity of labour, in order to cheapen commodities and, by cheapening commodities, to cheapen the worker himself." Braverman (1974) documents this process. In the early stages of industrial capitalism, workers "embodied the traditional knowledge and skills of their crafts" and maintained control over their labour process, participating in production from start to finish (59). To increase the value that could be extracted from workers' labour power, capitalists needed to bring the labour process under their control. This required a transformation from a social division of labour, characteristic of all societies and designed by workers for their own needs, into a detailed division of labour, wherein work was "systematically subdivided" into discrete tasks (Marx [1867] 1990; Braverman 1974, 70). This transformation of workers into "lifelong detail worker[s]," unique to capitalism, was accomplished through the incorporation of new technologies and principles of scientific management into production (Braverman 1974, 78). Technologies and management strategies have been used to divide the labour process into constituent parts and parcel piecework out to a range of workers, separating conception from execution and deskilling workers.

This process, not the autonomous forces of technology, enabled capitalists to reconstitute the labour process from one directed by workers to one controlled by management. Under this logic, Braverman argues that capitalism strives to reduce the majority of workers to a homogeneous group of interchangeable labourers who require little specialized training. He documents similar patterns of separating conception and execution in the office, a site of mental labour, where workers also experienced the progressive elimination of thought from their work in the name of efficiency and productivity. The office worker's brain, writes Braverman, came to be "used as the equivalent of the hand of the detail worker in production, grasping and releasing a single piece of 'data' over and over again" (319). From this analysis, labour process scholarship emerged to examine from various perspectives how work is organized at the point of production under capitalism and how management has historically employed a range of techniques to secure workers' consent (Thompson and Smith 2010; Peck 1996).

Much of the post-Braverman debate turns on the question of control and worker resistance to control. As Marx ([1867] 1990, 270) outlines, capital does not purchase a worker outright, but rather purchases her capacity to work – her labour power.[9] To earn profit, capital must put labour power in motion. Labour process theorists ask a key question: facing the "indeterminacy" of labour power (Braverman 1974, 57) and amid antagonistic relations between labour and capital, how does a capitalist realize labour power's potential? The methods by which control is acquired, maintained, and contested have been debated, but overall scholars suggest that capital draws on a variety of methods to gain and maintain control over the labour process, and that management does not and cannot wholly rely on control or coercion at the point of production: "At some level, workers' co-operation, creative and productive powers, and consent must be engaged and mobilised" (Thompson 1990, 101). There are many reasons why workers consent to even the most alienating and exploitative work – not all worker cooperation with management in production can be explained away by "the silent compulsion of economic relations" (Marx [1867] 1990, 899; Ursell 2000). I take up questions of consent and choice in more detail in later chapters, as they profoundly shape freelancers' experiences.

Despite some notable exceptions (Murphy 1991; Im 1997; Ursell 2000; Liu 2006; Smith and McKinlay 2009a; Örnebring 2010), labour process theory is relatively absent from research on media and cultural work, likely for several reasons. Labour process theory has predominantly been concerned with workers in standard employment who work on employers' premises, while cultural work is increasingly situated outside of these structures (Thompson, Jones, and Warhurst 2009, 57). Foundational and theoretical texts on the labour process were developed in the context of industrial manufacturing[10] and cultural work is usually described in direct contrast to manual labour in a factory, both in terms of how it is organized – flexible, project-based work for multiple clients – and in the persistent assumption that cultural work is creative, enjoyable, fulfilling work outside the purview of rationalization, work that has resisted the separation of conception and execution. Indeed, celebratory accounts of cultural work as that which cannot be controlled by capital's usual methods make this type of work appear as distinct from rationalized, automated assembly and service lines as work can be (Florida 2002; Deuze 2007, 51). More critical scholars offer accounts that draw on Michel Foucault's notion that power is not administered in a top-down manner but dispersed and exercised from innumerable points. From this view, workers are encouraged through discourse and institutions to self-monitor and self-discipline. They are "encouraged to believe that they (and not social structures) are the authors of fate; capable beings that script their own actions, and indeed, must actively do so in order to achieve the promise of a meaningful and rewarding life" (Banks 2007, 46). Researchers challenge the notion that workers are controlled or coerced by an external force completely separate from them. Rather, workers are disciplined via "technologies of the self" or "self-steering mechanisms" (Foucault 1988) that encourage them to "manag[e] the self in conditions of radical uncertainty" (Gill 2011, 249). Neoliberal conditions and discourse, as well as precarious employment, motivate workers to harness their "marketability and value-adding propensities" (Ursell 2000, 809–10), setting themselves to work, choosing to work excessively long hours for little pay, and embracing uncertainty and risk in order to pursue careers in culture (McRobbie 2002a, 101; Ursell 2000; Smith and McKinlay 2009c, 12). From this view, managers do not need to motivate cultural workers to increase productivity, and cultural workers are considered to self-exploit (Hesmondhalgh and Baker 2011, 140), internalizing the source of coercive power.

Finally, labour process theory carries little currency in studies of cultural work because the general tendencies of capitalist production – rationalization, deskilling, and separating conception from execution – are perceived as limited in cultural production. This view comes from the understanding that to have use values, cultural commodities – even mass-produced cultural commodities – must retain visible traces of the people who conceived of them, especially in instances of "person-specific" or "personalized labour," where the creator's name is attached to the work (Smith and McKinlay 2009c, 12; Ryan 1992, 136; Chanan 1983; Miège 1989). As Bill Ryan (1992, 45) writes, "Every book must have an author, every score a composer, every film a writer, director, and cast of actors, unlike cans of peaches, lines of cars ... where the direct producers of these commodities are entirely unknown to their purchasers. Artists must be engaged as named, concrete labour." Even cultural producers who are not "stars" – that small group for whom name recognition fetches high remuneration (Hesmondhalgh 2007, 199) – are valued because "of the identifiable, expressive abilities attributable to and inseparable from each and each alone" (Ryan 1992, 44).

The requirement for concrete labour limits the extent to which the idea creation process in cultural work can be broken down and divided up (although this does not stop capital from trying). Workers who create originating texts cannot be replaced with machines or with other people without altering the text (Chanan 1983, 318). This complicates the capitalist production process. Usually, capital's compulsion to lower production costs requires that concrete labour

– a particular worker's specific skills or tasks – be reduced to average levels so that it does not matter who performs the work. As Harvey (2006, 59) writes, "Skills that are monopolizable are anathema to capital." Ideally, individual workers are transformed into abstract labour: interchangeable inputs for production, their particular contributions congealed in and disguised by the commodity form. Capital is compelled to separate conception from execution and to reduce workers' specialized knowledge and heterogeneous skills to simple labour (Braverman 1974; Harvey 2006, 57).

Because certain skills or capacities are fundamental to cultural production and cannot be fully separated from the worker or "organized out of the creative labour process," some cultural workers have been granted relative autonomy at the point of production (Ryan 1992, 45). As Banks (2010, 260) writes, "There are limits to how far cultural workers can be divested of autonomy and recast as ordinary 'detail' labour; for to do so fully would compromise the potential for future profits." To compensate for this relative autonomy at the point of production, capital tightens control over the reproduction, distribution, and circulation of cultural commodities, creating divisions in status, job quality, and material conditions between workers in cultural industries (Chanan 1976; Miège 1989; Ryan 1992; Hesmondhalgh 2012). Recognition of structural requirements for relative autonomy has ejected labour process analysis from studies of cultural labour. For if, as these arguments suggest, cultural workers retain control over their work and its products, especially in the case of named labour, then it seems that labour process theory is not applicable in the cultural realm. Braverman's (1974, 107) definition of management – "the control over work through the control over the decisions that are made in the course of work" – seems incongruent with a notion of relative autonomy in cultural work.

Yet cultural workers do face pressures that undermine their autonomy. Evidence is mounting of principles of rationalization and deskilling in cultural, knowledge, and media work – forms of work previously assumed to be impervious to these techniques. For example, the work of translation, research, and design are broken into small tasks and farmed out to people working remotely for pennies an hour via digital piecework websites and apps. Newsrooms increasingly use sophisticated algorithms to create business, sports, and weather articles that are indistinguishable from those written by humans (Cohen 2015b). Technology and management practices in news media are transforming journalism from an occupation that requires skilled labour to one that "from a technical point of view might be done by anyone" (Deuze and Fortunati 2011, 112). Automation and deskilling processes are underway in screenwriting, animation, fiction writing, and video game design and production (Wayne 2003; Day 2007; Conor 2010; Dyer-Witheford and de Peuter 2009).[11] As Braverman (1974) argues, capitalist processes constantly pressure labour and seep into new areas of work. Cultural production is continually brought under capital's commodifying logic. Attending only to workers' autonomy limits the ability to identify the processes underway that are transforming or attempting to transform even aspects of cultural work that require skills that are difficult to wrest entirely from the worker.

CONTESTING CONTROL

Most freelance writers say they enjoy autonomy and thus experience control over their work and careers. For many, the very act of becoming a freelancer, or of refusing to enter an employment relationship, is a way to contest employer control. Being self-employed means that a writer does not have to accept work just because an editor assigns it, does not have to work on-site and according to workplace policies and schedules, and is not limited to writing for just one publication. In a freelance relationship, immediate control, considered to be "the authority to direct the labour process" (Fudge, Tucker, and Vosko 2002, 8), is under the freelancer's purview.

Within certain parameters such as genre and format,[12] freelancers have discretion over how to order words on a page, what information to include, how to frame an article, who to interview, what topics to tackle, when to sit down to work, and when to stop working, for example. Their relationships with editors, who mediate between writers and publishers (for whom writers actually work), are generally experienced as collaborations rather than as management-worker relationships. Freelancers' names are attached to their articles and to their invoices, which renders their labour not as waged labour that benefits an employer, but as work that benefits them directly.

Freelancers experience growing constraints in their work, but overall most retain control over their immediate labour process, which fuels feelings of autonomy and job satisfaction.

But freelancers do not have control in a broader sense, and their labour process occurs in a context where direct lines of exploitation are obscured, where publishers are much more powerful than writers, and where the way work is organized generates intensifying pressures and soft forms of control that are made possible precisely because freelancers are not employees. Although freelancers work outside of employment relationships, industry retains the capacity to tighten control over the conditions of production in which freelancers work. These conditions include what stories are possible for writers to produce, the contracts under which labour power is engaged, where (and how) articles are published, and the low rates of pay that require working longer hours to earn a living. As the freelance labour pool expands and publishers seek new ways to increase profits in the face of changing technologies and business models in flux, publishers gain increasing control over freelance writers as a class of workers. These contradictory experiences with control point to tensions ever-present in freelance cultural work, where it is precisely by relinquishing control over employees – transforming full-time work into self-employment, freelance, casual, or temporary work – that capital is able to increase the extraction of surplus value from workers.

In the narrowing space of freelancers' autonomy, relations of control do not disappear but are reconfigured. For this reason, Sheila Cohen's (1987) exhortation to attend to exploitation in the labour process is pressing. Cohen argues that the post-Braverman labour process debate focused on questions of control and coercion at the expense of examining exploitation. She argues that it is not control that "constitutes the principal dynamic at work in the capitalist labour process," but rather exploitation, ownership over the means of production, and class (35–6). Cohen recasts the lens of labour process theory onto valorization and exploitation, the motor of capitalist accumulation and production, which is fundamentally structured around the extraction and appropriation of surplus value from workers, methods of which can vary. The labour process is political not only because of an "ongoing power struggle over managerial domination," but because it is "the site of the central dynamic of ...

exploitation and the generation of surplus value" (39). Braverman, Cohen says, was not primarily concerned "with 'control' or even deskilling *per se*, but with the specifically capitalist logic which constructs these tendencies" (36). Exploitation is what requires capitalists to control the labour process, historically by intensifying work and lengthening the working day (Marx [1867] 1990, 645). Control over production can be surrendered if it is not an impediment to exploitation (Harvey 2006, 116).[13]

If valorization is understood as the fundamental structuring process of capitalist production, then how work is organized can be analyzed not just in terms of relations of control and contestation, but also as strategies for exploitation "patterned by the quantitative pressures of value production" (Cohen 1987, 43). Labour process theory returns to the study of cultural work crucial questions of social relations of capitalism, exploitation, power relations, and class. Attention to the labour process counters claims that cultural work is radically different from other forms of work and reaffirms a notion of continuity through change. Foregrounding a concern with patterns of capital accumulation, labour process theory opens a critical line of inquiry: if the continuity of capitalist production has thoroughly penetrated the cultural industries and if exploitation is fundamental to the capitalist labour process, how does this dynamic manifest in cultural work? If cultural workers enjoy a degree of relative autonomy and control, how does capital respond? Historically, firms have tightened control over workers whose work does not require relative autonomy (Hesmondhalgh 2012, 81), but these tactics are extending to workers engaged in more creative activities. This is especially the case for freelancers, who are at the forefront of capital's efforts to grant workers autonomy – in this case, freedom from an employment relationship – while simultaneously intensifying exploitation in specific ways.

FREELANCE JOURNALISTS AND EXPLOITATION

Because freelancers are not engaged in an employment relationship and are not paid a salary, it appears that they sell only a finished piece of work, or "labour already objectified in the product," not the labour time required to produce that piece of work (Marx [1867] 1990, 692). However, Marx argues that piece wages are another form of time wages and that the existence of this form of payment "in no way alters [its] essential nature," which is "the general relation between capital and wage-labour" (693, 696). Piece wages have historically been a method of lowering workers' wages and of lengthening the working day (699). Today, payments for freelancers, who are essentially doing piece work, function in similar way (McKercher 2014).

Marx argues that the origin of surplus value is obscured in labour-capital relations (Harvey 2006, 113), and freelance journalists provide an exemplary case study of this tendency. Whereas capital has historically increased surplus value by extending employees' working day and intensifying production (Marx [1867] 1990, 645), publishers reliant on freelance labour are freed from the obligations of an employment relationship and so require additional methods of extracting surplus value from workers' labour: the exploitation of unpaid labour time and the aggressive pursuit of copyrights to writers' works.

Exploitation of Unpaid Labour Time

Although cultural industries have a long history of freelance labour,[14] the precarization of cultural work has intensified since the 1980s. Now, more than ever before, cultural production is characterized by a "just-in-time" workforce (Barker and Christensen 1998, 1), and most people who want to work in media and culture have little choice but to accept freelance, contract, or temporary work. The rise of precarious employment is linked to firm strategies such as concentration, convergence, and outsourcing; the erosion of union power; and the spread and acceptance – by employers and by governments – of precarious forms of employment across labour markets. As firms make production flexible, a growing amount of cultural work shifts to tenuous freelance and project-based contracts. Whereas freelancing was once an occupational form chosen by a small segment of cultural producers with a monopoly over their skills, it has now become the only occupational form available to many as companies shed their workforces, resulting in a labour market flooded with freelancers, intensified competition for work, and lower wages.

This is the structural backdrop against which cultural work must be understood. Yet a concept of business risk is at the core of many accounts of the organization of work in the cultural industries. According to this view, because cultural commodities are consumed in "highly volatile and unpredictable ways," cultural industries must manage an element of uncertainty particular to capitalist commodity production (Hesmondhalgh 2012, 27; Miège 1989, 26; Garnham 1997, 58). Uncertainty around consumption translates into uncertainty throughout the production chain. Rather than continuously employing workers, cultural firms maintain loose affiliations with expanding networks of people constantly developing new ideas from which they can pick and choose. Increasing numbers of people enter cultural occupations to find limited employment options, joining the "vast reservoirs of under-employed artists" on which cultural production depends (Miège 1989, 72). This "reserve army"[15] of cultural workers (Murdock 2003, 22), ready to work when needed and underpricing the value of its labour to secure work, lowers labour costs. Thus, what may seem like an appealing move for workers seeking an exit from an employment relationship and some control over their work is at the same time an ideal arrangement for capital seeking to offload the risks of cultural production. Freed from the burden of employment and relieved of the costs of providing salaries, training, overhead, benefits, and pay for unproductive time, firms can hire a worker for a short-term project or purchase only completed works: an article, a piece of research, a design. Purchasing completed works ensures that publishers do not pay for the time workers spend developing and researching ideas, pitching stories, conducting interviews, or editing and rewriting. The arbitrary fees publishers pay freelancers do not account for the large quantities of unpaid labour of producing writing and maintaining a freelance career (D'Agostino 2010).

Feminist political economists have long argued that unpaid and flexible labour has always been an important source of value for capital, particularly the unpaid labour performed by women in the home (Dalla Costa and James 1972; Pollert 1988; Waring 1999; Weeks 2011). The task of social reproduction, or "the daily and intergenerational reproduction of workers," has historically fallen to women, who under the dominant gender contract – the assumed male breadwinner and female caregiver – have performed this work, unpaid, in the home (Vosko and Clark 2009, 27). The provision of unpaid labour lowers labour costs for capital while concealing the true cost of production (Weeks 2011, 121–2). Capitalism continues to find value in unpaid labour, instances of which are spreading into new forms and areas of work as labour time moves out of the office and into homes, stripping from working lives what Pierre Bourdieu (1998, 98) calls "temporal guarantees." Work in the social factory is, as autonomist Marxists argue, intensified exploitation of time, as capital continues to finds value from the blurring of work and home life, production, and consumption (Gill and Pratt 2008). Cultural work, like numerous forms of contemporary work, is marked by un-bounded temporality and the extension of working hours, many of which are unpaid but necessary to earn a living. The freelance labour process makes the logic of this arrangement clear.

Recognizing the value for capital of unpaid labour demonstrates that the *form* cultural workers' employment takes should be viewed as a site of struggle, underscored by processes of exploitation. Many note that discontinuous employment is a defining characteristic of the cultural industries, but fewer make explicit this process of low-ering labour costs through the structure of employment relation-ships. As I demonstrate in the proceeding chapters, freelance status deeply shapes writers' experiences, including their relationships with publishers, the kinds of works they produce, their economic and po-litical security, their conceptions of themselves as workers, the way they envision potential resistance, and what form that resistance takes. Troubling a taken-for-granted way of working in media in-dustries illuminates the tensions and contradictions that shape cul-tural work: freelance status simultaneously imbues workers with autonomy and limits autonomy.

Copyright as Exploitation

Because freelancers are not employees, publishers are not concerned with how works are created or with directly controlling the labour process. For publishers, what matters is not the time spent on a proj-ect or the pace of work or, at times, even the final product itself. Rather, what matters is that companies own the final product so that works can be republished across media platforms, relicensed, and repurposed (increasingly, media outlets demand moral rights to works).[16] Copyright grants to its owner legal rights to the expression of an idea and the ability to do anything with it (Owen 2006, 2; D'Agostino 2010, 16–17). This is a powerful method of controlling the works freelancers create, of generating surplus value from works already paid for, and of lowering labour costs.

Like most cultural commodities, written articles have always carried high production costs and low reproduction costs. Digital technologies have lowered the costs of reproduction to virtually nothing, and cultural industries' profits are increasingly generated from owning copyrights, which are exploited in multiple formats. Large, converged media corporations aggressively pursue bundles of rights to freelancers' works to recycle articles across media platforms and through syndication. These practices are carried out through stringent copyright regimes that present freelancers with complex and binding contracts. It is now standard for contracts to demand "all rights, in perpetuity, throughout the universe" (PWAC 2006, 35), rights for which freelancers are rarely paid.

A Marxist perspective views copyright as exploitation of labour power and as a way to reproduce capitalist class relations in media industries (May 2002a; D'Agostino 2010). Freelancers, who have negligible power to negotiate individually, are paid little for the works they create and then sign away copyrights to publishers, rendering their works publishers' private property. By owning the rights to writers' works, publishers can continue to extract surplus value from workers' labour power long after they pay for an article. Here again, exploitation persists at the core of freelance cultural work. The continuing relevance of property ownership in cultural work returns to the forefront of analysis asymmetrical power relations between labour and capital (May 2002b, 317).

"Reproduction of property relations" via intellectual property rights is a defining characteristic of the "information economy," anchoring this era to a long history of relying on information for capitalist accumulation (317). Capital developed by generating technological methods of extracting knowledge from workers to control production and increase efficiency (Braverman 1974), and continues this trajectory by claiming ownership of the information workers produce (May 2002b, 318; Fisk 2009). This is a crucial, under-examined link between cultural work and capital, overlooked either by a focus on cultural workers' autonomy or by a failure to acknowledge that human labour creates the texts, images, ideas, and symbols that are transformed into property (Ross 2009a, 166–7). The exploitation of intellectual property and copyrights is always the exploitation of labour, not "simply a matter of extracting the potential economic value from some inanimate thing" (Rossiter 2006, 145). Copyright and contracting practices challenge freelancers' abilities to earn a living and undermine the autonomy self-employed status generates. In most cases, with limited power, individual freelancers have no choice but to sign contracts, letting their rights slip away and, with each restrictive contract signed, normalizing practices that just a few decades ago were inconceivable. These relations mark the contested nature of freelance labour status.

FREELANCING AS A SITE OF STRUGGLE

Exploitation is a dynamic, dialectical concept that contains elements of worker resistance: publishers' methods of exploiting freelancers' labour power are a response to freelancers' efforts to gain control over their labour process, the products they create, and the terms of commodification of their labour power. The shift to freelance work cannot be understood solely as a top-down imposition by capital onto an unwilling workforce. While freelance employment gives publishers a way to offload the risks of production and take advantage of a labour force made flexible, it also presents a strategy for many writers who want to pursue their craft on their own terms and who seek creative and autonomous forms of work. However, under contemporary capitalism, networked media corporations harness workers' desires for freedom and control in their work by enabling freelance arrangements – outsourcing growing numbers of works to freelancers, for example – yet intensifying exploitation of freelancers' labour power through low pay and restrictive contracts. As Matt Stahl (2013a, 13) notes, new flexible forms of work in cultural industries and beyond "can be understood to incorporate new modes of labour control." Because freelancers are not organized collectively to confront and preempt publishers' strategies, individual freelancers face heightened precarity, deepening exploitation, and intensified commodification of their works. While individuals might experience control over their labour process, collectively, as a class of workers selling labour power to publishers, freelancers' control is constrained.

Attention to processes of exploitation reinserts cultural workers into the broader political, economic, and cultural conditions of capitalist production. Because antagonism lies at the core of Marx's concept of exploitation and because capitalist production is "inherently, structurally, a site of contestation" (Wayne 2003, 13), freelance cultural work should be understood as a site of struggle. This conception is acknowledged in some studies of cultural work, where struggle manifests as tension between "artistic desires for creative autonomy" and the requirements of profit-oriented cultural production (Banks 2007, 6; Ryan 1992). A broader conceptualization, however, views this struggle as labour focused, as contestation over the terms of commodification and the exploitation of labour power. Autonomist Marxist theorizing is useful here, as this approach begins from the notion that workers are active agents who resist capitalist exploitation and enclosure, and that capital reacts to worker resistance, which always has the potential to escape capital's control. This cycle, in turn, generates new strategies and tactics of struggle among workers that threaten capitalism anew (Cleaver 2000; Brophy and de Peuter 2007, 178). As capital persists, extending relations of exploitation into new areas, workers seek meaningful and autonomous forms of work. As workers resist capital's direct control, companies pursue new strategies to extend relations of exploitation into new work arrangements.

The spread of freelance work throughout the cultural industries has coincided with declining labour protections, limiting the benefits to freelancers of self-employed status. Traditionally, writers become freelancers to gain control over the terms of the commodification of their labour power, viewing an employment relationship as selling themselves wholly to employers, as having to submit to "routine alienation" (Stahl 2010, 285). Yet as I argue in the following chapters, under contemporary conditions of cultural production, this strategy has had an unanticipated side effect: freelancers find themselves having to submit, instead, to relations of commodification, not only by orienting the works they produce to the market – producing only what will sell – but also by selling themselves, engaging more intensely in self-promotion, self-branding, and self-marketing.

In the following chapters, I look at these conditions by taking seriously freelancers' agency and desire for autonomy, yet also con-

sidering the power relations that structure freelance work and how
freelancers respond to new challenges. I examine the underlying
contradictions of freelance cultural work both as having the potential for autonomous work and as a way for capital to reduce labour
costs and offload the risks and responsibilities of production. With
several possibilities for collective organization underway, freelancers
are at a critical juncture: adapt, or resist and try to shape the terms
under which they work. Many are adapting to the intensely individualized, competitive, market-oriented conditions of neoliberal
capitalism by operating in an entrepreneurial mode and learning to
manage precarity. Yet freelance labour has the potential to serve as
a model of independent, autonomous work that resists capitalism's
compulsion to exploit and alienate workers. Understanding these
conditions and envisioning ways to transform them is vital. Collective organizing among freelance media workers holds great potential to improve not only their lives and material conditions, but also
the kind of media journalists can produce.

2

A Labour History of Freelance Journalism

"It is not from choice that there are so many Bohemians in journalism.
They are forced into Bohemia by the men who buy their work."
"Working on Space," *Journalist*, 1888

By vocation, freelance journalists tell other people's stories. Their
own story, however – the evolution of freelance writing as an occupation and the conditions under which they have worked – remains
untold. Most historical accounts of magazines, where freelancers
have traditionally published, focus on famous publishers and editors. These men (and they are usually men) are portrayed as intrepid visionaries whose passion for a unique cultural form drove them
to create and publish magazines despite high financial risk (Barbour
1982; Sutherland 1989; Tebbel and Zuckerman 1991; Sumner 2010).
Research is generally celebratory in tone and relays tales of entrepreneurial zeal, high-profile business deals, and innovations in advertising and circulation practices. Rather than comprehensively
accounting for the development of the magazine industry and the
conditions of its workers, historical research on magazines selectively
profiles specific publications and their creators, and relays stories of
individual men, rarely of workers collectively producing magazines.
Historical tales pay detailed attention to the quirks of publishers'
personalities and of editors' visions, yet are for the most part silent
about the labour that produced the contents of these endeavours.
Contemporary studies of Canadian magazine publishing focus predominantly on policies developed to protect what has long been
understood as a fragile yet important cultural form. Researchers
scrutinize the range of government policies that have supported or
hindered commercial magazine production (tax breaks for adver-

tisers, postal subsidies, exemptions from trade agreements, and grants for publishers), but pay almost no attention to issues of work, especially the work of writing. The dominant trajectory of histories of the magazine industry has erased freelance writers' experiences.

Workers have long been erased from communication, cultural, and media studies. As critical historians of journalism demonstrate, media history tends to focus on dominant institutions, technological progress, and individual personalities, usually those of powerful publishers. Such an approach has marginalized the experiences of working journalists (Hardt and Brennan 1995a). Historical accounts of media in North America have included tales of consistent and unimpeded progress, of technological revolution, and of the unwavering democratic role of the press. Such a top-down approach to media history can be remedied through histories of newswork, or, as Hanno Hardt (1995, 25) writes, "By liberating media workers from the expressed inevitability of their condition." It is in this spirit of critical media history, which views media as sites of work and thus as sites of struggle (Hardt and Brennen 1995b, viii), that in this chapter I outline a history of freelance writers in Canada to contextualize contemporary writers' experiences. (My focus on print magazines and newspapers, the original sites of freelance journalism, will broaden to include digital publications in chapter 5.)

Little scholarly research about freelance writers in Canada exists, and historical research is particularly lacking. Most published works on the subject consist of how-to manuals and guides for professional writers. No one has written a labour history of freelance writers and, unlike in the United States (Hardt and Brennen 1995a; Smythe 1980), very little labour history of journalism has been published in Canada. Canadian governments have produced several studies on the magazine industry, but only one was explicitly mandated to examine the conditions of its freelance workforce (Harrison 1982). The fluid nature of the occupation poses a challenge for such studies. Freelancers have historically come from the ranks of novelists and poets, moonlighting reporters, teachers, politicians, lawyers, hobbyists, and people in occupations completely removed from media, including many who have not needed to earn a living from writing. Writers have always drifted in and out of freelance status, making it difficult to count how many do this kind of work. Apart from newspaper journalism, writing as an occupation has never been formalized, standardized, or regulated. Writers have always had to hustle for work, piece together a living, and be willing to write anything for pay, often to support the kind of writing – creative, experimental, political, enjoyable – they actually want to do. Payments for writers have always varied, along with occupational status and degrees of job satisfaction. There is no one history of writers as workers, but there is a history of underpayment and insecurity.

Understanding the trajectory of freelance writing as an occupation requires piecing together details from several literatures, investigating various histories, and learning from the gaps. In this chapter, I trace the occupational lineage of freelancers from the beginnings of publishing in sixteenth-century England to industrialized newsrooms in Canada and the United States in the 1930s, where many writers found employment and when journalists first began to unionize. The disparate yet overlapping histories of writing in these countries, as well as the development of the book, magazine, and newspaper industries, provides insight into contemporary freelance writers' experiences.[1]

The narrative I sketch develops my argument: as capitalism expanded and penetrated literary and media production, writers became proletarianized, or brought under the system of waged labour, predominantly by working for newspapers. This process intensified with the development of industrialized news production, which rationalized the work of writing, mired journalists in a complex division of labour, and made routine on a mass scale the once creative and smaller-scale process of gathering and writing the news. Journalists' desire for autonomy over their craft and control over their labour process – individually and generally – led many to pursue freelancing, severing ties with an employer to self-manage both the process of writing and the type of writing they could produce. This historical lens positions freelancing as writers' attempt to gain control over the terms of commodification of their labour power and the works they create. Thus, freelance writing can be understood as a challenge to the dominant form of journalistic production, namely news writing, which was rationalized to fit the commercialized format of mass newspapers and, increasingly, other journalistic forms. Viewing freelancing as an effort to gain labour and creative autono-

my is critical for understanding the contradictions that emerge when
it becomes a key corporate strategy to lower production costs and offload the risks of production onto individuals.

FREELANCE JOURNALISM AS AN OCCUPATION

The first freelance writers were English pamphlet authors, working
in the sixteenth century for stationers, the publishers of their day.
Pamphlet authors were paid very little for their work: a small sum
and a promise of printed copies of the pamphlets in which their
work appeared, or sometimes just the copies. They were not paid
royalties or reprint fees, and with no copyright laws – the first, the
Statute of Anne, was introduced in England in 1710 (D'Agostino
2010, 47) – publishers could legally do whatever they wanted with
authors' writing. Pamphlet authors understood their exploitation
by stationers, yet never organized to challenge stationers' power.
Even the most successful writers died poor (Clark 1983, 25–6). Pamphlet authors were the first group for whom writing for pay became
a primary occupation. They felt that any other work they performed
to earn a living was done to supplement their writing (27).

The first known periodical, *Mercurius Gallobelgicus*, was published
in 1594 in Cologne, followed by a variety of news summaries and experimental publications, many aimed at circulating booksellers' lists
and reviewing their books (Davis 1988, 4; Raymond 1996, 6, 9).
Newsbooks, precursors to newspapers, appeared in 1641 in Britain,
published by printers and booksellers (Raymond 1996). Some writers were hired by the court on retainer to write "formal letters of
news" (5), while others discovered they could earn money by writing for whomever would pay. An early example of the writer for hire
was Marchamont Nedham, who penned missives for both sides during the English civil war, representing a shift from writing based on
individual principles to writing anything for which someone would
pay (Hamilton 2008, 47). This practice was considered vulgar, and
those who wrote for pay were disparaged as hacks (Tebbel 1969, 28).
Still, with the emergence of commercial periodicals in Europe at
the end of the seventeenth century, writing came to be a "commercial enterprise" and writers were "remade into ... anonymous worker[s]" (Hamilton 2008, 47, 52).

These anonymous workers had several ways to make a living. Some earned income from writing what they desired and selling pieces to various buyers. Others, more commonly, were employed by publishers to perform nonwriting tasks. Some voluntarily contributed stories to newspapers as a hobby or out of a political or religious commitment, while others worked as translators for publishers. Into the early eighteenth century, writers worked as newsgatherers on retainer or on a freelance basis (52–3). They stumbled upon events and overheard conversations, wrote them up for newspapers, and were paid by the article (Sutherland 1986, 220–1).

In the eighteenth and into the nineteenth century, writing became more formal and less dependent on patronage as capital began to penetrate literary production and publishing grew into an industry, helped along by expanding populations, rising education levels, and increased literacy rates (Kingston and Cole 1986, 9–10; Heyck 2002, 236). A growing middle class sought reading material to fill its leisure time, and papermaking and printing technology improved, lowering the costs of producing magazines and journals. These conditions supported "a whole caste of professional writers" (Eagleton 2005, 30). The development of publishing and the growth of markets for periodicals, journals, and newspapers, conditioned by processes of commodification and commercialization, produced a tension that remains a key characteristic of the professionalization of writing. Increasingly, people could earn money from writing, some even a decent living, but fewer could do so by only writing what they chose. The market shaped writers' experiences as workers, both in the type of material they could write and sell, and in their style of writing (Mills 1956, 143; Kingston and Cole 1986, 12; Hamilton 2008, 52).

Publishers began to commission articles and demand more formulaic writing, a standardization of content that deepened as capitalism developed (Wilson 1985, 42; Heyck 2002, 243). Writers were brought into cycles of corporate commodity production and writing was brought under bureaucratic control as publications, which grew into or were purchased by larger companies, oriented cultural output toward the commodity form. This required the creation of predictable works, shaped by corporations "tightening [the] conditions of profitability" (Ryan 1992, 149), a practice that continues to

develop as publishers hone their business models. The process of
the commodification of writing corresponds to the history of the
development of magazines in Canada, which began primarily as cultural, political, or pet projects, but which transformed into large
businesses and important components of profitable, concentrated,
networked media industries.

WRITERS AND MAGAZINES

According to published narratives, magazines in Canada have historically been labours of love rather than moneymaking enterprises, founded to publish the work of Canadian writers, to unite a
disparate nation, and to foster the development of a distinctive Canadian culture (Desbarats 1991; Dubinsky 1996; Azzi 1999; McKercher
2001). The cultural importance assigned to Canadian magazines –
that they are the only truly national medium, that they protect local
culture in the shadow of American empire, and that they are key to
national culture's survival (Audley 1983; Desbarats 1991, 50) – has
been perpetuated by publishers, governments, academics, writers,
and other industry workers, often obscuring ever-present social relations of labour, including commodification and exploitation.

Magazines are described as important but risky endeavours, as "invaluable culturally but fragile financially" (Dubinsky 1996, 35). As
Richard Ohmann (1996, 354) writes, "Across the spectrum of mass
culture, in no other medium have economic fortunes been so
volatile, continuity so precarious." In Canada, with small markets,
two historically dominant languages, and geographically dispersed
readerships, "magazines have always been in trouble, it seems" (Desbarats 1991, 50). These sentiments run through most accounts of
Canadian magazine publishing, reaffirming it as a crucial yet fragile industry. Such a discourse has had a silencing effect, rendering
the working conditions and wages of writers unquestionable. Writers who ask for higher pay receive a refrain all too common in magazine publishing throughout the decades: we just cannot afford it
(Mott 1957a, 504; Woods Gordon 1984, 71; Wilson 2010). This dominant narrative can account for why writers are largely absent from
histories of magazines in Canada.

Canada's magazine history begins in 1789, with the launch of the
Nova Scotia Magazine and Comprehensive Review of Literature, the first

magazine published in English in Canada (Kesterton 1967). Like most early Canadian magazines, it reprinted material from British or American periodicals and newssheets – American magazines already reprinted much of their material from British periodicals – for little or no cost (Barbour 1982, 5–6; Desbarats 1991, 53, 55). By the second issue in 1789, its publishers declared that they could not afford to pay writers (Barbour 1982, 6). In 1867, the publisher of *New Dominion*, designed to compete with popular American magazines sold in Canada, encouraged Canadian writers to publish "original" works in the magazine but noted it could not pay them until its circulation reached 6,000. Early Canadian magazines were considered "free training school[s] for would-be writers," providing space for poets, essayists, and novelists to hone their craft and for book publishers to source publishable material and new authors – many early Canadian novels first appeared as serials in magazines (Barbour 1982, 37, 49, 150). Freelance writers have a long history of struggling to be taken seriously. In 1976, the Canada Council for the Arts responded to a funding request by the Periodical Writers Association of Canada by stating that funding such an organization would "require some turnaround in the thinking both of the council members, and the literary advisory panels," as the council's periodical officer believed that "the magazine writer, like the radio or television writer, has tended to be looked on as a poor cousin of the novelist or poet, or the academic" (Paré 1976).

Magazines that were not published or financed by book publishers were funded by subscriptions, which did not guarantee income: subscribers convinced to sign up would rarely renew and would not pay in advance of receiving issues, as is standard practice now, leaving publications with little money. Editors' salaries were generally paid in accordance with magazines' financial success (Mott 1957a, 198). Many magazines were pet projects of wealthy benefactors who did not need to earn a living, or printers who wanted to disseminate their own views on religion or politics and so had little need to hire writers. It was difficult to develop a market for Canadian magazines, as cheap American magazines were already being sold in the country by the 1880s. By 1819, many American magazines paid for contributions, so Canadian writers sold their work in the United States while publishing for no pay at home (Barbour 1982, 36; Mott 1957a, 197). Because they did not pay writers enough, Canadian magazines that intended to compete with American publications could not match their editorial quality, and successful writers encouraged fellow Canadians to publish their work in the United States (Barbour 1982, 63, 72).

It is difficult to determine definitively what writers were paid, or if they ever have earned their livings solely from magazine writing. The first Canadian study on this question was conducted in 1979 (Harrison 1982); earlier information comes from anecdotes scattered throughout published histories of Canadian magazines, which paid scant attention to writers. What is certain is that there was no consistency among publications and that payment practices varied widely. Some magazines paid nothing; others paid only their best-known contributors. No standard rates of pay and no guarantees of payment existed, but there was always the potential to be paid in the future, either as a book author or as a more established writer. As is the case now, the potential to earn a living or to gain recognition eventually (let alone wealth and fame) was a likely enticement for writers to write. Noel Roberts Barbour (1982) relays anecdotes about the payment of some writers – nine dollars for a column in one case, ten or fifteen dollars for a story in another – but does not ask why they were poorly paid, nor does he inquire into the material conditions of their lives. A typically colourful anecdote Barbour shares: "Frederick Paul, a reporter on the *Montreal Star* who contributed articles and stories to Canadian and American magazines, returned a cheque to a Canadian magazine with the remark that the editor must have sent the office boy's salary by mistake!" (70). What is clear is that most contributors to Canadian magazines had other sources of employment or income, even as magazines became less reliant on reprints and published more Canadian writers.

As magazines became commercialized and shifted to mass market and advertising models, more began to pay writers. Again, there is no thorough documentation of when or how much, just anecdotes. For example, Barbour writes that *Maclean's* and *Chatelaine* paid for established journalist June Callwood's research, on which she spent more time than writing; that in 1949, eight Canadian magazines spent $585,600 to purchase writers' works; and that magazine editors in 1950 complained that, while they wanted to pay for quality fiction, they could not find any good enough to print (145, 146). Published histories of magazines in the United

States, where it was rare for writers to earn a living solely from free-lancing for magazines, give further insight (Peterson 1964, 122; Mott 1957b, 14–15). In fact, as Theodore Peterson (1964, 123) writes, in the nineteenth century, "the freelance writer seems to have been much more myth than reality ... [yet the] myth of the freelance writer persisted tenaciously; it was encouraged by teachers of writing, by the books on magazine writing which rolled from publishers' presses ... by the roseate journals for amateur authors, by the correspondence schools which promised to make anyone a writer in ninety days, and by the editors themselves."

By the 1930s, freelancing was still considered a hobby or an avo-cation; most writers had "assured income from another source" (Rogers 1931, 247). Payments for magazine articles were nonexistent in the United States until 1819 (Mott 1957a, 197), after which writ-ers were paid only once their articles were printed, which could be up to a year after acceptance. Once articles were accepted, editors could alter copy without consulting the writer, exerting absolute control over what was published (Tebbel 1969, 28). The first Amer-ican magazine to pay for submissions was the *Christian Spectator*, whose proposed fee of one dollar per page became a standard in-dustry rate (Mott 1957a, 197). Still, payments remained inconsistent. Some writers were paid well for their work, others not at all, and still others refused payment (Tebbel 1969, 70; Mott 1957a, 197). As John Tebbel (1969, 29) writes, "Those who still considered writing a gentleman's amusement would not take money even when the edi-tors tried to bless the payment by calling it an honorarium." James Hepburn (1968, 5) links writers' long battle for compensation to this notion of "gentlemanly dignity," which he traces to Elizabethan authors who were not in "the 'habit' of asking for money" because writing for them was bound up in "the exalted character of art." He argues that "for another 300 years, [this attitude] helped to prevent authors from agreeing among themselves to establish principles of payment for their work."

In the twentieth century, a turn to advertising-based business mod-els enabled magazines to increase payments to attract talented writ-ers, who could in turn boost sales to attract advertisers (Peterson 1964, 123). *Graham's Magazine* set a precedent by paying from four to twelve dollars per page for prose, pushing up other magazines' rates. "Thus," writes Tebbel (1969, 71), "an author could expect to get from twenty to sixty dollars for a five-thousand word article – excellent payment by the living standards of the day." Publishers of general consumer magazines understood that raising payments could attract higher-quality work and increase circulations (67–8, 71). Still, magazines spent much less on editorial content than on paper and printing, and "for every magazine which paid $1,000 for articles, there were hundreds which paid $100 or less" (Peterson 1964, 124, 125). Payments to writers were distributed in an ad-hoc manner, and by the 1950s and 1960s, the industry could only support a few hundred writers; about half of them had other jobs (125–6). Ralph Allen, editor of *Maclean's* in 1955, observed that it was "almost impossible ... to make a living [solely] from Canadian magazines" (cited in Karr 2007, 140). A guide for aspiring writers published in 1954 encourages writers to "be provident enough, or have good enough credit, to live for months sometimes without income" (cited in Peterson 1964, 126).[2]

Magazines have always relied on freelancers to fill their pages, but many did hire staff writers, and these practices have existed simultaneously. In early North American magazine publishing, editors reprinted material or wrote it themselves (Mott 1957a, 193), either because magazines were launched to publish their editors' views or because there was a limited pool of writers. As Tebbel (1969, 28) argues, in the early nineteenth century, writing was not a way to earn a living: "It was still less a business than a leisure occupation for gentlemen," who may have written for "amusement and distraction," as the audience for magazines was still a small slice of the educated elite and writing was not yet a popular or respected occupation (see also Mott 1957a, 193; Wilson 1985, 8). At this point, editorial production was haphazard. Editors encouraged submissions and selected from contributions sent through the mail. Articles were not paid for and were often anonymous, printed without bylines (Mott 1957a, 196; Tebbel and Zuckerman 1991, 12). Following the lead of newspapers, some magazines hired staff writers, especially if they wanted to publish labour- and resource-intensive investigative journalism or high-quality writing (Nathan 1911, 414; Payne 1989, 349, 351). In the early 1900s, famed investigative journalist Ida Tarbell spent four years researching and writing muckraking articles on the Standard Oil Company for *McClure's*, for which she was paid nearly $50,000 (Kielbowicz 1989, 268). Samuel McClure, editor of *Mc-*

Clure's, recognized what it took to enable writers to produce high-quality writing: financial security. He paid writers salaries rather than by the word counts: "I decided ... to pay my writers for their study rather than for the amount of copy they turned out," he said. "To put the writer on such a salary that it would relieve him of all financial worry and let him master a subject to such a degree that he could write on it" (cited in Sumner 2010, 20).

Large staffs of writers, however, were rare. In Canada, the standard model has always been to source most of a publication's articles from freelancers (Audley 1983, 69), a model that persists today. But while production practices remain consistent, demonstrating continuity through change, magazines have become more established, more profitable, part of highly capitalized commercial industries, and able to draw from a much larger pool of freelancers, many of whom want to earn a living solely from writing. Magazines historically relied on freelancers for a range of reasons, but what developed as a tradition has become a business strategy critical to minimizing the costs of labour and of editorial material. A freelance-based production model dominates in media industries today more likely because of strategic management than tradition, and provides publishers with a steady stream of content for a fraction of magazines' operating costs. As Christopher Wilson (1985, 61) emphasizes, payments made to writers have always been decisions made for a variety of reasons, but decisions nonetheless. There is nothing natural or inevitable about the rates writers have been or could be paid for their work. The decision to use freelancers is highly cost-effective, as one magazine journalism textbook explains: "By using freelances [the British term for freelancers] the magazine can recruit enthusiastic newcomers and develop new talent, and if freelances become unreliable or temperamental, or their copy becomes dull, they can be dropped without compensation, apology or even explanation" (Davis 1988, 212).

Over the years, in its efforts to foster the development of privately owned, domestic cultural industries to counter the reach of American and British cultural output, Canadian governments have commissioned several studies to examine magazine publishing, and have proposed and enacted policies that have shaped the industry's development. Policies include postal subsidies, grants, tariffs on imported magazines, and tax breaks for advertisers.[3] Rarely, however, have writers' concerns as workers been addressed. The Royal Commission on Publications, chaired by M. Grattan O'Leary (1961), devoted a fraction of its study to writers. The commission was struck out of concern about the "relative underdevelopment" of Canada's domestic magazine industry, which at the time was dominated by foreign publications (Lorimer, Gasher, and Skinner 2008, 185), and was instructed to "investigate every aspect" of it (O'Leary 1961, 3). O'Leary notes that in 1961, some magazines invested twice as much in circulation and promotion as they did in editorial content, and that the top Canadian writers wrote for American magazines because they could not earn a living writing only for Canadian periodicals (68). He blames small Canadian markets and the challenge of attracting advertising revenue, but also mentions that writers faced unfavourable copyright laws (without specifying them). And while O'Leary suggests government policy changes to remedy the situation, he argues that issues of writers and of copyright were best "left to the individual responsibility in the workings of a free society" and therefore could not be dealt with in his report (95).

In 1979, Brian Harrison (1982, 13) conducted the first government-commissioned study of writers in Canada. He found that in 1978, some freelance writers earned a living solely from writing, but that 50 per cent of full-time writers surveyed earned less than $7,000 from writing alone.[4] One in five writers relied on newspapers and magazines for their principal earnings; most supplemented their writing with other work, including teaching and salaried writing (41, 13). At the time, Canadian magazines paid from twenty-five dollars to $2,500 for features (about 2,500- to 3,500-word pieces), and most paid less than $500 (65). Only 18 per cent of writers surveyed reported that periodicals provided their sole source of income (77). Overall, writers struggled to earn a living and felt underpaid and undervalued, despite the importance assigned to Canadian cultural production (65). As Harrison writes, "Many writers find it extremely difficult to maintain a reasonable standard of living and at the same time pursue their writing with the necessary vigor to produce creative works that maintain the level of quality to which they are capable" (73).

In its 1984 study of the Canadian periodical publishing industry, consultancy firm Woods Gordon (1984, 71) recognized that periodical writers were "insecure, unrecognized and ill-remunerated."

The report notes that a "top" freelancer working for the highest-paying Canadian magazines could earn around $19,000, but that fees for articles had not kept pace with inflation: "A major feature article of 2,500–3,000 words that in 1964 would have commanded $500 would pay $350 today" (69). The report links writers' low pay to the small amount magazines allocated to editorial: about 15 per cent of their budgets went to freelance wages, staff salaries, artwork, and other editorial costs (66, 70). Writers' remuneration is identified as a critical issue for the industry, but again is dismissed as an issue the government could not resolve; one best left to market forces. The report contains a revealing paragraph on the power relations between writers and publishers. The text is notable for the way it recognizes that writers' labour is fundamental to the production of magazines yet simultaneously undervalues their contributions:

> Because writers do not have a strong bargaining position, the money received by them often becomes one of the few discretionary expense controls available to publishers. For most of the industry, the position of the key supplier to their final product is of little concern. The overall view appears to be that the general quality of writing is unaffected by remuneration. Since many writers for smaller periodicals receive little or nothing for their efforts, the industry view may be justified. Most periodicals appear to sell largely because of their approach, style and reputation rather than on the basis of their authors. In fact, some periodicals do not publish authors' names and most people would be hard pressed to name a significant number of writers in their favourite periodicals. (69)

Although the report advises against state regulation of writers' rates, it does suggest that a portion of grant money given to publishers be allocated to writers, which would improve standards of writing and would "ultimately enable more publishers to justify paying more for editorial matter" (71).

Freelance writers in Canada have always struggled to earn a living, even during times of media industry expansion and profitability. Why, then, have people always wanted to freelance? For most, freelancing (or the idea of it) has been a way to claim some autonomy as a worker, to write for multiple publications, to explore a range of ideas and topics, and to exercise more creativity than other forms of paid writing – for journalists, predominantly newspaper journalism – allowed. The small number of well-paid, well-known freelancers who live by writing alone has always served as a source of aspiration, indicating the possibility of "making it" and of being the exception. Freelancing can be understood as a way for writers to resist, in some way, the commodification of their labour power, and to gain control over their labour process, particularly over their time and over the material they write (Murphy 1991). Here, autonomy represents for writers a refusal to be subservient to a single company, and a desire to unchain from a boss, to have freedom to self-organize their labour, and to work in a way that enables creativity and connection to their work. To understand this conception of freelance writing, it is necessary to consider the historical conditions of journalistic labour, which further transformed the nature of writing as an occupation. Research on newspapers provides insight into the working conditions of journalists, clues as to why writers may have chosen – and may still choose – to exit or avoid an employment relationship to become freelancers.

NEWSPAPERS AND THE DEGRADATION OF JOURNALISTIC LABOUR

The growth and expansion of newspapers in the eighteenth and nineteenth centuries provided the largest number of writers with steady, if insecure, employment, bringing them into the wage-labour system as they took up posts as reporters and journalists in newsrooms. Newspapers, which have been more thoroughly researched and contextualized than magazines, especially from a labour perspective, provide the clearest example of the commodification of writing and of writers' labour power.

Newspapers introduced the role of the paid reporter in the early 1800s, and salaried positions became the norm over the next several decades (Allan 1999, 22). As the market economy transformed North American newspapers from public service and partisan outlets to profit-driven enterprises, newspaper work – both editorial and the technical work of printing and typesetting – was transformed from craftwork into industrialized mass production (Rutherford 1982, 78). Industrialization brought about technological change that shaped workers' labour. Typewriters, telephones, and the telegraph were introduced to newsrooms and their use sped up both work processes and the news cycle. Journalistic labour began to mirror the organization of factory work, with specialized, complex divisions of labour, including layers of reporters, writers, editors, and copy rewriters working alongside large and growing advertising departments (Christian 1980, 262; Hardt 1995, 3; Salcctti 1995, 59). As technology was more extensively incorporated into news production, the cost of owning and running papers increased and ownership became limited to those with access to capital, such as venture capitalists and consortiums of bankers and investors, many of whom had little commitment to journalism beyond its role as a commodity. This development ended the tradition of writers, editors, and printers running their own newspapers (Christian 1980, 262; Salcetti 1995, 50–1). The business aspects of newspapers were separated from the work of printing and editing, and entrepreneurial publishers expanded newspapers into corporations and chains (Solomon 1995, 113). By the late 1800s, chain ownership spread and newspapers operated under an explicit profit mandate. News had become a commodity, its production organized around the corporate compulsion to lower labour costs (112–13; Salcetti 1995, 53; Sotiron 1997, 5, 6).

Through newswork, writers became fully integrated into capitalism and journalists underwent a process of proletarianization, transformed from independent workers in small enterprises into labourers in systems of mass production (Kaul 1986, 47; Murphy 1991, 142). In *Capital*, Marx ([1867] 1990) describes the process of proletarianization ushered in with the development of capitalism, which created a class of workers who had nothing to sell but their labour power. This process results not only in the extraction of surplus value from workers' labour power but also in the experience of alienation: once a worker sells her labour power, control over decisions about how to organize work is under the purview of whoever purchases it, and the worker loses control over the process and ends of her labour (Marx 1978a). In his discussion of the proletarianization of professional workers, Charles Derber (1982b, 14) defines this process as "a shift toward dependent, salaried employment, in which the labour of professionals becomes subject to the authority and management of others." For Derber (1982c, 169), key to this process is ideological proletarianization, which refers to a "loss of control

over the ends of one's work" and a "loss of control over the goals
and social purposes to which one's work is put." Creativity in the
content and process of work is reduced because workers can no
longer set the direction or objectives of their work (Derber 1982b,
16–17). Emphasis is placed on transforming skilled workers into
"technicians or functionaries" (Derber 1982c, 172).

Proletarianization, writes Arthur Kaul (1986, 48), "represents the
economic subordination of an occupation." Because they experience a loss of control, workers whose labour has undergone proletarianization become ideologically aligned "with the property
interests of the capitalist economy." Proletarianization accurately
describes the transformation of journalism as a profession: what
was once a form of intellectual labour produced independently or
sold on a freelance basis became standardized via industrialization,
marked by low status, poor working conditions, and, as I discuss in
greater detail later in this chapter, specific forms of ideological proletarianization (Leab 1970; Hardt 2005). Writers who were incorporated into mass media production experienced this acutely, as
their work became less about their own ideas and expression and
more about filling column inches with standardized copy. Paul
Rutherford (1982, 81) characterizes the early occupation of journalism as "a life of dependence and anonymity, as much drudgery
as excitement, long hours and low pay."

Much like other workers' wages, reporters' compensation was designed to extract the maximum amount of work for the minimum
amount of pay. Some newsworkers received salaries and some
columnists, specialists, and friends of publishers were well paid
(Leab 1970, 5), but the majority of reporters were paid by a space-
rate system, which paid fixed rates per column inch of printed copy.
Reporters who returned from an assignment without a story would
not be paid. If a story was written but not printed, a reporter received an hourly rate for time spent on the piece (Smythe 1980, 2).
This pay structure can be directly linked to the content of news in
the late nineteenth and early twentieth centuries, which was noto-
riously sensational, embellished, and long-winded. This style of journalism, often disparaged as "yellow journalism," is typically blamed
on unprofessionalism, but is more accurately accounted for by an understanding of reporters' working conditions: the longer the words
journalists used, the more extravagant their articles, and the more

column inches they occupied, the higher their pay (Smythe 1980; Wilson 1985, 19; Houchin Winfield 2008, 25). An anonymous writer in the *Journalist* in 1888 called the space-rate system "one of the most demoralizing features of newspaper work." Although this system was cheap for newspapers, it was "neither fair to the writer nor the public" and encouraged would-be succinct writers to write long, leading to an oversupply of "wordy" writers such that "space rates have steadily gone lower and lower" (*Journalist* 1888). The writer concludes with a call for change: "If the proprietors would put these men on decent salaries, the public would get better papers, the proprietors would make more money and journalism would have more earnest practical workers and fewer ink-wasting and debt-ridden Bohemians in its ranks."

Yet proprietors did not put journalists on salaries. The space-rate system meant that pay varied between newspapers, as some papers used different type sizes, column formatting, and editing styles (Smythe 1980, 3). Reporters often took money from sources – not because they were inherently corrupt as is commonly assumed, but because they earned so little (ibid., 5; Leab 1970, 8). These practices fostered competition among writers, further entrenching journalism's individualist spirit (Solomon 1995, 123). Journalists did collaborate when necessary: reporters working for different, often competing, newspapers would come to a consensus on the details of a story as a way to ensure "mutual protection" in the face of highly insecure employment – by being on top of the most newsworthy stories, reporters could appear indispensable to their papers (Birkhead 1986, 40). Newspapers' use of the space-rate system declined after World War II and wages increased as advertising developed on a much larger scale (although conditions did not significantly improve until collective bargaining was won), a reminder that writers' fortunes have historically been tied to processes of commodification (Salcetti 1995, 56).

In addition to low pay, journalistic work was arduous and insecure. Ted Smythe (1980, 5) describes writers working "long hours at a furious pace under extreme pressure." Reporters received no benefits, had no guarantee of a permanent job, and took little time off because they were only paid for what they could publish. Publishers hired and fired arbitrarily, spied on workers, were editorially overbearing, and drove seasoned reporters away to keep costs down

(Leab 1970, 7; Solomon 1995, 125, 126). This lack of respect, not only from employers but also from the public, meant that newspaper writing was considered by many to be a temporary occupation; a path to politics, business, literature, or more prestigious journalistic work; or just something to do to earn extra money (Smythe 1980, 8; Rutherford 1982, 78; Allan 1999, 21). As an editor of the Toronto *Globe* put it in 1919, journalism "is not exactly a profession, not exactly a trade, not always a means of livelihood" (cited in Rutherford 1982, 78). This notion that reporting was not a permanent occupation or that it was the vocation of young writers aspiring to something better served to keep work insecure and wages low, and perhaps even justified these conditions.

In 1928, the International Labour Organization conducted the first study of rank-and-file journalists, surveying media organizations in thirty-three countries in Europe and the Americas. The report found that since the industrialization of the press, newspapers had become difficult places to work and to write. Reporters complained not only about low wages, insecurity, and poor working conditions, but also about the quality of the journalism they were producing. They felt that the growing size and conglomeration of media companies threatened their autonomy and freedom of expression. They were frustrated by their dependence on large organizations that could determine their working and living conditions (Hardt 2005, 7, 8). Journalists' "horror of dependence," writes Marianne Salcetti (1995, 58), "reinforced the spirit of individualism that has characterized reporters and their work."

Journalism has long sustained a tension between poor working conditions and reporters' enthusiasm for their work (Brennen 2008, 151). Journalists' passion for working at newspapers was steeped in romanticism that at times excused difficult working conditions. Despite low pay and lack of security, newswork carried a spirit of excitement that persists today. Reporters viewed their work as "an intellectual calling," a service performed on behalf of the public and carried out by the institutions for which they worked (De Weese, 1898, 451, cited in Solomon 1995, 124; Salcetti 1995, 55–7). Devotion to the mythology of journalism led journalists to identify more strongly with their publishers than with other workers at newspapers, such as printers and typesetters, the effects of which have been lasting (Brennen 2008, 151).

Reporters' proletarianization involved not only rationalizing their labour process but also standardizing the content of their work, which for writers is a critical component of the labour process. Historically, management has gained control over the labour process by gaining control over workers' speed and output, among both manual and nonmanual labourers (Braverman 1974). Control over journalists' work extended beyond rationalizing the speed and output of news, manifesting in what David Murphy (1991, 146) calls conceptual technologies, which changed the form of reporters' writing and challenged their autonomy. This understanding of technology, which Murphy and Yung-Ho Im (1997, 37–8) use to apply labour process theory to the work of journalism, extends beyond machine technology to refer to principles of rationality, efficiency, and accuracy, which culminated in the invention of objective reporting in the late nineteenth century (Murphy 1991, 143). Objectivity represented a shift from journalism as a form of political persuasion to journalism as presumably politically neutral and nonpartisan, which journalists interpreted to mean "accuracy, fairness, balance" (Bennett 2009, 187). The invention of objectivity, however, was largely a commercial decision that aimed to attract profits by making journalism seem "neutral and unbiased" (McChesney 2008, 28–9). Objectivity, which has endured as a core principle of ethical journalism, was invented to attain mass-market appeal.

As newspapers developed an economic model based on mass advertising, publishers needed to draw the large readerships advertisers demanded. Newspaper content would need to become more commercial and accessible to a general, nonspecialized reading public, or "politically heterogeneous audiences" (Carey 1963, 32). Thus, the commodification of news intensified, transformed from its status as a public service or a form of political persuasion into a marketable good designed to be produced efficiently and sold to the widest possible readership (Im 1997, 39). Although the introduction of objective reporting was presented as a hallmark of professional journalism based on ethics and public service, it was, fundamentally, an economic strategy based on capitalist logic of rationality and profitability (Carey 1963, 32–3).

Objective reporting practices defined and reinforced a particular notion of professionalism that aligned reporters with management. Publishers regarded professional journalists as those who received formal training; who were able to make decisions about news that were not based on the opinions of owners and advertisers; and who prevented their own opinions from seeping into their work (McChesney 2008, 29). Professional journalists would draw on no explicit ideology or political party, and would present all sides of an issue, providing readers with all the information necessary to understand that issue and decide for themselves what to make of it (McChesney 2008, 33; Hackett and Zhao 1998, 29). Reporters had to learn to report news without "prejudice, colour, and ... style," erasing any traces of their own voices (Schudson 1978, 77). Practically, this meant that writing was rationalized into the generic form of the news story organized around the five Ws (who, what, where, when, why) to make editing and typesetting efficient. The inverted pyramid structure of news writing became standard: an overview of the most important information in the first paragraph, with the rest of the information organized in descending order of importance so that paragraphs could be excised quickly to accommodate advertising (Murphy 1991, 144; Salcetti 1995, 57).

The "formularization of story telling" is a conceptual technology that exerts social control over journalists, who learn to internalize practices of making news marketable (Murphy 1991, 146, 144). As Im (1997, 39) writes, objective reporting requires journalists to "lose the subjective nature of the craft" by "surrender[ing] control over the idea, conception, or goal of their work." Journalistic skill came to be defined by an ability to participate in the mass production of standardized news, objectively reported. As Peter Dreier (1978, 75) puts it, "The norms and procedures of daily journalism rendered the journalist little more than what one reporter labelled a 'glorified tape recorder,' with little ability to use his/her own expertise in deciding what was and wasn't news." As Robert Hackett and Yuezhi Zhao (1998, 36–7) note, this standardization, which they call "facticity," "could be a harsh discipline, often at odds with [journalists'] own desire[s] to develop a distinctive narrative style." Journalists were disciplined if they defected from the rules – for example, the use of words forbidden by editors and publishers could lead to docked pay (37).

The proletarianization of journalists and the standardization of their work provides a specific example of the degradation of the work of writing, what James Carey (1963, 32) calls "a conversion downwards" for journalists. Formulaic writing challenged writers' independence and encouraged them to produce "(interchangeable) technical expertise at the expense of (unique) intellectual contributions" (Hardt 1990, 360). Journalists began to transmit the news rather than serve a more intellectual or literary role as an interpreter or critic (Carey 1963, 32). This frustrated newsworkers, many of whom continued to be unhappy with their anonymity, wage dependency, and routine working conditions (Smythe 1980). Even as reporters gained more professional status and improved working conditions, the contradiction of professional writing was sustained: "The 'rise' of the reporter into an emerging professional class also meant their 'fall' into a white-collar industrial proletariat" (Kaul 1986, 47).

Such experiences point to the allure that escaping the drudgery of newsroom labour held for journalists, many of whom wanted to pursue the more creative or literary forms of writing found in magazines and books, or to reclaim the autonomy of writing and control over their labour process and the content of their work. For many journalists, freelance writing has long offered relief from the daily grind of newspaper reporting, along with the promise of "greater literary and personal freedom" (Drobot and Tennant 1990, xv). Catherine McKercher (2014, 219) emphasizes the "romantic cachet" of freelance journalism: "It promises no bosses, no shiftwork and no petty office politics. It holds out the possibility of writing about what you want and when you want, the prospect of a front-row seat on history, and the promise of a big payoff when you land the big story." In writer Val Clery's words, freelance magazine writing can be viewed as "a temporary limb of opportunity between the well-paid tyranny of daily newspapers and the ill-paid longueurs of literature" (cited in Sutherland 1989, 9). Writes Charles Rogers (1931, 246), it "provides the most precarious living, but it would appear from the testimony of some who engage in it, the most fun." Freelance work can also represent a more politicized conception of work and how it should be organized. For example, Andrew Beck (2003a, 4) notes that freelance cultural work could be viewed as "labour at the margins" or, at the same time, "a last space of resistance" in corporatized cultural production. As Bill Ryan (1992, 141) remarks, one of the rewards of freelancing is escaping the wage-labour relationship. Through Ryan's tracing of the transformation of art and artistic practice into the capitalist cultural industries, it is obvious that journalism has been severed from its historical ties to art forms, to writing as literary practice. Freelancers have tried to restore these ties by regaining their status as independent workers and remaining outside of an employment relationship.

Abandoning newswork for more autonomous forms of work was only one strategy. Many left journalism altogether (Solomon 1995, 126). Others found their way around rules and standard practices, relied on individual coping methods, or adapted to challenging conditions (Smythe 1980, 8; Solomon 1995, 126). A more effective strategy, following familiar patterns of labour unrest and dissatisfaction in other industries, was to organize collectively into unions.[5] And although unionization raised journalists' standards of living and improved working conditions, transforming journalism from a low-status job into a middle-class occupation, journalists struggled to define their occupational identity throughout this process, ultimately retaining a professional identity that has shaped contemporary organizing efforts. Rather than adopting a trade union identity that aligned them with the broader working class, journalists adopted a professional identity that they incorporated into their organizing efforts – often encouraged to do so by their employers – which, at times, eclipsed their identity as workers.

FREELANCERS AND THE REPROLETARIANIZATION OF JOURNALISTS

The 1960s brought about greater conglomeration in the cultural industries as industrial, financial, and business companies invested in media (Hesmondhalgh 2007, 58–9). Growth and conglomeration intensified in the 1970s and into the 1980s and 1990s, with the onset of increased globalization and internationalized trade; policy deregulation, privatization, and liberalization; flexibilized production; and corporate restructuring, culminating in the creation of contemporary "networked media industries," or large, concentrated companies with interests in a range of media products, platforms, and technologies (Winseck 2011). In Canada, magazines transformed from independent or family-run businesses to corporate-owned titles that belong to the largest media companies in the country. Changes in the way culture is produced and brought to market transformed the labour and social relations of cultural production. These changes include the massive expansion of the cultural industries, not only in terms of growth in the size of corporations and profits, but also in terms of their shift toward the centre of the economies of many Western capitalist states (Hesmondhalgh 2007, 1). Publishers now belong to large conglomerates with diverse media holdings. Since the 1970s, media firms of all sizes have operated in the context of intensifying globalized and internationalized trade, expanding consumer markets, flexibilized production, and a push toward lean production models. These are the conditions in which a growing number of freelancers now strive to earn a living.

Tracing a history of freelance writing as an occupation demonstrates continuities through change in media industries and freelance work. Freelance journalism is an old and historically insecure, low-paid, and low-status occupation for the majority of writers. Writers' opportunities for employment expanded greatly with the growth of industrialized newspaper publishing, but most experienced proletarianization and forms of ideological control in the employ of powerful newspaper publishers. The historical account of the degradation of journalistic labour in newspapers positions freelancing as a form of resistance, or at the very least, relief, from such conditions: a way for journalists to gain control over their labour process and the terms of commodification of their labour power. In a historical sense, freelancing can be understood as an attempt to resist proletarianization. However, from scattered historical accounts of freelancers as workers, it is clear that few were able to make a living from writing alone and that they have always occupied positions on the margins of the media labour force. The freelance labour model as a way to organize media production developed from a necessity or habit during the beginnings of Canada's magazine publishing industry into a core business model in contemporary media production, as companies grow, consolidate, and trim their workforces. In the contemporary era, freelancing is a strategy of offloading the risks of media production onto individual workers, and freelance writing as an occupation is returning to its historical conditions of low wages, insecurity, and control consolidating in the hands of powerful publishers. The term proletarianization, which refers to the way workers are brought under the system of waged labour, may seem incongruent in the case of self-employed workers such as freelance writers, yet we can see the pressures of proletarianization re-emerge in their working conditions in the form of declining material conditions and power and control in the occupation overall. As journalism is increasingly produced outside of newsrooms and without hard-won union protections, freelancers are, in a sense, being reproletarianized.

Contemporary freelance writers' experiences must be understood in the context of a history of being perpetually undercompensated and undervalued, yet simultaneously attempting to gain autonomy and control over their work. As capitalism expanded, drawing writers into wage-labour relationships and standardizing their craft, writers attempted to step out of formalized employment relationships to reclaim control over the terms of commodification of their labour power and of their work. Under contemporary capitalism, as publishing industries reorganize to remain profitable, writers are once again being squeezed.

3

Freelancers' Dues:
Wages, Contracts, Copyright

"It's much easier to be a writer now. It's much more difficult to make a living at it."

Larry Goldbetter, National Writers Union president
(personal communication 2010)

Competing discourses swirl around print media industries in Canada: magazines and newspapers are long-suffering but important cultural resources, yet are also lucrative brands that are part of large, profitable, and growing media corporations. While the first claim is used to justify low pay and rights-grabbing freelance contracts, the second is a more accurate reflection of contemporary Canadian media industries. Despite panicked accounts of declining advertising revenues and readership rates, newspaper companies in Canada remain profitable (Statistics Canada 2016). Canada's magazine industry has grown from a small sector run by individuals and independent companies into a vital segment of the networked media economy, fuelled by advertising revenue and government support and integrated into large media conglomerates. Media production in Canada is dominated by networked media industries, or concentrated firms run as "network[s] of media tied together through strategies, capital investment, ownership, technologies, uses, alliances, rights regimes and so on" (Winseck 2011, 3). Although Canada has a vibrant small magazines sector, constituted by hundreds of independently run publications that operate on small budgets, many of which are not-for-profit, sole-proprietor, literary, activist, or volunteer-run projects, the largest magazines in terms of circulation and revenue are owned by a few corporations with a diverse range of business interests and an aggressive focus on the bottom line. As I argue in this chapter, although magazine publishers remain profitable actors in Canada's media economy, the writers who fill their pages face stagnating and declining rates of pay and restrictive, rights-grabbing contracts, making it impossible for freelancers to earn a living writing just for Canadian magazines and signalling a deepening power imbalance between freelancers and publishers.

The concept of networked media industries captures transformations in the media industry, including the push by media firms beginning in the late 1990s to be "reconceived" as a "portfolio of assets," comprised of distinct departments competing with one another within single corporations (31, 33). Just as newspaper chains' business models rely on sharing content across publications, magazines play a strategic role as a source of material for networked media companies' range of products and services, which include digital advertising, syndication, and cross-platform activities. Commercial magazine publishing in Canada has been folded into large, highly capitalized corporations, yet magazines are still considered important cultural institutions rather than commodities produced primarily to deliver audiences to advertisers. A labour-of-love discourse tends to eclipse frank conversations about the publishers for which writers work.

The scope and revenue of the companies that own magazines stand in contrast to their appeals to government funding bodies, which continue to frame the magazine sector as a fragile industry that primarily aims to foster Canadian culture and is threatened by American competitors (TCI Management Consultants 2008). Consider, for example, one of the largest magazine publishers in Canada, Rogers Communications Inc., which produces media (over forty consumer and trade magazines, including the highest-circulating titles in the country; more than fifty radio stations nationally; major television broadcasting networks; and online publications), owns the Toronto Blue Jays Baseball Club and the Rogers Centre (formerly the Sky-Dome), and dominates television, Internet, and mobile telecommunications provision (Rogers Communications Inc. 2015). Rogers earned $12.9 billion in revenue in 2014, resulting in $5 billion operating profit (25). Although its media arm constitutes 14 per cent of

firm revenue (3 per cent of profit), media brings in $1.8 billion an-
nually. Publishing constitutes 11 per cent of that revenue (26–7), and
magazines provide the crucial material the company needs to meet
its stated goal of digitizing content to "offer advertising customers
more comprehensive audience solutions and reach" (Rogers Communications Inc. 2010, 41). Yet publishers across the industry continue to argue that magazines cannot afford to raise freelance rates
(Gardiola 2009).[1]

In a December 2014 roundtable interview about Canadian magazines on the public television program *The Agenda*, editors and publishers boasted of healthy circulations and stable profits. Steve
Maich, head of Rogers Media's publishing group, says that magazine readership is up but advertising revenue is down, which means
magazines publishers are strategizing new ways to monetize their
audience. Maich makes clear that magazines are commodities produced to generate audiences for advertisers and uses the term "consumer brand" in place of "magazine." In 2013, Rogers joined Next
Issue, a Netflix for magazines owned by the five largest publishers in
North America (Condé Nast, Hearst, Meredith, News Corp., and
Time Inc.) and private equity firm KKR & Co. LP. The all-you-
can-read service offers subscribers unlimited access to magazines
through tablets and smartphones for about ten to fifteen dollars per
month. Streaming or bundling magazines could prove very profitable for magazine publishers, as content is already paid for, and in-
tegrates magazine publishing into circuits of digital capitalism.
Notably, rates of pay for the original production of content have not
increased as freelancers' works get pushed to tablets, ereaders, and
mobile phones.

The other major corporations that dominate magazine publishing in Canada include TC Media, St Joseph Communications, Reader's Digest Association, and TVA Publications, a division of media
giant Quebecor Inc. Although these companies – along with
Rogers, known in the Canadian magazine industry as "the big five"
(Wager 2010) – earn more from their nonmagazine publishing
arms, their magazine ownership represents the largest slice of what
is still a profitable industry in Canada. Funding bodies and publishing association Magazines Canada promote the industry as
growing, profitable, and a generator of direct and indirect employment, rhetoric that is in part designed to attract advertisers and

shareholder investment and to confirm the necessity of government funding, but also is supported by industry-generated statistics (TCI Management Consultants 2008; Ontario Media Development Corporation 2009b; Magazines Canada 2010a). In 2011, Canadian periodicals earned $2.09 billion in operating revenue, with an operating profit margin of 7.1 per cent (Statistics Canada 2013), with the majority of industry profits going to the largest publishers (Magazines Canada 2010b).

As part of networked media firms, magazines are increasingly oriented to commercial interests and articles are purchased from freelancers to serve multiple platforms. Publishers' pressure to lower labour costs flows from magazines' lower profit margins compared to other media forms, volatile advertising revenues that fluctuate with global markets, high competition from American magazines sold in Canada, and the migration of advertising to digital media. Such challenges compel publishers to close magazines, lay off staff, and keep payments for freelancers low (TCI Management Consultants 2008; Ontario Media Development Corporation 2009a, 4). Publishers consistently lobby governments to increase funding and make claims about the importance of quality content to the industry's success, yet their requests for investment exclude paying the people who produce that content (but include paying for mailing costs, research, marketing and promotions, online presence, and "brand extension activities") (TCI Management Consultants 2008, ii). Publishers continue to draw on discourses of nationalism and economic uncertainty to keep payments to freelance writers low and to treat content as raw material for the ongoing generation of surplus value. Relying on freelancers is a central strategy for publishers to remain profitable in an industry contingent on technological change and consumer tastes and dependent on fickle advertising revenue.

The result is the devaluing and deskilling of freelancers' labour and the degradation of the works they produce. Freelancers for magazines and newspapers contribute to sectors of the economy that are profitable, highly concentrated, and, in the case of magazines, promoted as a key and vibrant aspect of Canadian culture (Magazines Canada 2011). Yet the industry is concentrated and highly competitive, resulting in heightened efforts to lower production costs, which puts pressure on freelancers' rates of pay, working conditions, and the terms under which they are contracted. Freelancers' circumstances are the result of decisions made about how to publish magazines as commodities, not the inexorable result of technological change or of individual freelancers' choices.

In this chapter, I trace the process and practices in print-based media that have shaped the work of freelance journalism in Cana da over the past few decades, primarily low rates of pay and restrictive contracts that demand escalating rights to writers' work without adequate compensation. (In chapter 5, I focus on conditions in digital journalism.) As a result, freelancers face low incomes, a diminishing capacity to produce journalism, and declining control over their work. Such precarious conditions undermine the autonomy freelance work promises. As freelance journalists demonstrate, exiting an employment relationship – or being denied one, as is rapidly becoming the norm – does not mean leaving exploitation and the labour-capital relation behind. Rather, freelance work arrangements permit capital to accelerate the exploitation of labour power.

FLEXIBILIZATION
AND THE SPREAD OF FREELANCE WORK

A major effect of transformations in cultural industries over the past few decades has been the spread of precarious forms of employment as firms outsource work that was formerly produced in-house, purchasing articles from freelancers or hiring workers on contract or as needed. As I demonstrated in chapter 2, these practices have always existed in magazine publishing and other cultural industries, but have become more entrenched in recent decades. Workers in precarious forms of employment now perform a growing portion of work in media, journalism, publishing, and the cultural and entertainment industries (Walters, Warren, and Dobbie 2006; Spilsbury 2013; Hill 2014). Precarious forms of employment have obvious benefits for employers, including lower labour costs; no responsibility for training, overhead, or benefits; and offloaded risk to a legion of skilled workers hustling to sell their works. A growing segment of cultural work is characterized by insecurity, intense competition, low wages, project-based work, dependence on social networks and connections, and fewer people doing more work for longer hours (McRobbie 2002b; Murdock 2003; Ross 2009a).

Although many say they freelance by choice, freelancing has rapidly become the only option available for those who want to work in journalism, particulary for those who want to write (McKercher 2009; Walters, Warren, and Dobbie 2006; Nies and Pedersini 2003). While many journalists report choosing to work freelance, others can only find freelance work. As one freelancer I surveyed notes: "After graduating from university and then a college course, I thought I would freelance 'until something else came along,' but there has been more and more freelance work and fewer other options ... Contracts that involve writing and research have been easy to get whereas other kinds of work (even full-time writing work) has been elusive at best." Some have found that although they did not choose freelancing, it has grown on them. Another freelancer I surveyed says: "Once I got the momentum going, I found I quite liked it – and I wasn't willing to take just any job for the steady salary." Whether by choice or not, however, the decision to work freelance must be understood in the context of the reorganization of labour in media industries and in the labour market in general, spurred by technological change, neoliberal policies, and deregulated labour markets, and evident in the ongoing shift from standard employment relationships to precarious forms of employment, including part-time, casual, temporary, self-employed, and freelance (Örnebring 2009; Lewchuk et al. 2014).

Although the freelance workforce worldwide is growing, it is difficult to accurately count the number of people who work as freelance journalists. The 2011 Canadian census shows 13,280 people working as journalists in Canada, 1,975 of them self-employed, with the vast majority not incorporated businesses – in other words, truly working for themselves (Statistics Canada 2011c). However, Statistics Canada's National Occupational Classification means that there are likely overlaps between those in the "self-employed journalists" and in the "authors and writers" categories (any nonnews journalistic writing falls into the latter). Of the 24,355 authors and writers working in Canada, 11,665 are self-employed. Statistics Canada tracks periodical sales, operating expenses, total wages paid, and profit margins in the magazine industry, but does not count the number of writers freelancing, nor the number of freelance contributions to publications. Claims about numbers of freelancers vary. For example, Magazines Canada (2008) estimates that 5,000 freelancers (including writers, editors, photographers, designers, and illustrators) work in magazines, while the Canadian Freelance Union estimates that there are around 10,000 freelance writers in Canada, contributing to outlets that extend beyond magazines (Michael OReilly, personal communication 2010). In the United States, the Bureau of Labor Statistics (unpublished tabulations from the Current Population Survey 2015) reports there are 80,000 "news analysts, reporters and correspondents," of which 8,000 are self-employed, and 221,000 "writers and authors," of which 90,000 are self-employed. Of the 60,000 journalists working in Britain, 28 per cent are self-employed, up from 21 per cent in 2001 (Spilsbury 2013, 7). The European Federation of Journalists (n.d.) claims that "in many countries the majority of journalists are freelancers," both through actual self-employment and through employers misclassifying employees as freelancers.

Technological developments have made it possible for anyone, in theory, to become a freelance journalist, and have made it easier than ever before for organizations to outsource writing and reporting. The tools required for journalistic work, such as access to press releases, newswire services and archives, interviews with experts, and other research tools, are now widely available to anyone with Internet access, no longer restricted to those who physically work in a newsroom (McChesney 2013). This development has made it easier for firms to contract out work and to expect freelancers to produce the same calibre of reporting as in-house journalists (ILO 2000). No certification or training requirements are necessary to work as a journalist. Unlike occupations historically considered to be professions, such as law and medicine, journalists are better conceived of as semi-professionals, for whom it is difficult to monopolize the labour market in order to establish occupational standards and control labour supply (Benner 2002, 134).

No specific technical training is required to work as a freelance writer. As Charles Rogers remarked in 1931, "a person becomes [a freelance writer] when he prepares a manuscript and submits it for publication" (248). Since technically anyone can become a freelancer provided they can write and negotiate the informal entry routes into the occupation, freelancers have no way to limit access via skills training, closed shops, or certification. Such an ultra-competitive climate makes it difficult for writers as individuals to ask for higher rates of pay and to collectively organize. Writers are acutely aware that many people, usually new writers or recent journalism-school graduates, are willing to work for low or no pay to gain the much-desired exposure required to build a reputation that can lead to paying work. One editor described this phenomenon as the "'if you don't want to do it at that price, I know others who will' syndrome" (cited in Tunstall 1996, 170–1). A journalist goes so far as to call new graduates "that fresh new crop of scabs the J-schools unleash each year" (Crysler 2005, 57). Many attribute the growing number of journalists looking for work to an abundance of post-secondary journalism programs. Despite tumult in the industry, journalism schools in Canada, the United States, and the United Kingdom continue to be oversubscribed, leading one journalism professor to describe them as "a growth industry" (cited in Charbonneau 2013). Currently, fifty programs at universities and colleges in Canada grant certificates, bachelor's, and master's degrees in journalism. In 2013, in Ontario alone, about 1,600 people were enrolled in journalism school (ibid.). Overall, journalism maintains low barriers to entry and many people want to work as journalists, challenging freelancers' abilities to demand higher wages or effectively withdraw their labour power. Someone else is always ready and willing to work, often for less pay.

The increase in journalism produced by freelancers in a time of media abundance is symptomatic of the deepening and normalization of precarious employment in media and cultural industries. And while cultural industries, especially magazines, have long relied on freelance and other nonstandard forms of employment, in recent decades these industries have grown in size and scope on a lean business model: production organized around a small core of secure workers and a larger, growing periphery of freelance, casual, and temporary workers hired as needed or for one-off projects. As the media industry responded to the 2008 economic crisis, advertising revenue declined, thousands of workers were laid off, and many turned to freelancing. While accurate numbers are difficult to obtain, reports show ongoing lay-offs in Canadian newspapers, broadcasting, and magazines in recent years, including at the Canadian Broadcasting Corporation (which cut 657 jobs in 2014), and Postmedia, Quebecor, and Torstar, which offered buyouts to 1,050 workers in 2011 (Dobby 2014; *Globe and Mail* 2011; Canadian Press 2011). The Canadian Media Guild estimates that 3,000 media workers were laid off between January and April 2009 (Hackett and Anderson 2010, 2). An American report on job loss in print media is extreme: "From 2003 to 2012, the American Society of News Editors documented a loss of 16,200 full-time newspaper newsroom jobs while *Ad Age* recorded a decline of 38,000 magazine jobs, which includes all jobs for the entire consumer magazine sector" (Jurkowitz 2014). The American Society of News Editors reports that 3,800 full-time positions in newsrooms were cut in 2014 and shows a dramatic decline in the newsroom workforce between 2005 and 2015, from over 55,000 workers to under 35,000 (Edmonds 2015). While many journalists find other work, some at new, expanding digital-first journalism organizations (several American digital media companies have set up shop in Canada), many more are absorbed into the freelance pool.

Magazine editors have offered many justifications for their historic reliance on freelancers, including an argument for maintaining editorial variety and quality: "Many editors believe that at least part of their magazines must be produced by freelancers because magazines produced solely by staff writers and contract writers often seem stale and lacking the freshness of view that outsiders can provide" (Rivers and Work 1986, 11). But what developed as tradition or habit has become a strategy critical to minimizing the costs of content as media companies shed already-lean workforces. Such conditions have increased the number of people who work freelance, intensified competition for work, and lowered wages, a pattern of labour oversupply and wage depression evident in a growing number of cultural industries (Smith and McKinlay 2009b, 40). In the United Kingdom, an organizer with the National Union of Journalists anticipates that soon the majority of media workers will be freelancers (personal communication 2010), and Canadian media unions have been strategizing for several years on how best to represent this growing yet unorganized segment of the media workforce. Workers' and journalists' organizations need to directly address the rise of a freelance labour force, as freelance work is a core component of publishers' business models, especially for online publications, which can be launched with small staffs and the knowledge that many skilled freelancers are ready and available to provide a steady stream of writing at low cost. The freelancers I surveyed report that there is no shortage of work available, as firms prefer outsourcing to freelancers over hiring employees. The commuter news-paper *Metro*, for example, is the most-read daily paper in Canada but does not produce its own articles nor employ "a single reporter or writer," relying instead on freelancers and copy from other papers and newswires (Brown 2011). As I examine in chapter 5, the *Huffington Post* employs very few journalists relative to its size and reach, and instead relies on free content generated from thousands of bloggers, wire copy, other news sources, and readers. Under new conditions of digital news production, freelance and unpaid work are becoming acceptable and normalized. As the saying goes, there are no jobs, yet there is a lot of work (Vosko 2000, 230). That there is a lot of work, however, does not alleviate freelancers' income and employment insecurity.

FREELANCE INCOME AND PAY

Despite its growth as an occupation globally, freelance writing is a form of precarious employment. The most recent comprehensive survey of Canadian freelance writers shows that incomes – historically low to begin with – are shrinking. The survey, conducted by the Professional Writers Association of Canada (PWAC),[2] finds that in 2005, freelancers earned an average of just over $24,000 before tax. McKercher (2009, 371) notes that this data was collected "in the midst of an economic boom and, one might think, the best of times for freelancers." Ten years earlier, writers' incomes were slightly higher, averaging $26,500 before tax. In 1979, freelancers' average income was about $25,000 (PWAC 2006, 12), which means freelance writers' earnings have been stagnant for over three decades. Accounts of low pay are reflected in my survey: 45 per cent of respondents earned under $20,000 (before tax) from freelance writing in 2009, 18 per cent earned between $20,000 and $30,000, 12 per cent between $30,000 and $40,000, 12 per cent between $40,000 and $50,000, 7 per cent between $50,000 and $75,000, and a combined 7 per cent between $75,000 and $150,000. Of the writers I surveyed, 71 per cent say that freelance writing is their main job. In the United Kingdom, the Authors' Licensing and Collecting Society (2014) surveyed 1,250 freelance newspaper and magazine writers with an average of eighteen years of industry experience. Its report finds that 58 per cent earn less than £8,200 per year from writing – about $16,000 in Canadian dollars (3) – while 77 per cent say their income is not high enough to support themselves and their dependents and 78 per cent have second jobs (2). As the report notes, "The majority of respondents felt that the initial fee did not fairly compensate them for the work undertaken in producing the article" (4).

Although all journalists' incomes in the United Kingdom, the United States, and Canada are in decline relative to inflation and overall wages (Spilsbury 2013; Bach 2014; Cohen et al. 2014), freelancers' incomes are considerably lower than those of staff journalists, many of whose wages are determined by collective agreements. As Catherine McKercher (2009, 371) points out, in the year PWAC (2006) conducted its research, a full-time reporter at the *Ottawa Citizen* or *Montreal Gazette* earned at least $63,500. A 2008 survey of salaries at Canadian magazines, conducted by Canada's Cultural Human Resources Council, indicates that staff writers can earn $45,835 at consumer magazines (Mercer 2009, 5). Wages for freelance writers, who were not mentioned in the report, are low in comparison, especially considering their typically high skill and education: 61 per cent of respondents to my survey hold a bachelor's degree and 27 per cent hold a master's degree. The National Union of Journalists reports that freelancers often have more experience and skill than the people for whom they work, yet a notion that freelancers are "amateurs or failed staffers" persists (Christie 2004, 8). A freelancer I surveyed notes that freelance pay is low because of "a stereotype that freelancers are amateurs, newbies, or hobbyists, rather than professionals, some with decades of experience."

Freelance writers' incomes have dramatically decreased amid rising costs of living and inflation and relatively consistent profitability in media industries (Winseck 2010; Statistics Canada 2011a, 2011b). As PWAC (2006, 12) notes, "Independent writers in Canada have watched their standard of living drop by more than 60 percent in one generation." Of writers I surveyed, 57 per cent report that low pay is a major issue of concern and, more broadly, 45 per cent note that economic instability is a major issue. One shares what is likely a widespread experience: being paid so little that her hourly pay works out to be less than minimum wage. An American investigative reporter with twenty years of experience describes his economic situation: "I exist only on social security, food stamps, Medicaid ... I live in one room and buy clothes at thrift shops. As a prize-winning investigative journalist,

I find this disgusting" (Project Word 2015, 12). In a survey of Canadian magazine industry workers, including CEOs, publishers, editors, staff, photographers, and freelance writers, respondents listed "insufficient pay for freelance work" as a top issue of concern (Scott 2009, 16). While commentary in popular media assumes that journalism is inherently low paid, freelancers' low incomes can be attributed to the form their payments take, the arbitrary nature of pay, and power imbalances between writers and publishers.

Arbitrary Payments

As pieceworkers, freelance writers are paid either per word, per article, per hour, per project, or, as the unfortunate joke goes, "perhaps" (Kingston and Cole 1986). The per-word form of payment, common among magazines, newspapers, and some online outlets, does not account for all the work that goes into the writing of those words, including research, interviews, developing a pitch (which could range from a short email to an in-depth query letter), editing, rewriting, and additional tasks magazines now offload onto writers, such as producing information packages for fact checkers. Investigative journalism requires time for "false leads, arduous data searches, voluminous emails and phone calls, formal requests to obstinate government agencies, and sheer patience for the hunt" – time media outlets do not pay for (Project Word 2015, 15). A freelancer I surveyed notes, "The pay often does not reflect the work you put into a piece. You are expected to come up with ideas, research and pitch without pay, yet are not adequately compensated when your story ideas are accepted."

Freelance writing careers depend on a growing list of nonwriting tasks, including pitching, researching, interviewing, transcribing, editing and revising, self-promoting, networking and socializing with potential clients, and attending meetings, as well as professional development and business-related activities such as bookkeeping, doing taxes, invoicing, and chasing late payments. One freelancer notes that tackling "the mountains of paperwork" and navigating different invoicing systems is the most "time consuming and annoying" aspect of freelancing (Who Organizes Writers? 2014). Freelancers are not paid for these essential tasks. For nonjournalism work (for corporations and nonprofits, for example), writers charge a per-hour rate that can include some preparatory work such as re-search, editing, and attending meetings. However, a flat per-word or per-article fee is the dominant media freelance model and one that writers and their organizations increasingly view as unfair. An in-terview with editors in *Scratch*, a magazine about writing and money, underscores the arbitrariness with which editors make payment de-cisions. Explains Dan Kois, a senior editor at *Slate*: "I view my job from a financial standpoint as finding all the different reasons I can *not* pay you $500 if I can possibly get away with it ... a lot of things go into that decision, and some of it has to do with how much work the piece will require, and how long it's going to be and how badly I want it from a writing standpoint and how badly we need it from a traffic standpoint and how badly you need the money as a writer, as far as I can tell" (quoted in Friedman and Martin 2013). Paying per word enables publishers to avoid compensating writers for the full value of their labour time, enabling the exploitation of their non-waged labour time. Publishers get much more than they pay for: not only the words on a page, but the time it takes to think up those words, arrange them into sentences, conduct research and inter-views, and the multiplying other tasks required to maintain a free-lance career.

The form of journalism that suffers most from the freelance model is investigative reporting in the public interest, which is particularly expensive and time consuming. In a survey of 250 freelance inves-tigative reporters, Project Word (2015) found that most freelancers can no longer afford to do investigative journalism, as they are not paid for the time necessary to do core reporting and research, in-cluding "pursuing documents, cultivating sources, and travelling to report the story close up" (12). Of reporters, 69 per cent wrote for media outlets that did not cover their reporting expenses (16). In gen-eral, freelancers argue that piece and per-word rates do not accurate-ly reflect the value of their labour power. For some, this is because the ideas expressed by the words should carry some weight. Says free-lancer Scott Carney: "Word rates are based on an idea that all words are worth the same. Saying that an interview with some celebrity is worth the same as a seven-month embed in Afghanistan is ridicu-lous, and it's disgusting that magazines have been able to get away with valuing things [that way]. I say the piece from Afghanistan is actually worth more per word" (cited in Sillesen 2015).

In Canada, only 44 per cent of freelance writers surveyed in 2009 felt that per-word payments work "reasonably well" (Scott 2009, 25).[3] This is because rates at magazines and newspapers have not been raised since the 1980s, when experienced, in-demand writers could earn one dollar per word from the highest-paying consumer magazines. Today, the rate most Canadian freelancers aspire to is one dollar per word, but publications pay as little as ten cents per word (PWAC 2006, 23). Rates are higher in the United States, which has a much larger media market and where top-level national magazines pay about two dollars per word (Shafrir 2008). In their study of American freelance writers, Brian Massey and Cindy Elmore (2011, 678) report that of 101 survey respondents, the average income was US$44,000 to $50,000 per year. Yet Doree Shafrir (2008), who has worked as a freelance writer, calculates that someone writing solely for magazines would earn much less: "Even if a fledgling magazine writer were to write one 1,500-word feature a month for a national magazine – which would in itself be a difficult feat to pull off – he or she would be pulling in $36,000 a year before taxes. That's also assuming that none of the stories were killed or held and that everyone paid on time." A freelance investigative journalist says, "Even places that will pay $1/word, plus expenses, still amount to $3,000–6,000 at most, which is a pretty small amount for a story that can take upwards of a year to report and write. Not to mention that you get paid on publication, so what are you supposed to eat during the year of reporting and writing?" (Project Word 2015, 17). In such conditions, it is increasingly difficult for most to earn a living from freelance journalism alone, and freelancers increasingly do corporate or commercial writing or find part-time work teaching or in retail or service industries, highlighting interconnections between various forms of precarious work.

Pay Differentials

Freelancers' pay fluctuates between writers of various experience, geographic location, and capacity to negotiate. Earnings are also gendered. Women constitute the majority of respondents to both PWAC's report and to my survey – 72 per cent – yet women freelancers are paid less than men. PWAC's report (2006, 28) reveals that men receive higher average pre-tax earnings than women, despite an increase in women's per-word rate from seventy-eight cents in 2002 to ninety-two cents in 2005 (men's rose from eighty-three cents in 2002 to ninety cents in 2005). The report notes, "Although the average lowest rates per word earned by men and women have increased overall, the lowest rates are still consistently paid to women." Of my survey respondents, women earned less than men in every income category. Just over 49 per cent of women I surveyed earn under $20,000 versus 35.8 per cent of men, while 1.9 per cent of men and 0.7 per cent of women were in the highest income category ($150,000 or more).

Researchers have various explanations for why women in freelance cultural occupations are paid less than men. Incomes may vary depending on what publications and clients freelancers write for; men who only write for corporate clients would earn higher annual incomes than women who write for magazines, for example. Kerry Platman (2004, 584) notes that men are more prepared to "argue systematically for higher fees," which reflects arguments in PWAC's (2006) report. Others argue that despite a long history women are not taken seriously as writers, that women face historic patterns of being paid less than men in most occupations, and that white men are in positions of power in cultural industries and their networks of contacts are comprised of people similar to them, namely other white men, boosting their chances of success and higher incomes (Bielby and Bielby 1992; Byerly and Ross 2006; Gill 2002; Madison 2012). Among self-employed Canadians, men are more likely to say that "independence, freedom, and the ability to be one's own boss" motivated them to become self-employed, whereas "women are as likely to cite balancing work and family obligations ... as they are to cite independence and freedom" (Cranford et al. 2005, 12). Studies of freelancers in the United States and Sweden find that many women choose freelancing to better balance childcare and paid work (Massey and Elmore 2011; Edstrom and Ladendorf 2012; McKercher 2014), which may account for the higher number of women than men in self-employment overall (Vosko 2010, 171). Women's lower earnings can be attributed to bearing a larger proportion of household labour as well as the persistent historical assumption that women are secondary wage earners "and/or ... have alternative sources of subsistence beyond the wage" (Vosko 2000, 42). In the case of freelance writing, a notion that women do not need to earn a primary wage can combine with the assumption that freelance work is something one does in addition to other work, not as a breadwinning occupation. These assumptions raise a contradiction, as freelancing is also presented as a way for women to pursue economic independence and avoid gender-based barriers in the workplace (Massey and Elmore 2011).[4]

Power Imbalances

Although PWAC has developed payment guidelines for writers and publishers, it has no ability to enforce them, and the highly competitive nature of the media labour market provides publishers and editors with little incentive to raise fees. Most writers report earning ninety-nine cents per word at the top end of the scale, and thirty-five cents per word at the bottom (PWAC 2006, 23). Writers are able to charge higher rates per hour for corporate work, and trade bylines, creative freedom, and copyrights for higher pay. One writer says that the aspects of freelance writing that he enjoys most – "being able to set my own schedule, the pace of the work, and the material about which I write" – are also "the elements most often sacrificed when lucrative assignments arise." Freelancers increasingly view the work they do for magazines or newspapers, work that motivated them to become freelancers in the first place, as a luxury to indulge in when time and money permit. One freelancer wants to write for "reputable" newspapers but they do not pay enough to make the effort worthwhile: "In the 1990s approximately 90 per cent of my work was for newspapers. By 2000, 0% of my work was for newspapers. Magazines are getting nearly as bad, which is why I am now constantly seeking out corporate and teaching gigs."

Without a collective agreement, freelancers have no way to negotiate, enforce, or regulate a wage-effort bargain, of which how much they are paid for their work is a crucial component. Most freelancers have very little control over rates of pay. Only 20 per cent of those I surveyed set their own rates for most of their work, compared to 44 per cent whose rates are mostly set by the publications for which they write. Rates can be cut without warning or explanation. Freelancers are not paid extra for edits, revisions, or rewrites, and many publications do not have kill fees (payment for work completed but not published). When outlets cease publication, writers' outstanding invoices remain outstanding.

Low pay is exacerbated by the rising costs of freelancing. Like other independent contractors, freelancers pay for their own overhead and expenses, the costs of which increase with the advancement of technologies required to do the job. According to one romanticized view, in the 1930s a freelance writer needed only "a typewriter, a sheaf of paper, envelopes and stamps, and a resourceful mind" (Rogers 1931, 247). By 2010 writers required a home phone, mobile or smartphone, Internet connection, computer, scanner, printer, photocopier, digital recorder, and transcription service (ILO 2000; Wilson 2010), not to mention invoicing software and a personal website. Increasingly, outlets will not cover the expenses of producing investigative journalism, leaving freelancers to front the money themselves. Of the 250 investigative journalists Project Word surveyed, 85 per cent reported subsidizing their own work; 30 per cent put up more than US$5,000 annually to finance their reporting, and 10 per cent put up $100,000. Of those, 55 per cent were unable to earn their expenses back and at least 67 per cent report being in debt for between US$5,000 and $30,000 (Project Word 2014, 5, 12).

Adding to their up-front investment, freelancers have no guarantee of timely payment after completing an assignment. As one freelancer notes, "I'm generally paid six to eight weeks after publication, which is often six to twelve weeks after the work was submitted." Payment schedules are inconsistent among publications, even between those owned by large chains. Some outlets pay upon acceptance of a pitch, some after an article is published, and some only after all other bills are paid. A 2009 study reveals that only 54 per cent of freelancers were satisfied with "receiving timely payment" (Scott 2009, 19). Writers must often chase late payments, making time-consuming phone calls and emails to editors. Delayed and missing compensation is so common that one freelancer describes being paid on time as "an amazing surprise" (cited in Dieker 2014).

Overall, freelance wages do not reflect the labour effort and time necessary to work as a writer. Many hours of unpaid working time go into the production of writing and the maintenance of a freelance career, which represents intensified exploitation of writers by media corporations. Media companies are able to decrease payments for writers' labour time, increasing the surplus value extracted from their works. The remuneration of those works does not account for the labour time or tasks necessary to produce them. Writers' compensation is based on an arbitrary valuation of a piece of work, delivered in piecemeal payments tied to word counts or column inches. Remuneration is also based on shifting notions of value itself. For media companies, especially major publishers, content is now valued more for its ability to attract advertisers, page impressions online, and potential cross purposing than for its quality of writing, ideas, or social function. These changes in publishing practices, many of which I review in chapter 5, affirm that the motor of profit propels freelancers' experiences, shaping the kind of writing it is possible to produce and the conditions under which freelancers work.

CONTROL AND POWER RELATIONS IN FREELANCE RELATIONSHIPS

Although it is often noted – indeed, assumed, accepted, and even embraced – that writers, artists, and cultural workers earn low wages, this statement is often divorced from any context as to why, which limits inquiry into how certain types of work are valued and remunerated. As Marx shows us, wages are not naturally determined, but rather socially determined, bound up in a labour-capital relationship wherein workers and owners struggle for control over surplus value, shaped by power relations, competition, and changing notions of value. Freelancers' pay rates stem from the political and economic decisions publishers make about how to value writers' work (D'Agostino 2010, 239).

Most writers neither have power individually nor are collectively positioned to demand increased payments that match their skill or time invested in their work. And writers are sensitive to this power imbalance: 83 per cent of those I surveyed believe that rates are low because publishers can get away with low rates. One editor was told by another that "we underpay [writers] because we can," making the point that unlike other suppliers (printers, landlords, the postal service, for example), freelancers do not contest low rates because they are acutely aware that they can be replaced (freelance writers' email list, 20 February 2008). Editors and publishers trade on writers' passion for their craft and desires for fulfilling and meaningful work. These power relations were made explicit to one experienced writer after a major magazine had not paid him two months after he submitted an invoice. As he recounts, "I complained yet again to the editor-in-chief who told me, in a peevish tone, that I should be grateful the publisher was willing to provide such a welcom[ing], high-profile outlet for good journalism" (freelance writers' email list, 12 March 2007). This is a common example of what freelancers face.

Existing writers' organizations can only advise on pay, leaving individual writers to negotiate on their own behalf. Only 13 per cent of survey respondents do negotiate; most accept the fees editors or publishers offer. Some writers do not negotiate because they lack the confidence needed to push for higher pay. Due to the isolated nature of freelancing, many freelancers do not know what others earn or what they could potentially be paid. Many are reluctant to negotiate because they do not want to risk damaging relationships with publications, either because they have friendly, collaborative relations with editors or because they are aware that securing assignments, especially repeat assignments, depends on personal relationships (Ekinsmyth 2002). No one wants to be marked as "difficult" in a small, competitive industry built on reputation and social ties. This fear is especially prevalent among new writers. As one says, "I feel as if I could never negotiate rates because of my newbie fear that no one will want to work with me ... I have recently run into a problem of not being paid two to three months after the article has hit newsstands. It's really awkward, because it is such a small industry and people do talk. I never want to upset anyone or have my name start to be attached to phrases like 'difficult to work with'" (freelance writers' email list, 22 November 2007). Ekinsmyth (2002, 237) argues that rate negotiations between freelance writers and editors are particularly fraught, oscillating between relations of friendship and business. The freelancers she interviewed disliked negotiating pay because it embarrassed them to discuss such matters with people they considered friends. The embedded nature of freelance-editor relationships, or the fact that social and collegial friendships are mired in business relationships, serves to maintain unequal power relationships between labour and capital, with freelancers in a weaker position (237).

Overall, freelance writers I surveyed report having "total" control over their writing process (80 per cent), their workspace (81 per

cent), and their time (55 per cent). They have "some" control over the
stories they write (66 per cent), the publications they write for (48
per cent), their income (70 per cent), their rates of pay (64 per cent),
and the way their final piece is published (78 per cent). Although
few report having no control over these aspects of their work, these
responses demonstrate that control and autonomy is contested in
freelance relationships, shaped by power relations that structure the
industry. Writers' rates are constantly under pressure, both from a
"culture of employment insecurity" (Ekinsmyth 2002, 235) in media
industries that encourages them to undervalue their labour and consent to low or no wages, as well as from changing corporate practices
and new business models made possible by developing technologies. In particular, digital technologies are putting new pressures on
copyright and contracting practices, enabling media companies to
gain unprecedented control over writers' works.

CONTESTED COPYRIGHT AND CONTRACTS

Freelancers' livelihoods in a digital age are built on the shaky foundations of copyright protection, which are being eroded by corporations' escalating demands for control over writers' intellectual
property. Copyright has emerged as a high-stakes site of struggle for
cultural workers across a range of industries, as digital technologies
provide new ways to extract surplus value from workers who have
relative autonomy in the labour process. Although copyright
regimes have always embodied tensions between protecting the
rights of those who create original works and the companies that
bring those works to market, the balance of power is shifting as publishers aggressively pursue rights to writers' works as a key component of firms' accumulation strategies.

As independent contractors, freelancers own the copyright to the
articles they write. Under Canadian copyright law, unless they stip-
ulate otherwise, authors own their intellectual property. Publishers
are granted a limited licence to publish articles in designated outlets
for specified periods of time, but authors retain outright ownership
(Canada 1985, s.13; D'Agostino 2004, 6). In contrast, staff writers are
employees. In exchange for salaries and other benefits associated
with an employment relationship, employees do not own the rights
to the works they produce while employed (D'Agostino 2010, 4).

Traditionally, this arrangement has been one of the benefits writers gained from freelancing and has enabled freelance writers to resell articles in various markets and formats to boost their incomes, in some way compensating for low rates of pay (Lorinc 2005, 37; PWAC 2006, 41). Even if writers did not resell articles, the right to do so at the very least gave them a sense of agency over their works, over where their articles are published, over the results of their creative labour, and over their careers. However, traditional practices are being undermined by new uses of technologies and publishers' aggressive attempts to control copyrights.

The practice of demarcating ownership over intellectual property emerged in Europe in the sixteenth and seventeenth centuries at the behest of book publishers seeking to retain control over printing and distributing books, which at the time were being widely copied, cutting into publishers' profits (D'Agostino 2010, 42). Since its beginnings, copyright law has served primarily as a protection for publishers, giving the right to own and exploit literary works to the media-owning capitalist class (Bettig 1996, 17). Although copyright laws "firmly fix[ed] the idea of copyright as an author's right" (23), they have, historically, been primarily rights for publishers (Drahos 1996, 100; McLeod 2001, 26). This history, outlined by Martha Woodmansee (1984), Ronald Bettig (1996), and Giuseppina D'Agostino (2010), demonstrates ongoing unequal power relations between publishers and writers, whose livelihoods depend on consenting to copyright laws and the market logic on which they are based. Unequal power relations are especially clear when copyright is considered through the lens of labour relations, which, to be sure, is not a dominant approach in the majority of debates over copyright and intellectual property.

A form of intellectual property, copyright is the legal protection of "the expression of one's ideas" (D'Agostino 2010, 16). Economists view copyright primarily as providing economic incentive for creators to produce intellectual and artistic works (Bettig 1996, 7); however, under the capitalist mode of cultural production, copyright's primary function is to guarantee its owner exclusive right to exploit the work. Copyright is a process of commodifying writers' labour and the works they create. It makes tangible the immaterial, transforming intellect, knowledge, ideas, and expressions into inputs for production (May 2002a, 41). As Christopher May (ibid., 73) argues, copyright enables employers in high-tech and information- and knowledge-intensive industries to continue historic patterns of Taylorization by using technological methods to gain ownership over workers' knowledge and skills.

For publishers, copyright has become a key source of surplus value from workers granted relative autonomy at the point of production. As I argued in chapter 1, publishers willingly grant freelancers control over most elements of how they work because the real value for corporations lies in the continued exploitation of completed works. As a respondent to my survey confirms, "No one cares where I am, just as long as I get the work done." Control over copyright enables media firms to expand their market power. Intensified competition in an era of globalized media production, the pressures of lean production, and opportunities for convergence presented by new technologies in networked media industries have compelled the publishing industry to develop into a "rights-buying business" whose primary concern is to "produce as much copyrighted material as possible" (D'Agostino 2010, 18, 25). For once an original work is created – and, as freelance rates demonstrate, for as little payment as possible – the cost of reproduction for publishers is minimal (Bettig 1996, 2). But the rewards are virtually limitless.

Many researchers, editors, and writers have blamed the development of the Internet and the growth of online publishing for limiting writers' abilities to resell their work in secondary markets. With information flowing freely across borders, it is difficult for writers to resell articles in different jurisdictions. The ease of cut-and-paste digital reproduction means that writers' works are often reprinted online without notice, consent, or attribution, let alone payment (Lorinc 2005, 39; PWAC 2006, 41). But technology alone is not to blame for writers' losses in the ongoing struggle to control and be fairly compensated for their work. Media corporations have used technology to transform the business of writing.

COPYRIGHT AND DIGITIZATION

The growth and consolidation of media and entertainment firms over the past twenty years is linked to the rapid development of technology, especially digital communications and the process of digitization. Digitization provides a universal language for media content and enables convergence across platforms, and as a result corporations can deepen the commodification and exploitation of communication resources and the labour that produces them (Mosco 2009). Digitization enables quick transmission of information and simplifies duplication, especially online, so publishers can repackage information in multiple formats. In this context, copyright enables publishers to extract profit from writers' works far beyond the initial fee, especially in the case of current contract regimes under which publishers claim the rights to "future freelance works in any media now known or unknown" (D'Agostino 2010, 241), which effectively expands possibilities for commodification and the generation of surplus value indefinitely.

Publishers began to harness the power enabled by digitization in the 1980s by placing writers' work in electronic databases, then licensing or selling the articles to third parties without additional compensation. Once in a database, works become "universally available with no further rights to the writer" (Woods Gordon 1984, 70). In the 1990s, faced with rapidly developing digital technologies and uncertainty about the future, publishers began to introduce contracts that claimed future rights to writers' works, even when publishers had no immediate use for them and even if the technologies required for extracting profit from those rights had yet to be invented (D'Agostino 2010, 25). This move took freelancers by surprise. Most were used to controlling their works and enjoyed cordial relationships with publishers. Suddenly, however, they began to see their works reproduced without their consent and without compensation, marking a troubling shift in the power relations between writers and publishers. Most periodical and newspaper publishers in Canada have grown into or been swallowed by converged media corporations that control a range of integrated media properties, hungry for content that can be repurposed for a range of platforms. This power shift is evident in rights and rates negotiations, which used to be conducted between writers and editors, who had amicable and mutually dependent relationships. Now, contracts are drafted in legal departments and handed down to editors from publishers.

Digitization helped corporations realize their ambitions of concentration and convergence, aided by and fuelling the push to obtain as much copyright from writers as possible, directly affecting freelancers' earnings (D'Agostino 2010, 20). Media concentration and chain ownership have shrunk the number of markets in which writers can resell work. A publisher that prints several editions of a magazine, for example, can purchase a story once for its Canadian edition and reprint the piece in editions worldwide, with no extra payment to the writer. Or, in the case of Canadian-owned media chains, publications purchase an article once and run that piece across the chain's platforms. These practices have grown more pervasive as they have moved online. An early example was revealing for freelancers. In fall 2010, Rogers Media began to syndicate articles that freelancers wrote for its magazines to Yahoo! and MSN. Writers were unaware that their articles were being republished as they either had not signed contracts permitting republication, or had only granted permission to reprint material for forty-five days (Scott 2010; Story Board 2010). Although Rogers editors were unaware that stories were being reprinted, executives had begun syndication as an initiative of Rogers Digital Media, which promotes access to its vast range of content to advertisers. Rogers Digital Media claimed the syndication was covered under the "promotions" clause in Rogers's newly introduced standard contract, which stated that Rogers can "publish the Work and/or an edited version thereof in any promotion of the publication and/or its brand in all forms of media" (Story Board 2010). Writers' organizations, however, claim that this was a broad interpretation of the contract: "Most contributors would not read 'promotion' as syndication on [websites] many months after their story first appears in a Rogers publication," argues Derek Finkle, founder of the Canadian Writers Group (Scott 2010). Finkle further notes that syndication without consent infringed on writers' moral rights, as writers' bylines appeared on versions of their work with which they may not have wanted to be associated. This example represents corporations' growing desires to own outright the rights to writers' works and to use them as they please. Contracts stipulating new copyright terms began to appear in Canada in the mid-1990s, a time when the industry standard meant printing a work once and negotiating all other rights – in other words, asking for permission and paying for what was published (Bettig 1996, 238; OReilly 1996; D'Agostino 2010, 201). The industry standard has changed and contracts have become more demanding and complicated.

COPYRIGHT AND CONTRACT REGIMES

Media companies' aggressive approaches to copyright have been developed and deployed through "non-negotiable standard form contracts" (D'Agostino 2010, 16) that can demand, for example, "all rights, in perpetuity, throughout the universe" (PWAC 2006, 35), rights for which publishers do not pay. Depending on the company and its media holdings, these rights can include translations, digitizations, adaptations, reprints, relicensing, promotions, and storage in electronic databases. In January 1995, British magazine chain EMAP Metro included a particularly shocking clause in its contract, claiming "ownership of the freelance[r]'s notebook, interview tapes, and the right to order all material connected with the commission deleted from the freelance[r]'s own work processor" (National Union of Journalists 2004, 17). Demands can be outrageous. One writer received a contract from "a major Washington, DC, media outlet with a global partner" that required freelancers to "acknowledge and respond to all e-mails within 48 hours" (Hutchins 2014). Another writes, "I've seen contracts that ask for theme park rights" (cited in Davis 2015).

Signing restrictive contracts – or any contract, for that matter – is a change for Canadian freelance writers. Freelance writing used to be governed by what Caves (2000, 14) calls "implicit contracts," based not on formalized terms but rather on "practices that are common knowledge in the community." Before the advent of digital publishing in the mid-1990s, writers rarely signed contracts; assignments were given with informal agreements on deadlines and word counts, under the assumption that unless otherwise negotiated, first publication rights were the only rights purchased (Lapointe 1996; D'Agostino 2005, 166). Even by the mid-2000s, contracts were uncommon (PWAC 2006, 37). In 1996, Southam Inc., which then owned most major daily newspapers in Canada, drew up a contract that asked freelancers for "one-time publication in all its newspapers in all its forms," which included emerging digital forms (Lapointe 1996). Writers' organizations, led by PWAC, began to pay attention to contracts, urged members to refuse to sign Southam contracts, and demanded higher payment for increased rights requests (Diamond 1996). This attitude was a far cry from the 1970s, when the former president of PWAC summed up how most writers at the time felt about copyright: copyright, he said, "is the most boring goddamned word in the world" (cited in Drobot and Tennant 1990, 117).

Although some publications still ask only for first publication rights, the dominant practice among large, converged media corporations is to purchase rights to articles as a bundle, which means paying a writer once to publish an article in print and online and then reusing it across the chain in various platforms and formats, including those yet to be invented (D'Agostino 2005, 166). One freelance writer refused to sign a contract with a newspaper that demanded not only all copyright, but also her moral rights, which grant authors the right to be identified by name and the "right to the integrity of the work," as noted in the Copyright Act, 1985. Under Canadian copyright law, moral rights cannot be assigned, but they can be waived, which effectively grants companies the ability to reconstitute works, remove bylines, and edit articles as they see fit without needing to consult the writer. The freelancer was offended by the demands. As she explains: "I don't want to lose control of my stories. I don't often resell stories, but I want to be able to have the option to say where my work is printed, and I also feel a sense of obligation to my interviewees, whose words are part of the story and therefore I want to be accountable to them about where their words end up. I am not sure how much longer I can freelance with this kind of market restriction" (personal communication 2012). She tried to negotiate the moral rights clause with her editor, but was told it was not negotiable. She refused to sign and lost the income from her assignments and the possibility of future work from the paper.

The contracts freelance writers are presented with are lengthy – sometimes longer than the articles they are drafted to cover – and written in complex, difficult-to-parse legalese. They are generally non-negotiable. Publishers enjoy powerful advantages over individual writers, who do not have access to legal departments and who depend on publishers for future work (D'Agostino 2010, 253). As Laura Murray and Samuel Trosow (2007, 135–6) note, "The increasingly standard publisher demand for an exclusive grant of all rights represents a unilateral change to traditional industry practice. It is backed by bargaining power, not by anything in the Copyright Act." Indeed, in a thorough review of the legal theory of copyright law, D'Agostino (2010, 251) recognizes that at the heart of the struggle over copyright lies "inequality [in] bargaining power" between freelancers and publishers. Freedom of contract, which has been the foundation of copyright law, assumes that both freelancers and publishers willingly enter into a contract and that freelancers are "capable of entering into their own bargains to maximize their self-interest" (251). These assumptions do not account for the imbalance in power relations between individual freelancers and publishers, rendering freedom of contract an "illusory" concept for freelancers, who depend on publishers to bring their works to market and who have little choice but to sign non-negotiable standard form contracts that strip them of their rights and potential to earn income from their labour (251). In the context of a growing supply of freelance labour, publishers wield considerable power and the onus remains with freelancers to "'opt out' of giving away rights that were theirs to begin with" (281).

The power imbalance is most explicitly demonstrated in the practices of the largest publishing corporations. In September 2009, Transcontinental Media, which at the time published over thirty magazines,[5] introduced a new contract for its magazine writers. Called the Author Master Agreement, the contract notes that the creator "retain[s] the copyright ownership of each Work that you provide subject only to the rights granted to the Publisher below," but goes on to grant to the publisher:

The ongoing non-exclusive right to do in respect of the Work any other act that is subject to copyright protection under the Canadian Copyright Act (including, without limitation, the right to produce and reproduce, translate, develop ancillary products, perform in public, adapt and communicate the Work, in any form or medium) as well as to authorize others to do so on behalf of or in association with the Publisher ... the ongoing non-exclusive right to edit and otherwise reasonably modify the Work. (Bad Writing Contracts n.d.)

The contract does not mention any compensation for these rights, and further notes that the above rights apply to "all media," "(including, without limitation, all digital and electronic media now known or hereafter created) and also includes the Publisher's ongoing nonexclusive right to archive the Work (including in digital data-bases and abstracting/indexing services) and to make the archived Work available to the public, either directly by the Publisher or through third parties" (ibid.). Publishers "unilaterally impos[e] non-negotiable terms" (D'Agostino 2010, 25) and writers effectively sur-render their right to sell their works, to which they own the rights, to other publications and in other formats. The Transcontinental contract demonstrates publishers' power to strike licensing agree-ments with third parties that can generate revenue for the company but not for writers. Freelancers were so offended by the contract that a coalition of fourteen writers' groups organized a Transcontinental boycott and set up a website called Bad Writing Contracts to publi-cize their effort and to encourage readers to cancel their subscrip-tions to the publisher's magazines. Despite several high-profile writers publicly signing onto the boycott, the Author Master Agree-ment remained intact and Transcontinental continued to publish magazines, pages full. Then, in 2013, it introduced a new freelance contract that would take outright ownership of writers' works, and included moral rights and the right to delete a writer's byline from her story. Critics of the contract argued that it effectively turned free-lance contributions into works made for hire without compensating the freelancer as such. One freelancer explains why she refused to sign: "It rankled because the worldwide rights are overreaching, to say the least ... To be told that as a writer you're giving up all your publishing rights, print, digital, audio and any other media yet to be invented for the entire universe and that they can make changes without discussing with the writer, that's just disheartening ... I have to walk away from this, because it's just wrong ... I don't want to be bullied. I don't want to be in an abusive relationship, it's time to go" (Story Board 2013). Rather than walking away, many freelancers fought back. After a campaign by freelancers' organizations and unions, Transcontinental amended its contract in 2013 (see chapter 5 for more details).

The struggle over contracts continues. The *Toronto Star*, a newspa-per famously guided by a set of social justice–oriented principles that include acknowledgement of "the rights of working people" (*Toronto Star* 2008), introduced a demanding new contract in 2011. The con-tract "grants to the Publisher and to each of its affiliates, an irrevoca-ble, perpetual, worldwide, royalty-free non-exclusive license," without specifying who or what these affiliates are. It demands use of the work for "marketing purposes," which writers fear could mean worldwide syndication under the guise of "promotion," and requires some free-lancers to permit the *Toronto Star* to sell their work to third parties. The terms do not include additional payments to writers for such uses (Story Board 2011a; Douglas 2013). "The bottom line with all these contracts," argues Canadian Freelance Union founding president Michael OReilly in a 2011 personal communication, "is that publish-ers want to be able to treat freelance work as if it had been produced by staff writers. They want to do this without all the bother of paying a living rate or providing annoying things like health benefits, pen-sions, vacation, desks, computers, office space or even pens." Work-for-hire contracts – which give media companies ownership over freelancers' work, treating them like employees without providing the security of employment – are proliferating in journalism, particularly in online journalism (Laskow 2013). The Canadian Freelance Union fought a similar contract at the Halifax *Chronicle Herald*, an inde-pendent daily that in spring 2011 introduced mandatory contracts claiming ownership to writers' print and digital rights, forever. While the union was not able to get the paper to amend its rights clause, it was able to push back on the paper offloading liability onto freelancers and pressure it to increase freelance wages slightly. However, many free-lancers simply stopped writing for the *Chronicle Herald* (Soroka 2011).

The new contract regime is a powerful method of extracting sur-plus value from writers. Indeed, copyright and control over rights is one area in which writers have indicated that they are willing to sup-port collective bargaining (PWAC 2006, 41). With little bargaining power, most writers either sign publishers' contracts or lose work. Al-though some freelancers manage to negotiate some changes to their contracts, these instances are rare and are usually available only to those with power behind their names or with personal ties to edi-tors. Due to her friendships with editors at a national newspaper, for example, one writer refused to sign a rights-grabbing contract and was presented with a friendlier "marquee" contract, reserved for columnists and star writers (freelance writers' email list, 26 March 2008). Others are not as fortunate. Writers who refuse to sign restric-tive contracts or who strike out select clauses have columns and as-signments revoked or are barred from writing for an entire media chain (Diamond 1996; National Union of Journalists 2004; Lorinc 2005, 38; D'Agostino 2010, 28). Some writers who refuse to sign away all of their rights find their opportunities for magazine work shrinking. In a particularly insidious move, several British magazines issued cheques to freelancers that were impossible to cash until "the free-lance[r] had put a signature to copyright assignment [written] on the back [of the cheque]" (National Union of Journalists 2004, 13).[6]

Copyrights and contracts have been the source of contentious battles in the cultural industries, most notably in the field of screenwriting for film, television, and digital media, demonstrated in 2007 and 2008 when the Writers Guild of America went on strike for three months to win a greater share of residual money from DVD sales and revenues from digital downloads of movies and television programs (M.J. Banks 2010). Lacking collective organization, freelance writers in Canada have relied on other strategies to fight copyright, including public campaigns led by PWAC, boycotts, and, most effectively, class-action lawsuits. With the help of PWAC, freelance journalist Heather Robertson settled two class-action lawsuits against publishers that infringed upon freelance writers' copyrights. The first, *Robertson v. Thomson Corp.*, launched in 1996 after the *Globe and Mail* published Robertson's articles in three electronic databases without her permission, was settled in 2009 with $11 million paid to Robertson and other freelancers. The second, *Robertson v. ProQuest, CEDROM, Toronto Star Newspapers, Rogers and CanWest*, was settled for $7.9 million in May 2011.[7]

Freelancers received some benefits from these lawsuits. The lawsuits forced companies to compensate writers for illegal use of their works, putting some money in some writers' pockets. They represent an acknowledgment that writers should receive compensation for multiple uses of their works – an acknowledgment that media companies must take seriously. Freelancers effectively challenged publishers' notion that websites and databases (and mobile platforms) are extensions of print publications and therefore require no additional compensation (D'Agostino 2010, 25). The results of these lawsuits gave freelancers a taste of victory and an example of how effective collective action can be. Although different from member-driven collective action, any instance where freelancers come together to address publishers' power could be a significant motivator as they work to address other issues.

Yet legal action has limitations. Class-action lawsuits are lengthy and expensive endeavours that, for the most part, address past practices, specifically the practice of writers not signing contracts with media companies (D'Agostino 2007). Both lawsuits discussed above were settled out of court, so they did not set legal precedent (Impresa Communications 2011). And critically, they spurred the proliferation of contracts that demand multiplatform, multiuse rights, including rights for platforms yet to be invented. A Torstar executive editor said as much to freelance website Story Board (2011a) when asked about the *Toronto Star*'s new contract: "The terms are broad because we are trying to ensure that potential future business initiatives are not unduly encumbered, and to avoid issues such as the recently-settled lawsuit." Although a victory for freelancers, the class action lawsuits entrenched and codified publishers' powerful practices.

The struggle over copyright makes obvious freelance writers' lack of power. D'Agostino (2010) proposes several mechanisms to improve freelancers' status under copyright law, including a legal framework that brings the rights of freelancers more in line with those of publishers, who the law has traditionally protected, as well as education through writers' organizations, raising awareness, encouraging writers not to sign all-rights contracts, and developing model contracts for industry use (286, 280). D'Agostino affirms the need for publishers to fully compensate writers for the use of their works in new media and proposes the establishment of freelance grievance boards and collection societies, which could "control the electronic distribution of freelance articles and maintain effective license schemes to distribute freelance articles to the public" (283, 282). As I demonstrate in chapters 6 and 7, writers' organizations have pursued many of these strategies. What they have not yet achieved, and what could address the root of power inequities in writer-publisher relationships, is organizing for the purpose of collective bargaining for minimum rates and copyright agreements. Collective action, as I show, will be the most effective way for freelancers to resist exploitative contracts and improve their material conditions.

THE CONTRADICTIONS OF FREELANCE WORK

Many writers seek freelance work to gain autonomy and control over their craft. For others, freelancing is the only option, as the spread of precarious employment accelerates throughout media industries. Whether freelance by choice or not, however, freelancers' autonomy is undermined by political economic conditions of media production as large media corporations lower labour costs by off-loading the risks and costs of production onto individual workers. Freelancing has become highly contested terrain between journalists who seek greater freedom and corporations that seek more efficient ways to exploit workers. In this chapter, I documented transformations in the publishing industries that are shaping writers' work, primarily publishers' strategies of intensifying exploitation of freelancers' unpaid labour time and seeking escalating control over writers' intellectual property. Under these conditions, precarity undermines freelancers' autonomy and control over their work, demonstrating that the experiences of cultural workers under contemporary capitalism cannot be fully understood without an understanding of the dynamics of exploitation.

Although freelance work is often presented as the ultimate in flexibility, freelance writers and the media corporations that purchase their works experience the benefits of flexibility differently. The dominance of a freelancer-based business model means that workers have little choice about the form their employment can take. As Ekinsmyth (2002, 235) observes, the British magazine industry "requires an insecure workforce who are willing (or have no choice but) to work in a climate of uncertainty and personal risk, but who nevertheless have a level of commitment to the quality of their work that sells magazines." Canadian freelancers are highly committed to their work. Despite rampant insecurity and the precarious nature of freelance writing, and despite a growing need to find paid writing work outside of journalism and paid work outside of writing, freelancers display a strong commitment to Canadian magazine publishing (and other forms of print and digital media), which they view as having the potential to appease, if not sate, their career and creative ambitions. This tension is evident in a survey of working conditions in the Canadian magazine industry that found that although only 20 per cent of freelancers felt they were paid enough to live comfortably, 87 per cent "found it very satisfying or satisfying to work with, in, or for magazines" (Scott 2009, 19).

What can we make of this contradiction? Why do freelancers express satisfaction with their work for Canadian media while experiencing declining material conditions? As I demonstrate in the next

chapter, the way that freelance work is structured generates particular material conditions that shape writers' understandings and
experiences of their work.[8] And as I argued in chapter 1, a major
source of freelancers' contradictory experiences flow from their self-
employed status, under which they are encouraged to experience
freelancing as entrepreneurial labour. Freelance writing is highly
individualized, which makes it difficult to address labour-capital
power relations. Although it is an industry dictum that journalism
attracts individual-minded people, structural competition fuelled
by the fleeting promise of success and the attendant rewards can
encourage the notion that if one works hard enough, they will succeed (Kates and Springer 1984, 247). The organization of freelance
work prevents writers from recognizing that they face common
challenges linked to structural conditions. Most freelancers link
low pay to personal or professional experience, or accept it as inevitable rather than identifying it as exploitative – although thanks
to the collective campaigns, writing initiatives, and new forms of
collective organizing I examine in the following chapters, this may
be changing.

In Canada, the cultural importance assigned to magazines, freelance writers' traditional domain, also shapes how writers respond
to work-related challenges. As I examined in chapter 2, the discourse
around magazine publishing positions magazines as primarily cultural endeavours designed to support Canadian culture, removing
them from the realm of commodity production so that the magazine industry is not recognized as a source of worker exploitation. In
addition, a large segment of Canadian magazines are small arts, activist, or not-for-profit publications run by volunteers or activists out
of a political, social, or community commitment. In this context,
many freelancers report feeling lucky to be able to make a contribution to Canadian culture, which effectively undermines claims
they feel they can make to be treated well as workers. Says one
writer: "Magazine journalism is a high-prestige activity. That is likely why it pays so poorly ... I guess I just don't expect anyone to provide me with a good living doing what I most enjoy or think looks
best on a cv" (freelance writers' email list, 22 December 2006). Such
a "do-what-you-love" mantra enables exploitation (Tokumitsu 2014).
As I argued in chapter 1, questions about job satisfaction have limitations, yet responses to my survey point to tensions in freelance

writing that must be interrogated. In chapter 4, I examine these tensions as they are expressed in writers' feelings about their work and contextualize some of the challenges involved in organizing freelancers, extending my claim that the political economy of freelance labour – or the social and power relations that constitute the production of freelance media work – is at the root of freelancers' conflicting experiences of precarity and freedom.

4

Hustle, Write, Cope:
The Microautonomy of Freelance Work

"I got out of the freelance game because I was tired of the hustle, not because I was tired of the pay."

Cited in Sicha et al. 2013

When asked what they most like about their work, freelancer writers respond with the word "freedom."[1] Sometimes the word alone answers the question; other times, they specify the kinds of freedoms they enjoy: to work when and wherever they like, to write about topics they find interesting, to choose which editors or clients to work with, and to control how they perform their work. They enjoy freedom from fixed schedules, from commutes, from cubicles, from bosses. These responses, drawn from my survey of Canadian freelance writers, suggest that freelance writing is a satisfying and creative occupation that grants workers a sense of autonomy and control. But freedom is tempered by precarity. Material conditions top the list of things freelancers like least about their work. Examples include financial insecurity, work instability, the persistent undervaluing of skills and experience, a lack of paid time off, and late or absent payments. One writer I surveyed speaks of "the terror of not having reliable work or reliable income." Another reports that she can cope with inconsistent pay cheques but is frustrated that "so few places are willing to pay me to do my job." Many are unable to plan their finances or their futures and have little control over when or for how long they work.

The work of freelance writing is marked by conflicted and contradictory experiences. Many enjoy freelancing and cannot imagine doing anything else. Others dislike the instability of being a writer for hire and would prefer full-time work. Many express disappointment in the media industry, noting a decline in the quality of journalism and a lack of respect for writers. Others think writers should stop complaining and work harder, or quit. "I turn down work all the time," reports one freelancer. "There is plenty of work out there, and anyone who has the skills can negotiate a good rate. Maybe it's not $100,000 a year, but it might net them $60,000 if they work at it." Yet for some, low pay and insecurity have become unbearable. Others find balance in intangible rewards. Some writers earn good livings, while others admit they could not freelance without a partner's support or income from another, often unrelated, job. Some aspire to write only for magazines and newspapers, while others believe this is a limited, even romantic view of freelancing, as most writers' incomes come in part or solely from nonjournalistic writing. Some feel lucky to be paid to do work they feel passionate about; others are outraged that after years in the business they still scramble to earn a living. As one freelancer notes: "At this point in my career I am very disheartened. More than twenty years of dedication to my craft doesn't seem to have amounted to very much in terms of my marketability or financial future. Thanks to my determination to make a go of freelancing, I will never own a house, have racked up huge debt ... A handful of journalism awards doesn't seem like a lot of compensation in the face of that reality." These varied accounts point to tensions at the core of freelance media work: a knot of desire and disappointment, satisfaction and sacrifice, mediated by conflicted feelings of choice and control. Like other cultural workers, freelance journalists sacrifice economic and social security for intangible rewards: the opportunity to do work they care about, to be a part of exciting industries, to attain recognition or social status, or to gain autonomy in their work (Ursell 2000; McRobbie 2002a; Neff, Wissinger, and Zukin 2005; Ross 2009a). For many, intangible rewards can serve as "compensation for more difficult and troubling aspects of creative work" (Hesmondhalgh and Baker 2011, 124). Freelancers simultaneously experience enjoyment and frustration, a sense of freedom and the anxiety precarity brings.

While many view journalism as work that has inherent social value, media and cultural work is also fuelled by an ethos of pursuing one's passion and engaging in meaningful and fulfilling work

(Svendsen 2008; Tokumitsu 2014). Work, for writers, can serve as an expression of one's "true" self, a key identity marker. In contemporary capitalism, such views have combined with a generalized elevation of creativity to "the most desired of human qualities" (McRobbie 2002a, 109), sought by workers resisting alienating work and celebrated by capital and governments alike. Creativity, writes Angela McRobbie (2002a, 98), is regarded as "a sovereign space for finding pleasure in work," generating desires for jobs that enable us to be our full, creative selves. Freelancers often describe writing in such terms. "You see," says one freelancer, explaining why she sometimes writes articles for no pay, "there's this huge rush that comes with finishing a piece that thrills you to the pit of your writer's core" (Lucianovic 2013).

The excitement and enjoyment of creative work comes from producing the work itself, but also from the form of employment. Freelancing has always been linked to a desire to escape the drone of corporate office life, rigid nine-to-five schedules, and stifling management structures. Self-employment is viewed as an escape from work itself (a common refrain on the Toronto freelancers' email list I belong to is a variant of "if you do what you love, you'll never work a day in your life"). But in recent decades, freelance journalism has been recast under an emergent "socioeconomic common sense" of entrepreneurship (Szemen 2015). Taking up contemporary society's fixation on the entrepreneur as a remedy for broader political, economic, and social problems, freelance journalists are being repositioned as entrepreneurs: independent, self-reliant individuals forging careers independently, innovating, and "disrupting" traditional journalistic practices to make work for themselves in a time of job scarcity. While a discourse of entrepreneurial journalism has emerged as a way to cope with precarity (Cohen 2015a), as an ideology, enterprise further dilutes an understanding of freelance journalism as work. Structural challenges are understood as personal failings to overcome through innovation, hard work, and individual strategizing, the implications of which are manifold.

It is vital to take seriously workers' desires for control over their time and their work, sought via flexible arrangements. Andrew Ross (2009a, 46) warns that it "would be misguided to dismiss the hunger for free agency as a mere product of market ideology; the flexibility it delivers is a response to an authentic demand for a life not dictated by the cruel grind of excessively managed work." And Ross Perlin (2012) writes: "Precarious labour is not exploitation *tout court* – the flipside is greater independence, flexibility, self-direction, and agency." Yet we must also take seriously the way that workers' desires for autonomy, control, and flexibility are recuperated by capital, generating tensions between workers' desires for and experiences of work and their material conditions. Precarity is a double-edged sword in contemporary capitalism: "It enables the attractions of flexibility – the escape from the Fordist time of the factory and the firm – yet accompanying these relative freedoms and expressive potential for new forms of organization is the dark side of ... risk, uncertainty, complexity and insecurity" (Rossiter 2006, 27). The freelancers I surveyed speak of this double-edged nature of freelance work. For most, freedom from an employment relationship comes at a price. Many seek freelance work to escape constricting employment relationships, where creativity and autonomy can be subsumed by the pace and routines of large media organizations. Yet amid the spread of precarity in media industries, freelance status is no longer a choice for most, challenging freelancers' autonomy and power.

Freelance journalists may have autonomy to decide which publications they pitch articles to and which clients to work for, yet overall their autonomy is undermined by the structure of compensation, the processes of contracting work, and the social policy context in which all employment is regulated and supported. Although writers can decide the hours and pace of their work – the manifestation of coveted flexibility – control is challenged by the feast-or-famine nature of freelance cultural work: an avalanche of work tempered by stretches of time with no work at all, resulting in persistent insecurity and stress. As one freelancer explains:

> No matter how good my receivables are looking, there are long stretches when no payments arrive and I have to dip into my line of credit or overdraft or even credit card, the consequence is paying interest because my clients dragged their feet on their payments; the other side of this is that sometimes $10,000 will arrive in a day or two, so there is absolutely no way to build any kind of routine budget or bimonthly mortgage payment plan with that kind of uncertainty.

Part of freelance work is learning to cope with such instability. One freelancer describes life in this mode:

> All the good things happen at once and all the bad things happen at once. You get the ball rolling, you have some awesome momentum and people will start asking you to write stuff and you'll be really stoked on your career. Like, "oh this is so awesome!" But then maybe the next month, you haven't heard back from an editor, you pitch something and it got rejected and you kind of start to get a little depressed about it. You kind of have to take those ups and downs as part of your life. (quoted in Iddamsetty 2014)

Critically, individual writers have little power to change their circumstances. Carol Ekinsmythe (2002, 240) argues that freelance journalists experience a form of "powerless autonomy," but these workers do have power in a very limited sense compared to many others in precarious forms of employment. Freelancers' experiences are better encapsulated by the term microautonomy, or the experience of strategically navigating conditions over which one has no control. Microautonomy points to constrained choice, contested flexibility, and fluctuating power.

In this chapter, I interrogate the structure and organization of freelance journalism as a form of self-employment and its consequences, which are expressed in freelancers' contradictory accounts of their work. I argue that these contradictions flow from the material conditions of freelancing and its organization as a form of self-employment. The structure of the work produces particular subjectivities and occupational identities – those of artists, professionals, individuals, and entrepreneurs, for example – that freelancers adopt as a requirement for finding work and for success. For many, freelancing is a calculated trade-off, and to survive means to embrace the very characteristics that can undermine freelancers' working conditions.

EMPLOYMENT STATUS

"A freelance writer is someone who has a typewriter and a working mate" (cited in Harrison 1982, 11). While intended as a joke, the statement speaks to many writers' historic and enduring financial dependence on partners or family members. PWAC's survey (2006, 10) found, for example, that the "typical" freelance writer in Canada is married and lives with another wage earner. A respondent to my survey reports that she can only freelance "because I have the emotional and financial support of an encouraging partner. I rarely have to depend on this financial safety net, but knowing it's there has allowed me to take risks with my career that I may not have otherwise." In addition to family, many freelancers – just over 70 per cent, according to PWAC (10) – depend on other work to earn a living, including journalism and nonjournalism work, teaching, retail, and food service. Only 36 per cent of my survey respondents report having no other employment, even though 71 per cent state that freelance writing is their main job. Many freelancers cannot afford to have children (43).

Freelancers' financial insecurity is linked to their employment status. Although freelancers differ in terms of the kinds of writing they do, their incomes, their hours, and how they feel about their jobs, a common connector is their employment status, which is legally defined in terms of what it is not: an employment relationship. Much of what freelancers experience – the challenges and joys alike – flows from their status. As own-account self-employed workers in media industries, freelancers "lack ownership of the means of production and also experience very limited autonomy and independence," despite their ongoing characterization as entrepreneurs (Stanworth and Stanworth 1995, 221).

The growth of self-employment in the labour market and in media industries has fuelled the spread of individual payment systems and contracts, under which individual workers negotiate terms of their engagement for each assignment (Antcliff, Saundry, and Stuart 2005, 3). While journalistic work has always been characterized by a mix of employment statuses, with some people in secure employment relationships governed by union-negotiated contracts and others on contract, the scales have tipped in favour of short-term contracts and freelance work as print-dominated unionized workplaces shrink. Although individual contracts in media industries enable some journalists to negotiate beneficial terms and conditions, they have ultimately resulted in greater insecurity for most, depressed working conditions, and lower pay, and have encouraged the broad flexibilization of journalistic labour (Gall 2000). Individual and flexible freelance contracts result in free-lancers experiencing vastly different working conditions – includ-ing pay rates – from one another.

By definition, freelancers have no job security. Some are contract-ed for a single assignment and others for ongoing work, but they generally have no guarantee of future work. Publishers have no legal obligation to provide freelancers with sufficient notice or with sev-erance payment for terminating working relationships. Being fired can mean just not hearing from an editor again. To mitigate such uncertainty, freelancers must work on multiple projects for multiple outlets simultaneously and must constantly look for work. "I'm al-ways selling myself," says a freelancer I surveyed. "[I] have to always be pitching stories and looking for markets. So I never know when the next pay check is coming, or from where."

Like all precariously employed workers, freelancers have much less social protection than workers in standard employment relationships (Vosko 2000). They do not have income security, benefits, pensions, or access to paid leaves and employment insurance. Some report that fluctuating incomes make it difficult to access other forms of insur-ance, such as disability insurance, or to secure apartment leases, lines of credit, and mortgages (The Born Freelancer 2015). In 2009, the Canadian government launched a program that enables self-employed workers to enrol in Employment Insurance and, as of 2011, access maternity or parental leave, compassionate care, and sickness benefits (Neil 2010, 19). Yet the program does not accommodate the particular working conditions of freelance cultural workers, whose earnings fluctuate greatly year to year and who may earn income from royalties even while unemployed. Once benefits are claimed, a worker must stay enrolled in and continue to pay into the program, making it unaffordable for most (20).

Only 39 per cent of writers I surveyed report that a lack of social benefits (maternity leave, employment insurance, and vacation pay, for example) was a major issue of concern, yet 57 per cent said that "better social benefits" would be helpful to their career. Many writ-ers do receive some benefits through their partners, private services, or group insurance plans accessed through unions or writers' organ-izations.[2] Freelancers' responses signal a shift in general expectations about work and the social protections and stability historically associated with a standard employment relationship, which have altered what workers expect from employers and from themselves under new work regimes. Says one freelancer: "I don't expect an organization to provide me with true financial benefits. Nor do I think benefits like vacations, etc., can be mandated. That should be a part of one's payment rate and it is up to me to set some money aside to cover periods of illness and desperately needed vacations." Joel Dullroy, organizer of the Freelancers' Movement campaign in Europe, explains in a 2015 personal communication that social security, such as retirement, is something that young freelancers especially are not concerned with:

> For me [retirement] is more of an abstract concept that I don't
> ever believe will ever affect me. I just accepted the fact that I will
> never have [a] good retirement plan, and I will just work until I
> die – and most people I know are kind of resigned to that reali-
> ty. When we turn sixty, we might feel quite differently about it.
> I'm not happy about it, but I also can't seem to do much about
> it except work as hard as I can ... and hope that works out, but
> there is no plan B.

Writing in the United Kingdom context, McRobbie (2011, 33) observes that undertaking creative work requires one to consent to "shun" notions of social protection and entitlements in favour of "self-reliance, ambition, competition and 'talent.'" She argues that creative industries policy in Britain – a front-runner in responding to deindustrialization by promoting culture as a "driver of economic development" (Ross 2009a, 17) – served as a vehicle for the state to download responsibility for workplace protections and social security onto "the individual freelance person" (McRobbie 2011, 33). Under these conditions, where the state and industry encourage people to become entrepreneurs and where a growing number of industries outsource and contract work, "ideas of the social become emptied of meaning" and "work is promoted as the sole means of ensuring personal security" (McRobbie 2002a, 99–100).

The decline since the 1970s of job-for-life work patterns has changed not only the nature of the employment relationship but also how we feel about work: we no longer feel attachment to a single firm or harbour expectations of climbing internal company ladders, but rather identify with "an occupation, a skills cluster, or an industry" (Stone 2004, 3, 70). Workers expect to change employers frequently or, as is the case with freelancers, to have no employer at all. In this "brave new world of work," argues Beck (2000, 2), workers are inculcated into a "political economy of insecurity," expected to replace their notions of lifelong work with a normalized conception of short-term, interrupted work and underemployment. Individualism and entrepreneurialism have been presented as "alternatives to traditional careers," requiring self-reliance and self-sufficiency (McRobbie 2002a, 112; Beck 2000, 3).

Many of the freelancers I surveyed express ambivalence about state or employer protections. Some willingly exchange security and social protections for flexibility and some believe workers should be responsible for their own social security. One writer describes the trade-off: "I do have a full-time 'staff' gig but I am not on the payroll and am technically a freelancer; I do not get benefits or anything like that. But, the job afforded a creative opportunity that I wanted to take. Plus, the ability to make my own hours and decisions about the work I do is more important than stability."[3] Others demonstrate more conflicted feelings, linked to their perceptions of how freelance work is structured. For example, some women would like to take maternity leave but worry about the difficulty of rebuilding a freelance career after returning to work, as editors may forget writers whose bylines they do not regularly see. Whatever writers' individual attitudes toward social security, it is clear that the protections journalists won through collective organizing efforts have faded as individuals bear increasing social risk for undertaking journalistic work.

CHOICE AND (IN)SECURITY

The contradictory nature of freelance writing, evidenced by the discord between writers' challenging experiences with work and their high job satisfaction, must be considered alongside a notion of choice. If one wants to work as a writer in Canada, freelance is generally the only form of work available. As one freelancer explains:

[Freelancing] was supposed to be a temporary thing, while looking for a fulltime magazine job. I had just moved to Toronto

from Yellowknife, where I had a great magazine gig for five
years. But now that I've been freelancing for a year, I've grown
to like many aspects of it. But ... there are weeks that I get fed up
with the uncertainty, the thankless nature of the job, the endless
tug of guilt when I'm not busy/compulsion to always be busy.
Bottom line, I want to be a magazine writer, and being a freelancer is the only way at this point in my career.

Freelancers choose their occupation, not necessarily the form the
occupation takes. Yet the act of choosing creates a powerful subjective lens through which writers interpret their experiences. The ability to choose to engage in precarious work, for whatever reason –
what Lorey (2009, 187) calls "'self-chosen' precarization" – constitutes "deciding for oneself what one does for work and with whom;
consciously choosing precarious forms of work and life, because
more freedom and autonomy seem possible precisely because of the
ability to organize one's own time, and what is most important: self-
determination. Often, being paid well hasn't been a concern as the
remuneration was enjoying the work. The concern was being able
to bring to bear one's many skills" (196).

Degrees of choice are present in freelance media work. Although
the practices and processes that shape freelancers' experiences are
deeply linked to the political economies of media and publishing in
Canada, and while freelance work is spreading and is often the only
form of work available for those who want to write, freelancers must
actively decide to keep writing freelance rather than leaving the industry altogether. They must decide they can afford to take what is
an economic and, at times, psychological risk. For many, the act or
sense of choosing to pursue exiting, fulfilling work despite the insecurity is empowering, even thrilling. As Gina Neff (2007, 33)
writes, "People accept and welcome risk because taking risks offers
a semblance of choice in an era when many things seem out of ordinary employees' control."

The conditions under which freelancers choose self-employment
are highly gendered (McKercher 2014). Women face different structural constraints than men, particularly the uneven division of social
reproductive labour. And so, women may be pressured to engage in
flexible work forms such as freelancing to balance paid work and
unpaid domestic work, which undermines a normative conception

of self-employment as entrepreneurial work undertaken purely out of a desire for autonomy (Vosko and Zukewich 2006, 67). Feminists challenge the unequal gendered social relations that shape people's abilities to choose self-employment, arguing that choice is always bounded by the scope of options available. As Jill Murray (1999, 13) writes, "Workers with family responsibilities … might be said to choose part-time work voluntarily only in the sense that this is the only form of paid employment possible." Melissa Gregg (2008) argues that under neoliberalism, women are offered the "choice" to work freelance as a way to balance work and family in lieu of states developing social solutions to gendered divisions of social reproductive labour, such as childcare policies. Therefore, Gregg argues, in fields such as technology, the choice for women to work when and where they want is positioned as liberatory but in fact reinscribes gendered divisions of labour, as such work can conveniently be organized around domestic labour. One freelancer I surveyed notes the conflicts around the blur of paid labour and social reproduction, including the gendered construction of freelancing as not "real" work: "People mostly assume what I do isn't 'real work' because I don't go to an office or have a direct boss. Even my significant other gives me mixed messages: on the one hand, he thinks work takes over my entire spare time; on the other, he expects me to run errands, clean the house, and take care of practical matters during the day, when I'm working."

The choice to freelance despite the known risks reflects shifting notions of security and work generally. Many freelancers feel that they have job security, if not a steady pay cheque, as their income is directly related to how hard they work, or the number of assignments, words, articles, or reports they write. If a writer needs to increase her income, she will take on more assignments. Typically, writers work on multiple projects for multiple clients at any time, so if a writer loses or stops writing for a client here or there, she will not lose all her income at once. For many freelancers, job security feels entirely self-directed. Says one freelancer: "I think there is more financial security in receiving pay cheques from multiple sources than in relying on only a single employer for my livelihood." Freelancing is, for many, an inverted form of job security, reflecting the broad individualization of employment and widespread insecurity that makes even salaried workers feel precarious. Freelancing gives media workers a sense of control in an ever-changing industry where opportunity is promised and seems possible, even if it has yet to manifest. As one writer notes, "Corporate lay-offs have shown me there's no such thing as job security. I prefer to be my own boss."

Entrepreneurial Labour

The sense of being one's own boss imbues writers with an ethos of entrepreneurialism, about which discourse is spreading. In the face of lay-offs, precarious work, changing technologies, and uncertainty about journalism's future, commentators, journalists, industry, and journalism schools have latched onto a notion of entrepreneurial journalism as a way to remedy the industry (Cohen 2015a). While targeted toward all media workers and institutions, entrepreneurial journalism discourse takes on a particularly disingenuous patina when deployed in conversations about freelancers. An age-old form of work, freelancing is recast as an innovative and inevitable option for individuals who want a place in the brave new world of journalism. Swapping the word "entrepreneur" for "freelancer" often does little more than gloss over workers' lots, where struggles are turned into opportunity for enterprising go-getters who can make their own work.

Journalists are not the only workers interpellated into entrepreneurial discourse. Cultural work generally is positioned in contemporary capitalism as "entrepreneurial labour," a useful term for describing work done by self-employed workers that takes on a *spirit* of entrepreneurship, including self-investment and self-responsibility; high personal risk; and the lure of fortune, status, and fame (Neff, Wissinger, and Zukin 2005). While work is infused with a spirit of enterprise, most freelance cultural workers are generally not imbued with the power and agency that entrepreneurs traditionally enjoy. While they may appear to take on the characteristics of entrepreneurship, and while they may share employment status classification with entrepreneurs, self-employed workers are often "much more like employees than they are like entrepreneurs" (Fudge 2003, 36). Still, the veneer of entrepreneurship encourages workers to embrace risk, has helped normalize flexibility, and presents challenges for collective organizing (Neff, Wissinger, and Zukin 2005).

The way that freelance media work is structured compels free-lancers to embrace entrepreneurial sensibilities. For one, the informal nature of freelancing engenders utter self-reliance. Formal mechanisms such as job postings or mediating organizations that help freelancers secure work are uncommon, and so informal connections, personal contacts, and social networks are crucial. Normally, writers pitch story ideas to editors, which can involve unpaid work ranging from typing a short email to completing detailed research and interviews to develop an in-depth pitch. The work of obtaining work is less onerous for those with industry contacts, such as formerly employed journalists or journalism school graduates. What this means, however, is that the ad hoc distribution of work relies heavily on individuals' cultural capital and ability to network and make key connections. This work is easy for those whose family and social circles gravitate around powerful people in media, and can shut out those who could not afford to do unpaid internships, those who did not attend journalism schools in expensive, media-industry-saturated cities, racialized immigrants, and those who do not share a social location with the people in power: middle- to upper-class university graduates who are overwhelmingly white and male (Women's Media Center 2014). Fifty-three per cent of my survey respondents say they find making contacts with editors difficult, yet know that doing so is crucial. Says one: "I feel like I could be more successful if I was better at networking, both online and in person. So [much] of the work I've gotten has come after an introduction to an editor by another writer or editor and oh so rarely purely on the merits of a pitch or submitted work."

Freelancers must sell themselves and their ideas based on previous work, including amassing writing samples and cultivating a reputation as reliable and skilled. As competition for work intensifies, so does the importance of networking and self-promotion, and writers are pressured to devote increasing unpaid working time to marketing themselves and their work by managing websites and building social media followings. Such promotional necessities, and pitching stories to editors, are the aspects of the job that many freelancers like least, though they are now core to freelancing. "I am first and foremost a writer," says one freelancer I surveyed. "I am a reluctant marketer." The hustle, or the unpaid time and effort of pitching, looking for work, and self-promoting, can be relentless and exhausting. Every social interaction becomes a possible story idea and each new person a possible contact or source, transforming writers' whole lives into sources of potential productivity (Gill 2011, 249). Rosalind Gill further argues that in a culture (and economy) of "radical uncertainty," freelancers are pressured to become "a new ideal worker-subject whose entire existence is built around work" (249). This ideal worker-subject is ready to work anytime, social, and self-directing, embodying the traits of neoliberal subjects: flexible, adaptable, and enterprising. As one young freelance journalist explains: "In an ever-expanding economy of freelancers, you are required to have a social media presence. You don't get to say that you are unpublished, because you can always self-publish; you don't get to say that no one knows who you are, because you can self-promote. Basic HTML, search engine optimization, and knowledge of some kind of content management system are all 'life skills.' No work? You're out of excuses, lazybones" (Jung 2014, 49). Freelance media work is characterized by this frenetic pace of skills upgrading (on your own time and dime), managing multiple projects, hustling for work, and self-branding via social media, resulting in blurred work and nonwork time.

Some freelancers report thriving under current conditions and desire temporal flexibility, considering it a trade-off for the other, more negative aspects of freelance work (Ross 2009a; Hesmondhalgh and Baker 2011). Many freelancers say that the pay is low and the work stressful, but at least the hours are good. In interviews and in their own writings, freelance journalists often cite the ability to go for a run in the middle of day as evidence of control over their time. For the most part, however, flexible arrangements as they currently exist put power in the hands of already-powerful publishers. Under conditions of flexibility and insecurity, media corporations can operate on a "supremely flexible basis" (Ekinsmyth 2002, 237), drawing on a vast pool of skilled workers ready and available to work who bear all the risk of cultural production. Outsourcing work means offloading onto individuals full responsibility for securing work, self-discipline, training and keeping up with new technologies, making connections, and maintaining networks. The underside of freelancers' flexible schedules – the ability to go for an afternoon run, for example – is the need to be available if and when work arises. Freelancers must "subsume their own specific needs beneath a mantle of availability and acquiescence" (236).

"This is not the career path I envisioned when I graduated from college and applied for an internship with *The Nation* in 2003," writes one journalist (Adler 2012). "My father was a senior editor at *Newsweek* at the time, and I set out on the traditional path to national magazine writing: intern for at least a small stipend, freelance for at least a small fee, and apply for staff jobs until you got one. Today's aspiring magazine writers might be better advised to start their own websites, promote them on their Twitter feeds, freelance for no paycheck, and hope for good things to happen." In a tweet on 25 January 2015, Kyle Chayka (@chaykak) advised fellow freelancers to "above all, treat writing like a business, because that's what it is until you have the luxury of pretending it's not." Freelance work arrangements encourage freelancers to consider themselves entrepreneurs, despite the fact that the vast majority do not experience true entrepreneurs' power.

HUSTLE

Many freelancers' sense of freedom comes from the ability to determine their own hours. Most of my respondents cite control over their time as the primary reason for freelancing. Such control means being able to set a work schedule, to choose when to take time off, to spend time with family and friends, and to have time to develop story ideas. Yet one of the biggest challenges most freelancers face, after a lack of steady income and low pay, is time. Freelance writers report working varied and unpredictable hours, having a lack of control over when there will be work to do, experiencing a blur between work and the rest of life, and not having enough time to do the work, or do it well. Paradoxically, while time is at the centre of many writers' choice to work freelance and, importantly, is at the core of a desire for autonomy, it is experienced as a source of stress and anxiety in ways that undermine the yearning for freedom from its binds. Many writers cite long hours – 55 per cent of survey respondents report working upward of fifty hours a week at their busiest – and intense workloads as aspects of the job they like least. One describes the temporal stress of freelancing: "I hate being contacted by a frantic editor to whip up a story on a very tight deadline. It's thankless at times. [I dislike] not being able to enjoy my time or money (when I'm not working, I feel guilty about it. When I have money, I don't want to spend it). Mostly, I hate that I can never relax."

Writers' conflicts with time flow directly from publishers' low rates, which compel writers to take on more work to earn enough income. Both PWAC's (2006, 15) and my survey indicate that writers who earn higher incomes work longer hours. But more broadly, conflicting experiences of time speak to what is becoming a general condition under contemporary capitalism: the spread of paid work into all aspects of life, seeping out of the confines of offices into homes and leisure time, occupying moments that had, for many, been separated from wage labour.[4] The term social factory describes the blurring of work and leisure time, wherein a growing number of social and nonwork activities become productive for capital or are placed under pressure to create value (Dyer-Witheford 1999, 80). In the social factory, activities pursued in nonwork time become used for paid work, muddying the lines between "personal and professional identities," what Gregg (2011, 2) calls "presence bleed."

Presence bleed is intense for freelance journalists, for whom every social interaction and life experience serves as a potential story idea. They must constantly seek new work while engaged in other projects, a relentless search that necessitates always being "on." A freelancer describes how she experiences the work-life blur: "Your career is who you are. You are a walking brand in a way. And so the work/life balance gets very convoluted ... when you're interacting with the world ... you're always on the hunt for stories ... and so every interaction, even with friends, could be potential fodder for work ... it's a little bit embarrassing to have so much of your personal identity consumed by how you make your money" (quoted in Iddamsetty 2014). Securing work requires constant self-promotion: making contacts, networking, participating in group email discussions and writer communities, keeping one's name in the public mind, and building a reputation, all of which conflates work and leisure in a deeply personal way. This labour also takes time, and time is precious, intense, and pressurized, as freelancers skip from one deadline to the next. In practice, freelancers' experience time as never enough. A freelancer I surveyed notes: "Sometimes I take on jobs even though I should be sleeping just because I need the money. Yet, there are only so many hours in the day and if I was paid more I could concentrate properly on a few jobs, rather than juggling so many to the point of exhaustion." Another notes her conflicting experience of time: "If travel opportunities come up, I don't have to skip them the way I would if I had a desk job, but at the same time I will most likely be spending those 'vacation' days glued to my laptop." It is often a point of pride among freelancers that they either do not take vacations or work while on holiday (Sanders 2015b).

The number of hours freelancers work per week fluctuates depending on their projects. Thirty-five per cent of respondents to my survey work on average thirty to forty hours per week, and 33 per cent work on average twenty to thirty hours per week. The range can be extreme. Some weeks writers work less than ten hours per week, and some as many as one hundred hours, reflecting Ekinsmyth's (2002, 235) observation that "the freelance escape route ... offers no respite from long hours." The freelance media workers Kerry Platman (2004) interviewed, for example, report working to deadline when sick, risking their health for long stretches of work, and putting off vacations to meet clients' needs. These practices, Platman argues, often mirror the "flexibility and 'instant' solutions demanded by employers" (583). McRobbie (2002a, 101) notes that young cultural workers "now normatively self-exploit themselves by working hours no employer could legally enforce." Like most aspects of freelancing, experiences of time, including long hours and a crunch to meet deadlines, are mediated by writers' feelings of choice. As one freelance writer says: "Even if I have to work Sunday during a busy week, it's because I made the choice to and all the profit and benefit is mine."

When I asked freelancers about the aspects of freelance work they like best, one replied: "The sense of owning my own time; the sense of control and possibility that comes with it." And although many writers express a desire for and enjoyment of control over their time, most work irregular hours that fluctuate from week to week. Freelancers' control over their time is constrained, as editors or clients determine deadlines, and juggling multiple projects can place unexpected demands on their time. An alternate interpretation of flexible working hours, in the sense of choosing when to work, means being available to accept work when it is offered, even if a writer does not have the time for it – overwork in the present is preferable to no work in the future (Ekinsmyth 2002, 237). Freelancers may have control over their immediate labour process, but the contested nature of flexibility demonstrates the limitations of control in a broader sense.

INDIVIDUALIZATION AND OCCUPATIONAL IDENTITY

As one of several processes that structure the work of freelancing, flexibility helps shape a particular occupational identity among freelancers – as artists, individuals, professionals, entrepreneurs – that eclipses their status as workers. Karen Ashcraft (2007, 12) defines occupational identity as the way a person understands their work, derived from a combination of actual working practices and an "image" of that work, or "larger, public discourses of occupational identity, manifest in popular, trade, and even mundane conversational representations of the essence of a job and those who perform it." She notes that people often adopt "sweeping representations of an occupation's spirit, often strategically manipulated," (13) as their occupational identity. Such identities are constructed through historical association, popular discourse, and a person's own desires for their work and their life. Freelance writers have strong occupational identities despite having no workplace or shared employer. In fact, their occupational identities as professionals, independents, and creative free agents are strong precisely because they do not have a workplace or organizational identity to adopt and must build an occupational identity based on a conception of themselves as individuals. In my survey, 75 per cent of freelancers say they have the strongest allegiance to their own work, over other freelance writers, the publications they write for, their editors, journalism as a craft, a professional association, the media/publishing industry, or Canadian culture.

Freelancers demonstrate a high commitment to their work, a craft mentality long held by writers. The craft element of journalism is reinforced by the fact that a writer's name appears on a published article, which represents a self-identification with and attachment to a particular piece of work (despite the fact that multiple people play roles in readying articles for publication, including the invisible work of editing, copyediting, fact checking, proofreading, and other editorial tasks). Indeed, a longstanding act of resistance among journalists has been to withhold a byline from an article to protect the integrity of the work or to protest working conditions (Ritea 2003). This deep connection to the work is exploited by employers and leads to writers discounting their labour – often to zero pay – with the expectation that current sacrifices will lead to future rewards (Ross 2000).

Individualism has long been core to journalists' occupational identity, fostered over centuries and reinforced through practices such as competition for scoops, bylines, merit, and rewards for individual effort; the potential for fame; the recognition of individual creativity afforded by copyright; and the cultural myths of journalism as the pursuit of intrepid individuals (Elliott 1978; Bettig 1996, 19; Aldridge and Evetts 2003, 560). All workers, argues Michael Burawoy (1979, 81), are inserted into the labour process as individuals "rather than as members of a class distinguished by a particular relationship to the means of production." Although media production is collaborative, the system of rewards and recognition "is based on individual rather than collective effort" (81). Individualism is reinforced and intensified under neoliberalism, which emphasizes competitive individualism, self-sufficiency, itinerant work biographies, and entrepreneurialism (Couldry 2010; Ong 2006, 11). In neoliberal conditions, individualism takes on a shaper edge, becoming what McRobbie (2004, 197) calls "hyperindividualization."

Freelancers develop occupational identities through navigating the flexible conditions of a neoliberal economy, where workers are wholly responsible for sourcing and securing work, training and skills development, and self-motivation, and for running households, lives, and businesses with no job or income security, in fiercely competitive conditions where seeking support and solidarity from others is discouraged. These are the requirements for successful participation in media and cultural work today. Although freelance journalism as an occupation long predates neoliberalism and its enterprising culture, neoliberalism has exacerbated conditions of insecurity and reinforced the importance of individual initiative for success. Many of the characteristics of freelance writing, traits workers must adopt to survive, reflect the characteristics of an idealized neoliberal worker: while a freelancer provides valuable, low-cost labour, she has no formal ties to any company and rarely interacts face to face with the people who pay her. A freelancer is an independent, atomized worker solely responsible for her own output, productivity, training, and discipline. She pays for her overhead, workspace, and tools; locates sources of income; is responsible for her own health benefits and social security; and, as a requirement for participation, must embrace the individualized identity of the independent, entrepreneurial subject. Mark Deuze, Phoebe Elefante, and Brian Steward (2010, 228) argue that today's media workers "have to construct, reproduce, and give meaning to an increasing rootless or 'liquid' professional identity." Precarious conditions push many freelancers to double down on a notion of themselves as entrepreneurs, businesses, or "companies of one" (Lane 2011).

In this context, the tensions that underpin freelance writing are clear: freelancers can be seen as participating in a refusal of work, strategically avoiding alienating work and seeking autonomy, or they can be seen as ideal neoliberal subjects, flexible, unattached, and adaptable, absorbing the risk of cultural production and learning to cope. Ross (2001, 144) argues that the "free agent" and the "ideal ... post-industrial knowledge worker" have much in common: they are both "comfortable in an ever-changing environment that demands creative shifts in communication with different kinds of employers, clients, and partners; attitudinally geared toward work that requires long, and often unsocial, hours; and accustomed, in the sundry exercise of their mental labour, to a contingent, rather than a fixed routine of self-application." Indeed, when I asked the writers I surveyed to list words that best describe freelance writers, their top choices included "independent," "entrepreneurial," "flexible," "hard working," "adaptable," "self-motivated," "creative," and "dedicated." The structures that shape freelance work and the subjective experiences that freelance work produces influence how freelancers respond to challenges.

COPING

Freelance writers rely on individualized responses to problems that are systemic, pervasive, and flow from the structural logics of the organization of media production. Rather than identifying issues of low pay and restrictive contracts as patterns of exploitation and unequal power relations in media industries, they turn inward, identifying personal flaws or weaknesses in skills or career approaches and adjusting how they work. This reflects a longstanding practice in journalism: "Journalists ... take their own institutions as they find them, and work within them" (Fulford 1981, 4). Some writers identify the source of their challenges as linked to publishers' practices, but often accept these practices as "the nature of the business" that must be individually negotiated. As one freelancer explains in a 2011 personal communication:

> The reaction [to a problem] is always, "I'm on my own, what am I going to do about this?" You may have a couple of friends who are writers so you'll consult with them to see what they recommend. Maybe you're part of [an email list], you might look and see if someone can offer advice there ... Writers look internally because ultimately we're running our own show ... Those of us who chose to be freelancers, we like running our own business and having that personal responsibility, and so I think we tend to make decisions on our own.

When asked about the most effective way for freelance writers to address challenges, 46 per cent of respondents to my survey selected "learn how to adapt and best manage as an individual." When freelance journalists are confronted with low, stagnating pay and restrictive contracts, few turn to organizations or seek collective forms of action. Most take on more work to increase their income, which usually results in longer hours but not always higher pay. As one writer reports, "Since entering this business thirteen years ago, my average annual income has gone up, but my average fee per hour has remained pretty constant and I'm working more hours" (PWAC 2006, 14).

Of respondents to my survey, 33 per cent report that when their income from freelancing is not enough to cover their costs, they write more to earn more. They also reduce spending in other areas of life (54 per cent); cease to work for publications that do not pay well (37 per cent); and increase financial dependence on a partner or family members (37 per cent). Only 20 per cent of writers have asked editors for higher pay, 26 per cent have considered giving up freelance writing altogether,[5] and 21 per cent have sought out a writers' organization to help them address declining income. Others depend on savings, look for a staff job, or increase their nonwriting work. One survey respondent reports marketing herself "more vigorously" to attract more work. Many freelancers undertake professional development, participating in workshops such as Getting to

Yes: How to Pitch Stories to Editors and Making Your Narrative Non-fiction Dazzle! (Story Board 2011b). Such approaches reinforce expectations of a typical freelance career progression, an unspoken but widely accepted assumption that writers must put their time in and gain experience to later be assigned "more substantial work," be able to reject low-paying work, and "credibly" request higher fees (PWAC 2006, 14) – a narrative that shapes freelancers' understandings of the value of their labour.

Turning inward for solutions in the face of uncertainty is a symptom of and reinforces the fact that work-related challenges experienced on an individual level are difficult to recognize across the occupation and locate as part of broader structural changes (McRobbie 2002a; Banks 2007, 11). Freelancers' individualized coping strategies are linked to their self-employed status and fortified and sustained by the individualizing structures of freelance work, particularly the construct of choice and a spirit of entrepreneurialism. Individualized structures, under which freelancers are required to act as competitive individuals to secure work and survive, generate an individualized occupational identity that is more aligned with a notion of a professional or an artist than with that of a worker. These experiences encourage freelancers to seek individual coping methods rather than confront issues in a more systemic and collective way. And as I argue later in this book, this strategy is reinforced by freelance writers' tendency to create professional associations, which reinscribe relations of entrepreneurialism, self-sufficiency, and individualized strategies.

Self-branding and personal promotion can be seen as part of a broader entrepreneurial spirit freelancers embrace to cope with challenges. Robert Gehl (2011) identifies online self-branding as an "Internet-mediated remedy" for the anxieties of precarity. He defines personal branding as the "metaphorical expansion of the practices of marketing of branded goods and services into the realm of individual workers, freelancers, and entrepreneurs" (ibid.). Personal branding has intensified with the rise of social media, and is used by established and aspiring workers to stand out in the crowd, to sharpen their competitive edge, and to broaden their reach in order to obtain work. A good reputation has become the "currency" (Hearn 2010) required for success in flexibilized labour markets, particularly in the status-oriented cultural industries. These efforts, while clearly mimicking corporate marketing behaviour and in many ways acceding to neoliberal pressures, should also be taken seriously as a tool workers use to feel as though they have some control over their careers and as though they are actively working to address the precarity that can make them feel so powerless. As Gehl (2011) writes, "A properly maintained brand [can feel like] a bulwark against an uncertain future."

Freelancers' default self-reliance strategies point to some of the larger challenges involved in collective organization, challenges that flow from the highly individualized organization of freelance work and the subjectivities it produces. In neoliberal times, workers' efforts have shifted from collective resistance and organization toward self-sufficiency, adaptability, and intensified attention to their individual careers. The precarious nature of the labour market focuses workers' concerns on self-improvement and becoming more competitive, which is thought to be accomplished through more effective self-branding and self-promotion. Aspiring and emerging media workers embrace such modes of labour: in his assessment of bleak career options for journalists, a journalism school student calls for more entrepreneurial training. He accepts the precarious nature of the industry and implores journalism schools to better prepare students to face a job market with no jobs through an ethos of promotionalism (Ligeti 2012). Amid declining conditions of work and the growing importance of building an audience independent of any media organization, journalists are doubling down on individual professional identities as survival tactics.

The organization of freelance work makes it difficult to identify the source of freelance writers' challenges, which are rooted in the power imbalance between freelancers and publishers, or the labour-capital relationship. Class differences – workers versus capital – are difficult to identify because of the obfuscating effect of piece wages I describe in chapter 3 and because of the mediated nature of cultural production. Editors mediate between individual freelancers and the corporations they write for; executives and legal departments create writers' contracts; and managers determine the budgets editors are allocated from which to pay writers. The writer-editor relationship is usually creative, collaborative, and cordial, a relationship of mutual dependence that must be fostered over the long term to sustain a freelance career (Baines and Robson 2001). Although writers work alone, they closely collaborate with editors, an experience many find enjoyable. The pair works together from a story's conception to the published piece, a process that can take months. Because of the close nature of this relationship and the fear of damaging it, many writers find it difficult to negotiate fees with editors. Even an experienced writer who is an outspoken advocate for writers' rights says that he hesitates to risk straining his relationships with editors: "[I worry] that I might alienate valuable existing clients in an industry that is so very, very small" (freelance writers' email list, 3 September 2008). The "embedded" nature of the writer-editor relationship masks underlying economic relations (Ekinsmyth 2002) and encourages an affective attachment to certain publications, which can stifle desire to push for change. As one writer I surveyed says, if she were to join a writers' organization or union, it "would have to be legitimate in the eyes of publishers and editors."

A lack of standardized compensation and working practices and the individualized nature of work means that freelance writers, an amorphous group to begin with, have different working experiences and material interests, and therefore have different stakes in collective organization and resistance. Freelance writing means different things to different people: some consider themselves journalists, literary writers, content producers, or writers for hire. Some want to write in-depth magazine features, others are willing to write whatever someone will pay them to write. While some freelancers revile the notion of being considered a content producer, others embrace it, adopting monikers such as "contentpreneur." Competing and sometimes conflicting versions of what a freelance writer *is* can make it difficult to organize. To paraphrase Dorothy Cobble (1991, 15), often the only commonality is that all writers write. Freelancers' individualized experiences can prevent them from recognizing that they belong to a class of workers with similar interests.

Whereas the difficulties in organizing workers in nonstandard forms of employment often stem from state, policy, and legal issues (Cranford et al. 2005), many of the challenges involved in organizing freelance writers are linked to their conceptions of themselves as workers. Subjective experiences are shaped by material conditions that flow from the organization of freelance work, its precarious nature, and the modes of being that freelancers must adopt to survive and thrive. Successful organization requires addressing these challenges directly to build membership and, ultimately, free-lancers' power.

MICROAUTONOMY AND ITS CONFLICTS

Despite the enjoyment many freelancers report from their lack of an employment relationship, the structure of freelance writing – with its informal yet collaborative nature, the constant pressure to pitch and to market oneself, the relentless self-promotion, and the constant stream of ideas and talent from which editors may choose – serves media companies well, as do freelancers' self-coping strategies. The way that freelance work is organized, especially when it becomes a taken-for-granted labour model, blocks recognition of how power operates in the process of media production. While many consider flexibility a trade-off for other more negative aspects of freelance work, such as low pay (Ross 2009a; Hesmondhalgh and Baker 2011), over-all, flexible work arrangements as they currently exist in media consolidate power in the hands of already-powerful publishers, many of whom have fired salaried, unionized journalists and rehired them on precarious contracts (Gill 2014a, 14). Media companies have been unburdened from the costs of training and maintaining a workforce. Content is made cheap, as publishers do not pay for a large portion of the work that goes into each article, and because they benefit from a large pool of workers competing for work, which puts downward pressure on wages. Publications are granted operational flexibility to quickly respond to changes and to end relationships with writers without financial obligations. The structural conditions of freelance writing produce highly individualized subjectivities among free-lancers and challenge their ability to collectively address problems.

Drawing on Marx, Giuseppina D'Agostino (2010, 245) argues: "The term freelancer is arguably an artificial definition used to maintain control and keep freelancers ... vulnerable and exploitable ... The very appellation of *free*lance may add to the obscurantism, denoting in-dependence." Yet many of the freelance writers I surveyed report having autonomy in their work and enjoying the flexibility of their occupational arrangement, emphasizing the contradictory nature of freelance cultural work. The contradictions emerge in freelancers' descriptions of their work in interviews and in their own writings. One freelancer describes his life to the *New York Times*: "It's great, it's scary, it's worrisome, it's stressful, it's exciting ... It's every extreme adjective I can think of. You really don't know what to expect. Every day, you're hit with something new" (Swarns 2014). An Australian freelance writer network surveyed its members, asking about the "best" and "worst" things about freelancing: 79 per cent report that the best aspect of freelancing is "flexibility to set my own hours and choose when/how I work," while 59 per cent report that the worst is that "it's feast or famine and the financial insecurity does my head in" (Smith 2013). Even successful freelancers struggle with the yo-yo of "freedom and uncertainty" (Swarns 2014), demonstrated in an article about an American freelancer deemed a success story:

> For [Kyle] Chayka and other winners in this economy, freelancing is both a career in its own right and a calculated risk, a bet wagered in the hopes of winning something better – whether that something is a staff job, a book deal, a larger professional network, a more prestigious beat, or some other means of advancement. The gamble is whether you can make enough money to survive in the near-term while producing work that's strong enough to significantly improve your professional standing. The task of today's digital freelancer is to build a business and grow as a writer in an environment where pay rates don't seem to amount to a living wage. (Meyer 2015)

The author interviewed several "established freelancers," inquiring about the possibility of earning a living freelancing online. Responses ranged from "I make a pretty good living" to "it's pretty challenging, I must admit" to "there is no way you can survive on just writing alone" (ibid.). He concludes, "Even excellent writers with established reputations on the Web have to work very hard to make a living in this environment" (ibid.) The microautonomy of freelance media work plays out in conflicted and contradictory ways.

As I argued in chapter 2, many writers pursue freelance employment in an effort to gain some control over their working conditions and autonomy over their craft. Indeed, the things that freelance writers like about their work are things that many of us desire and that align with politicized visions of a post-work world (Weeks 2011). The trade-offs freelancers make for self-employment can be read as a broad vision of work where control remains with workers and where time is organized primarily to benefit social life. The ability to "go running in the middle of the day" is, for one writer, a "conscious trade-off" for "the lack of long-term stability" (Davis 2013). Yet reports of weariness and exhaustion, presence bleed, and perpetual work undermine the breeziness with which many freelancers cite the ability to go for a midday run (this justification appears in my survey, too). As freelancer Noah Davis (ibid.) writes, "It's possible to succeed in this gig economy. It's also exhausting." As the freelancer I cited in this chapter's epigraph states, the hustle, more so than the low pay, is what propels freelancers out of freelancing.

For many, freelancing is a temporary gig, a way to break into journalism and land a staff job – a more preferable tryout than the unpaid internship – but many see no end to the temporariness they anticipated, and so must strategize on how to make freelancing work. Under conditions of media concentration, stagnating pay, and an intensified struggle over copyright, freelance writers are losing control over their work and works, and are challenged to earn decent livings, to produce the kind of writing they would like, to have a say over where their works are published, and to retain ownership over their intellectual property. For many, this amounts to having little control over their career. As one writer reports, her career has not been the result of any conscious planning: "I have basically done what people called me up and asked me to do" (PWAC 2006, 16). Structural conditions of self-employment lead to freelancers enjoying their work yet feeling frustrated, dispensable, and precarious.

The challenges of freelance labour in an expanding media industry demonstrate the importance of interrogating self-employment status and how self-employed workers are inserted into a labour market that remains structured to benefit those in standard employment relationships. Such recognition does not call for a return to standard employment, but rather points to a pressing need to introduce policies and legal regimes that better support workers in a range of employment relationships and to detach social and economic security from employment relationships (Vosko 2010). Supporting self-employment in journalism, which carries the potential to generate autonomous, critical, or innovative journalism, requires more than expecting individuals to go it alone and cope with precarity. It requires attending more broadly to policies that can mitigate precarious work, such as proposals for a universal basic income or the ability for self-employed journalists to unionize and collectively bargain for higher rates of pay and improved contracts. Collective organization in some form is, for some, urgent. "[Writers] have been unable to act together for our collective best interest, so we remain the easiest to squeeze," says Michael OReilly, founding president of the Canadian Freelance Union, in a 2011 personal communication. "Until we find a way to collectively push back, we will continue to watch our profession decline. It's not about the economics of the industry, nor about the latest technological challenge, it's about power. [Publishers] have it, and until we learn to act together, they will always have it." Freelancers are undertaking several efforts to collectively push back, and in the final chapters of this book I examine these efforts and their potential to resist structural and entrenched individualism in the most individualized occupation. First, however, I turn to the contemporary conditions of freelance journalism for digital outlets, which are extending the unequal power relations and devaluation of writers' labour power into the online realm.

Work in the Content Factory: Doing Digital Journalism

Articles that describe the vagaries of freelance life have proliferated online in recent years. On platforms that range from personal blogs to the *New York Times*, writers offer sharp critiques of freelance labour, pushing freelancers' concerns into debates on the state of media industries. The articles freelancers write about their work are a form of worker testimony: firsthand accounts of otherwise silenced experiences that turn private frustrations and disappointments into a public burden. "I'm only getting paid two and a half cents per click on this story," opens one article about trying to earn a living from online writing (Biba 2014). The writer declaims media companies' use of algorithms to determine what freelancers should be paid: "The algorithm ... cares not at all how well written this story is or how much experience I have," she says. "All that's important is how many times you guys click." Another complains about young writers' routes into digital journalism: "You might start out by writing an unpaid piece for HuffPo or The Awl (and hope it goes viral), or blogging 12 times a day, as a job I interviewed for at Curbed last year required. You might be working from home, without an editor to mentor you. You might be earning no money, or never knowing what you will earn, month to month" (Adler 2012). Most freelancers' accounts of their work begin by noting their own credentials (such as an expensive journalism degree or years of experience), outline what it is like to work freelance (the word hustle frequently appears), and foreground how unfair their circumstances feel (see for example Magary 2014; Salario 2014). Some express resignation to the status quo of an industry in flux, and others are angry: "Exposure doesn't feed my fucking children," goes one notorious blog post (cited in Coscarelli 2013).

Such accounts describe lives marked by economic uncertainty and financial instability linked to low pay and mounting pressure to work for free. "They're waving 'exposure' at me like it's a cheque," writes Jennifer Mills (2013). In a high-profile op-ed in the *New York Times*, veteran writer Tim Kreider (2013) states, "it's not any one instance of this request" – the request to write for no pay – "but their sheer number and relentlessness that make them so tiresome." Kreider was motivated to air his frustrations after three requests in one week to prepare an original piece of work for free. He conjures the image of a club promoter offering a band of twenty-somethings a gig not for money, but for "exposure": "This same figure reappears over the years, like the devil, in different guises – with shorter hair, a better suit – as the editor of a Web site or magazine, dismissing the issue of payment as an irrelevant quibble and impressing upon you how many *hits* they get per day, how many *eyeballs*, what great exposure it'll offer. 'Artist Dies of Exposure' goes the rueful joke" (ibid.). In a blog post that was read by tens of thousands (and which has since been deleted), US writer Nate Thayer railed against an *Atlantic* editor who requested he repurpose one of his articles for their website for no pay. The request was familiar to freelancers the world over: "We unfortunately can't pay you for [the article]," wrote the editor, "but we do reach 13 million readers a month" (cited in Coscarelli 2013). Thayer responded on his blog: "I am a professional journalist who has made my living by writing for 25 years and am not in the habit of giving my services for free to for profit media outlets so they can make money" (cited in ibid.). In a more confessional tone, Susie Cagle (2014) describes the challenges of writing blog posts for pennies, waiting for delayed cheques, and trying to live on US$17,000 a year. She makes public what freelancers discuss privately: "Our low, late pay, our inherent insecurity, and the dual pressure to appear productive and successful while also available for hire." A rash of similar articles have been published since 2012, many of them spurred by the question at the core of Thayer's blog post: should freelancers write for free?[1] Regardless of their position on this question – yes, no, or sometimes – the articles generally concur that a lack of full-time, secure jobs in journalism results in poorer-quality writing and that, despite the growth of online journalism, it is more difficult to earn a living as a freelancer now than it was in the past.

Taken together, these accounts challenge persistent hype about journalism in a digital age: that journalism is in its "golden age," that the expansive online media industries offer boundless chances for anyone with a Wi-Fi connection to succeed, and that the insatiable need for content (a word I address later in this chapter) means untold opportunity for emerging writers. Freelancers' accounts of their work challenge this vision by inviting us into their version of what Marx ([1867] 1990) calls "the hidden abode of production," where "the secret of profit-making" lies (279). Such accounts expose the secrets of digital journalism's financial success, evident in the proliferation of new media companies, new journalistic formats, and new avenues of (often speculative) profit-making (Mangalindan 2013). Freelancers' writings about their work make visible the usually invisible labour of writing: individuals producing endless streams of articles for low or no pay under exploitative contracts or no contract at all. Such accounts demonstrate that journalism's labour challenges persist and deepen in the digital age, and that freelancers' labour troubles require more than a technological fix.

As has long been the case with journalists, freelancers' explanations of their conditions often begin and end with technology (Örnebring 2010). Most blame the Internet, specifically the way the Internet has facilitated an unquenchable thirst for new material produced at a dizzying pace, which circulates through links and shares and for which readers do not pay (unlike, say, when they purchase a print newspaper or a magazine). The Internet has also enabled thousands of citizen journalists, amateur writers, and aspiring media workers to produce high-quality journalism, often outside of a wage relationship and expectations of payment, expanding the crowded pool of writers and normalizing the assumption that people willingly choose to write for no pay (Kuehn 2014). The Internet, argues novelist and critic Jonathan Franzen (2013, 12), is "accelerating [the] pauperization of freelance writers." While the use of the Internet in media production has undoubtedly and drastically changed the way journalism is produced, circulated, and consumed, blaming technology or the Internet alone for freelancers' challenges renders their circumstances inevitable and therefore unchangeable. Blaming technology, rather than how media companies use technologies in the process of capital accumulation, neglects to consider the power and social relations that structure the production of journalism online, and the attendant labour processes being put into place.

The shift from primarily print-based to digital journalism has taken two forms: traditional news organizations are integrating digital technologies in the production and circulation of journalism, and born-digital or digital-first organizations are producing journalism specifically for online or mobile platforms. The shift to digital, spurred by technological development as well as transformations in capital accumulation strategies, means that media organizations old and new are experimenting with new revenue and production models. The traditional business model of print-based media – which included generating mass audiences and selling advertisements for specific issues (including classified ads), reader subscriptions, and newsstand copies – can no longer reliably return immense profits to media owners (McChesney 2013). Advertisers are spending less on print media and more online: in 2014, advertisers spent US$50.7 billion on digital ads, including advertising for mobile devices (Olmstead and Lu 2015). Yet digital advertising is complex and fickle. Online advertising is targeted, sold via "real-time bidding," and spread over many niche spaces online (Turow 2012). To appeal to advertisers, media outlets must attract large readerships (or in industry terms, generate high traffic). Ads are sold on a cost-per-click or cost-per-action basis (so, advertisers only pay if and when consumers click on their ads or purchase their product), or more commonly, via CPMs, or a cost-per-thousand-impressions basis (an impression is counted when an ad loads on a person's screen). The more desirable an audience, the more a media company can charge for CPMs. This means tracking and collecting data on readers to build profiles to pitch higher fees to advertisers, and a relentless drive by media firms to boost traffic (Turow 2012).[2] Digital newsrooms pay web analytics companies to track readership and reader behaviour in real time so that editors know what stories, topics, or writers will boost ad sales (Petre 2015). And so, while the Internet offers new places for journalists to publish their work, it also presents new challenges.

The Internet offers journalists "speed, immediacy, interactivity, boundless capacity, [and] global reach" (Massing 2015), and enables new ways to gather, report, and circulate information. Yet challenges arise, foremost being the need for unprecedented amounts of writing generated rapidly and continuously, independently of the deadline-driven structure of a single print newspaper or magazine issue. Digital media outlets produce innovative and important forms of journalism, such as investigative or activist journalism, critique, and perspectives from those historically shut out of traditional mainstream media, yet they also depend heavily on aggregation, repurposing, summary, outsourcing, branded content, metrics to track what people are reading, and, more recently, automating the writing process with sophisticated software that can mimic the writing style of a sports or business reporter. These practices are, in the words of one writer, are "degrading authorship" (Benton 2012). He writes: "Degrading authorship is something the web ... does spectacularly well. Work gets chopped and sliced and repurposed. That last animated GIF you saw – do you know who made it? Probably not. That infonugget you saw on *Gawker* or the *Atlantic* – did it start there? Probably not. Sites like Buzzfeed are built largely on reshuffling the Internet, rearranging work into streams and slideshows" (ibid.). Such practices, the lifeblood of emergent media companies making huge profits online, have implications for journalistic labour with which researchers are just beginning to grapple. In this chapter, I examine some of the challenges freelancers face in this milieu by drawing on freelancers' accounts of their work published in various media outlets over the past few years and surveying some emergent digital publishing practices, many of which put immense pressure on freelancers. While it is clear that in general, freelancers struggle to earn a living from journalism, find meaningful work, and get paid for that work, such challenges are not the result of technology alone. Rather, following labour process theory I outlined in chapter 1, they result from the ways technologies are used in the process of capital accumulation in media production.

Freelance journalists are on the forefront of the broad devaluing of journalistic labour and journalism itself, a process that began before journalism's move to the Internet but has accelerated since. Freelancers' challenges with low and no pay reflect a shift toward contentification, or the transformation of journalism into "content": raw, undifferentiated material needed for the endless cycle of media production and for capital accumulation online. Driving this transformation is the ongoing process of commodification (Mosco 2009), or diminishing journalism's use values – its capacity to entertain, inform, educate, politicize, or comfort, for example – as it is produced expressly to generate profit for media companies. Journalism has been commodified since the nineteenth century (Borden 2007), but its potential as a commodity has deepened and extended in contemporary, digital capitalism. The most profitable and fastest-growing digital media outlets, such as *Buzzfeed* and the *Huffington Post*, make most of their money through advertiser-sponsored content, often called brand journalism or native advertising, which makes paid-for-by-advertisers articles indistinguishable or nearly indistinguishable from the rest. Although digital-first media companies produce reporting and investigative journalism, too – many are expanding their news departments and hiring news reporters – their bread and butter are short blog posts, repurposed material, GIF-animated lists, and other made-to-go viral content. New media outlets are often fuelled by large infusion of venture capital, and according to one investor, venture capitalists do not want to fund journalism: "'Journalism' is indeed a word that scares off investors, who prefer publishing models that leverage user-generated content instead of paying a full-time editorial staff to create stories from scratch" (cited in LaFrance 2014). This model, which is proving profitable, sets the context in which freelancers work. In such a thoroughly marketized milieu, individual articles are viewed by as mini profit centres by new media capitalists, putting pressure on writers and their works alike and giving rise to some of the examples I consider in the rest of this chapter: content farms, media companies that do not pay writers, and low fees. New journalism production practices call attention to the contradictory nature of digital journalism: while many online media companies are growing in size, scope, and profitability, freelancers face precarious conditions and a shrinking ability to earn a living from journalism alone.

DIGITAL PIECEWORK:
CONTENT FARMS AND JOURNALISM ASSEMBLY LINES

"There's a rise in demand for content [online], but the pay is not rising along with that [demand]," says Manjula Martin (personal communication 2015), a freelancer and founder of *Scratch*, a magazine about writing and money that published from 2013 to 2015. High demand and low pay result from digital media companies pushing freelance labour models to the extreme. Motivated by an expansive global pool of precarious workers and "the ... premise that for online content to be profitable, it has to be produced at a truly massive scale" (Shaver 2010), companies have emerged to farm out quick content production to freelancers, paying extraordinarily little. The rise of content farms, described by critics as virtual factories or digital sweatshops, has signalled to freelancers the challenges that the Internet poses to their livelihoods. Content production companies like Demand Media, Associated Content (now Yahoo! Voices), and dozens of others are organized as journalistic assembly lines. These sites produce thousands of articles and videos per day, cheaply, to attract keyword advertising. Companies publish articles on their own websites or sell editorial content to papers and websites operated by large, traditional newspaper companies such as USA *Today* and the *San Francisco Chronicle*.

Content farms use algorithms to identify queries people search online, then commission freelancers to produce articles and videos to match keyword searches, optimized to appear at the top of search engines. Anyone can sign on as a freelancer through companies' websites by submitting a résumé and writing samples, and many contributors are un- or under-employed freelance journalists (Basen 2011). Freelancers are paid a small fee (between three and fifteen dollars per article; in recent years some offers increased to twenty-five to thirty dollars per article) and give up all copyrights to their works, which companies own outright (Ingram 2010; Spangler 2010). To earn significant income doing this type of piecework, a writer must work extremely quickly. Demand Media also hires freelancers to perform copy editing (for which it pays $2.50 per article), fact checking (one dollar per article), screening video quality (twenty-five to fifty cents per video), and transcription (one to two dollars per video) – a tiny fraction of what professional freelance copy editors, fact checkers, and transcribers would charge (Roth 2009). Content farms were set back in 2011 when Google changed its algorithm to deprioritize search results from sites producing mass content, which Google considers "junk" or "spam" (Wallenstein and Spangler 2013), and have not marked the end of professional journalism that some critics anticipated. Yet content farms remain profitable and are made possible by the expanding, expansive global freelance workforce.

The debate over outsourcing bits and pieces of digital journalism to precarious workers exploded with the arrival of a company named Journatic. Deploying a combination of computer algorithms and human labour, Journatic outsourced the production of hyper-local news (news focused on a specific geographical area, such as a neighbourhood or town) that was published in dozens of newspapers across the United States, including the *Chicago Tribune*, the *San Francisco Chronicle*, and the *Houston Chronicle*. Stories about town council meetings, school cafeteria lunches, and local sports teams were written and edited by freelancers in the Philippines, various African countries, and throughout the United States in assembly-line fashion – broken into bits, parceled out, produced quickly – for payments ranging from thirty-five cents to twenty-four dollars per story (Smith 2012; Wasserman 2013). When radio program *This American Life* (Koenig 2012) revealed that Journatic used fake by-lines for its writers in the Philippines, newspapers using Journatic's content pulled out of their agreements. One of these was the publisher of the *Chicago Tribune*, which had believed in Journatic's model enough to invest in the company and lay off a portion of its reporters, whose work Journatic could perform much faster and in larger quantities (Miner 2012).

Journatic has been described as a "globalized, Internet-based informational assembly line" that was able to produce tens of thousands of articles per week by scraping data sources "for micro-news of appeal to neighborhood-sized audiences," such as Little League scores, house sales, and school lunch menus, then assigning articles to low-paid freelancers overseas, or having US-based freelancers add quotes to a press release and file local news from afar (Wasserman 2012). As with all outsourcing, low pay is key to Journatic's business model, particularly the ability to take advantage of racialized and globalized divisions of labour. Journatic paid its US writers "$24 for an 800-1,000-word story ... $12 for 500 words" while writers in the Philippines earned 35 to 40 cents "per item" (ibid.). Journatic's CEO boasted of the economics of this business model: "Compare what we do to the single reporter model. I can go into a town of 25,000 and give you 50 news briefs a week for $250. If you hired a reporter to cover that town, will they touch as many people as my 250 briefs? No" (cited in Carlozo 2013).

Although a failed experiment, Journatic serves as an important harbinger for the future of journalism and freelance media work in a digital age. As media companies face shrinking profits and expanding demands for content, the pressure to publish more for less could be met by companies like Journatic, which use digital technologies and lean business practices to cheapen the costs of news production. Journatic – whose name is a portmanteau of journalism and automatic – represents an alarming prospect for media work, as it demonstrates the ease with which it is now possible to separate work from workers who have traditionally been thought resistant to the rationalization of production, or the separation of conception and execution as a strategy for deskilling workers and cheapening labour (Braverman 1974).

Consider another experiment in providing hyperlocal news: California-based Journtent, which purports to revive the "legman/rewrite man" model of news production that arose with the advent of the telephone. Aided by digital tools, Journtent aims to deploy hundreds of "observers" into a community to record local events and send video and audio to the headquarters, where editors or writers piece together an article. As founder James Macpherson (2012) writes, "This division of labour fields inexpensive 'eyes' and 'ears' on the street, directed by the veteran 'brains' back in the news room." Editors assign the writing of the story to freelancers in the Philippines and Mexico and quickly move on to "manage" another story. Like content farms, this model depends upon the existence of a large pool of freelancers – a far cry from the legmen and rewrite men of the past, who may have performed smaller tasks for a bigger article, but whose employers provided jobs with steady pay. Macpherson developed the model at his local California paper, *Pasadena Now*, which outsourced coverage of Pasadena city council meetings to workers watching via webcam in India (Roderick 2010). As Macpherson notes: "We have to cover a lot ... Sometimes as many as seven interviews in a day. This is how I solved the problem of time: I outsource virtually everything. I'm primarily looking for individuals who I can pay a lower rate to do a lot of work" (cited in Sheffield 2012). Newsrooms have always run on complex and strict divisions of labour, but digitization makes possible virtual work spread across the globe, which means increased freelance work that is low paid.

NO PAY:
WRITING FOR EXPOSURE AS BUSINESS MODEL

"Every piece I write has the potential to be a paid piece ... but the messed-up reality is that it just doesn't always work out that way," writes one freelancer (Lucianovic 2013). As freelancers' accounts attest, pressure to write for free is mounting. The no-pay model came to mainstream attention when the *Huffington Post*, which began life as a news aggregator and gossip website, was sold to AOL for $315 million in 2011 (Verizon purchased AOL, including the *Huffington Post*, in June 2015). The *Huffington Post* has since become a network of high-profile news sites that claims 214 million readers per month (Berman 2015, B3). "The once-scrappy start-up now has an editorial staff of about five hundred in its New York headquarters and another forty in its Washington office, plus thirteen international editions stretching from Brazil to Japan, with more on the way," writes Michael Massing (2015). *Huffington Post Canada* runs regional sites for Alberta, British Columbia, and Quebec. While it employs professional editors and paid reporters, the *Huffington Post* draws heavily on free content contributed by thousands of writers and bloggers – its stable of contributors is estimated to include 9,000 bloggers, but site namesake Arianna Huffington puts the number at 100,000 globally (Gustin 2011; Peterson 2015). Huffington (2011) says that her publishing model provides high-profile exposure for writers and argues that people who blog for the *Huffington Post* do not want to be paid. Rather, they contribute for free "for the same reason they go on cable TV shows every night for free: either because they are passionate about their ideas or because they have something to promote and want exposure to large and multiple audiences. Our bloggers are repeatedly invited on TV to discuss their posts and have received everything from paid speech opportunities and book deals to a TV show." She argues that the *Huffington Post* provides exposure for writers without the constraints of a deadline or specifications on what to write about, and that contributing to it is similar to posting on social media sites or updating Wikipedia entries. But unlike social media participants – not to mention Wikipedia, which is a nonprofit organization – *Huffington Post* bloggers are expected to adhere to "regimented and employee-like" standards and editors must approve their work (Elk 2011b). Bloggers cannot use anonymous sources and posts are fact checked for accuracy before publication. The *Huffington Post*'s "exposure" model primarily benefits people who are employed or who have other sources of income at the expense of those who need to be paid for their writing to earn a living.

The sale of the *Huffington Post* to AOL and its expansion into Canada in May 2011 ignited vigorous debate among freelance journalists about the value of their labour. Many writers argue that publishing models that turn on unpaid or low-paid labour are degrading the craft of writing, cutting into professional writers' livelihoods, lowering entry-level requirements to become a professional writer, and, critically, depressing writers' fees. Others embrace the *Huffington Post* model, arguing that it is a high-profile outlet to promote work that can potentially lead to paid work in the future. One survey of twenty-six *Huffington Post* bloggers found that while bloggers viewed writing for the site "an unpleasant experience," they found it "an effective outlet for reaching a wide audience and promoting their own personal brand" (Fuller et al. 2011, 8). One Canadian freelancer pitched the value of the *Huffington Post* to fellow writers this way: "The site has incredible reach, read as it is by 1.5 million Canadians per month (and growing). If you are trying to build your brand but don't have access to a regular column, I honestly can't think of a better platform. (How many times you had something to say/rant about a current event and realized that you wouldn't be able to pitch it to an editor and have it published in a timely fashion?)" (freelance writers' email list, 30 June 2011). Shortly after writing this message, the freelancer stopped writing for the *Huffington Post* because of its no-pay policy, signalling growing dissent. A week before *Le Huffington Post Québec* was set to launch, nine writers who had signed on as contributors quit over criticism about writing for free (Heinrich 2012). In the United States, after the sale to AOL, *Visual Arts Source*, an art publication representing fifty *Huffington Post* contributors, called for a strike and was joined by the Newspaper Guild and the National Writers Union, which represents American freelance writers. The groups organized an electronic picket of the *Huffington Post*, carried out primarily via blog posts and online discussion (Neilson 2012). In light of its $315 million windfall, journalists demanded that the *Huffington Post* pay bloggers and give them greater editorial control over their work, including not posting editorial content beside advertiser-sponsored posts (Lasarow 2011). Sports journalist Dave Zirin participated in the strike because "Huffington is creating a new editorial business model built on the desperation of the 21st century journalist. It's a business model that enriches itself by selling the snake-oil that, for a writer, 'building your brand' is an end unto itself ... I think it's dangerous for the future of our craft and I ain't gonna work on Arianna's farm no more" (quoted in Elk 2011a). Although the strike was called off in October 2010 – the National Writers Union (2011) argued that it had "run its course" – the action spurred a campaign called Pay the Writer!, focused on establishing fair payments for all freelancers writing online.

In April 2012, journalist and activist Jonathan Tasini, who blogged for the *Huffington Post* until its sale, filed a class action lawsuit against Huffington, the *Huffington Post*, and AOL for US$105 million on behalf of the thousands of bloggers who wrote for free. Tasini argued that the bloggers should receive a portion of the site's sale (Sabbagh 2011). While writers had originally contributed to the *Huffington Post* for free because they agreed with the cause (promoting progressive politics), after its sale to AOL, many felt exploited (Cherry 2013, 383). Tasini's lawsuit was dismissed by a district court in New York and then the United States Court of Appeals for the Second Circuit when a judge ruled that "the bloggers had been fully aware that their work was to be unpaid when they signed up for it, and so any compensation would be to rewrite the terms of their engagement retrospectively" (Pilkington 2012). Although the ruling bolsters the argument that freelancers willingly write for free as an investment in social capital or future work, Tasini views the lawsuit as part of a larger effort to challenge unpaid writing online: "We're using the lawsuit to spark a movement and an organising effort among bloggers to set a standard for the future because this idea that all individual creators should work for free is like a cancer spreading through every media property on the globe" (cited in Pilkington 2012). While the movement has lost steam, unpaid writing remains central to the *Huffington Post*'s business model.

Variations on models of monetizing content provided for free are becoming normalized across the digital media sphere, where growing numbers of websites develop large networks of unpaid contributors, often based on a promise of paid work in the future. *Bleacher Report, Forbes, Gawker,* and others rely in whole or part on unpaid writers, many of whom are established or aspiring journalists working under the assumption that eventually they will be paid. In 2014, *Entertainment Weekly*, owned by Time Inc., established the Community, a "contributor network" where bloggers will be "compensated in the form of prestige, access to the brand's editors and a huge potential readership audience" (Moses 2014). A week after announcing this network, *Entertainment Weekly* fired three long-time (and likely expensive) writers. As Julia Wong (2014) writes: "If you don't see the connection between these two moves, you're not paying attention."

Medium, a writing platform that grew out of blogging platforms, launched in 2012 to enable anyone to publish professional-looking articles with which readers can interact (articles are circulate and promoted by readers via social media). *Medium* is cited as evidence that journalism's golden age has arrived, as thousands of people, no matter their occupation, experience, or social location, can publish aesthetically pleasing pieces of writing to immediate audiences, who then pick and choose articles they like to circulate and promote (helped along by an algorithm). *Medium* is popular among journalists, academics, activists, politicians, media organizations, and corporations (established media organizations like *Mother Jones* and the *New York Times* have set up blogs on *Medium*, and companies and politicians, including Barack Obama, use it to publish press statements). Yet "more than 95 percent of the 1,000 to 1,200 posts a day come from nonprofessionals" trying their stakes in the platform's attention economy (Carr 2014b, B1). In this model, the infrastructure a publisher would provide – editors, layout, photography, packaging, distribution – is left up to the individual. The more you work to publicize your piece, the more chances you have of people reading it.

I asked Evan Hansen, a former *Wired* editor whose apt new job title is head of content labs at *Medium*, about the platform's business model and if contributors are paid.[3] He says that *Medium*'s existence depends on thousands of articles being published as a way to amass content, a "user base," and revenue, meaning that *Medium* is still experimenting with revenue models. The company has raised at least $25 million in venture capital funding and can rely on the deep pockets of founder Evan Williams, who cofounded Twitter (Isaac 2014). The vast majority of writers who publish their work on *Medium* are not paid. Hansen views this arrangement as a "win-win": writers get a platform and *Medium* gets content. *Medium* also runs a few "publications," curated sections of the site where editors and some writers are paid. But these publications draw from already established and well-paid writers with name recognition who can boost *Medium*'s profile and encourage people who are not writers to use the site as "an arena for self-expression" (Isaac 2014). *Medium* is developing in a manner similar to most tech start-ups: first grow an audience or a user base to a massive scale, then determine how to monetize it. Hansen acknowledges that paying writers would be "transformative for creativity" and promises to "build tools that creators can use to monetize their work." He thinks *Medium* can be the first online start-up that figures out how to pay writers because of its ability to monitor and track how articles are read and shared online. That this is a model that some journalists are pinning their hopes on is worrisome. Writing for exposure as business model trades on writers' willingness to write for no pay to build a portfolio that can later secure paid work, and further normalizes unpaid labour as a ticket into a writing career. Sites such as LinkedIn's *Influencer*, *Condé Nast Traveler*, *Entertainment Weekly*, and *Forbes* follow suit (Carr 2014b, B1). While these sites may provide opportunities for anyone to publish their work, they also expand the thickening layer of writing – often high-quality, worthy of professional rates – that is produced for no pay and must compete with the glut of writing online for attention, readers, and, what matters most to media companies, advertising dollars. New digital publishing models can be considered at once empowering and exploitative.

Martin found through her own research that many freelancers find it difficult to transition from writing for exposure to writing for a living (Who Organizes Writers? panel 2014). It turns out that for most writers, as Zirin notes, building a brand is not an adequate end unto itself. The logic fuelling the write-for-exposure model contributes to the commodification of writing. Writing, or doing journalism, is now viewed by many as a future investment or brand-building exercise rather than work or labour, which carries with it a particular set of social relations, namely the exploitation of that labour for profit. In the write-for-free model, media companies view journalism as content: raw material for the profit-making process. The surplus of writing online is increasingly harnessed for venture-capital-fuelled experiments, which claim to make money through technological innovation alone. As writing is transformed into content, power inequalities deepen between freelancers and the media corporations that profit from their work, and it becomes increasingly difficult to demand payment. Tai Neilson (2012, 6) notes this inequity: "Institutions such as the *Huffington Post* develop means to convert attention (audiences) into revenue through advertising, but writers are deprived of this direct revenue opportunity" in the form of wages. Kathleen Kuehn and Thomas F. Corrigan (2013) argue that online business models increasingly capitalize on people contributing their labour for free "as a future-oriented investment" in the hope of attaining paid work later on. They call this "hope labour, or un- or under-compensated work carried out in the present, often for experience or exposure, in the hope that future employment opportunities may follow" (10). Hope labour is core to digital journalism business models, which present unpaid writing as a "moral choice" that individuals must struggle with, rather than a structural feature of digital media publishing (Mills 2013).

LOW PAY AND PERFORMANCE-BASED COMPENSATION

"I now contribute to some of the most prestigious online publications in the English-speaking world," writes Tim Kreider (2013) in a *New York Times* op-ed. Yet Kreider is "paid the same amount as, if not less than, I was paid by my local alternative weekly when I sold my first piece of writing for print in 1989." While many freelancers steer clear of content farms and others refuse to write for free, even established writers like Kreider face low pay at media outlets ranging from independent start-ups to large corporations. The expansion of digital journalism presents a conundrum for freelancers: large, profitable media corporations pay similar rates for articles as small start-ups, and almost all publications justify low pay with the argument that no one yet knows how to make money online. The editors of independent journal *n+1* explain the contradictions and inconsistencies that emerged as digital-first publishing became a viable space for working writers:

> [When print publishing dominated] a "longread" could come from *Vanity Fair*, where it would fetch $20,000, or from *n+1*, where it would fetch more like $300. These disparities, which

had once been par for the course (*Vanity Fair* was a profitable corporate entity whose editor in chief made more than a million dollars a year; *n+1* was a money-losing operation whose editors lived primarily with roommates), began to seem suspicious, especially once the big corporate magazines started producing more online content, and paying online rates for it. The Awl, a shoestring operation, might pay $150 for an online piece, but so would well-financed xoJane and *Vice*. Other magazines that fit the same broad category might pay nothing at all. (*n+1* 2014)

Freelancers' accounts of their work make clear that there are many media outlets for which to write, yet rates of pay remain extremely low and contribute to a precarious existence. Writes one freelancer: "How depressing did the paydays get? Why, last spring I published a 1,500-word news story for $20 – and had to play hardball just to get *that*" (Alexander 2015).

In general, freelancers do not know what online publications pay for freelance articles or how much others earn. Martin set out to change that in 2012, after discussing rates with other freelancers on Twitter. She envisioned a place for writers to list which publications paid and how much, and created a tumblr called Who Pays Writers?,[4] "a crowd-sourced blog of actual rates paid by publications to writers" (personal communication 2015). Browsing the site – which consists of short entries, published as submitted, that name the publication, rate of pay, type of piece, and information about copyrights – is revealing. The following is a sample of reports displayed on the front page of Who Pays Writers? on a randomly selected day in May 2015: "$300 for a 1,000- to 2,000-word criticism piece online" for the *Hairpin*, "$200 for a 500- to 1,000-word reported piece online" for *Mashable*, and "$50 for a 1,000-word essay online" for *xoJane* (the writer had been waiting four months to be paid). Some publications' rates are higher, as this report on writing for sb *Nation* indicates: "$2,000 for a 6,000-word feature profile online, 2014. Payment within two weeks. Heavy reporting. Pre-existing relationship with editor or publication ... You'll work very hard for your money at sb Nation Longform. (I'd estimate I put in about 250 hours for this story.) But the check will come on time, and you'll have one of the most fulfilling experiences of your career, from a creative standpoint." Another writer shares that Yahoo! paid print-like rates, or one dollar per word for a 500- to 1,000 word article, but that it retained all copyrights. Rates for print publications remain higher (one writer was paid two dollars per word for a 1,200-word personal essay in *Cosmopolitan*), but print-based media companies also pay low online rates (one writer was paid $100 for a 500- to 1,000-word news story for one of the *Washington Post*'s sites). Who Pays Writers? and other online discussions of writers' rates confirms that rates are arbitrary and varied, and depend greatly on the writer, the topic, and perceptions of value rather than a set fee schedule. An editor for the independently owned website *Boing Boing* shares how he determines what to pay: "'A little bit more than whatever the writers you want are prepared to write for' seems right, but maybe too ruthless? So we end up with wild stabs in the dark, nailing decent word rates without thinking too hard about it" (cited in Sicha et al. 2013).

As usual, the debate over how much (and if at all) to pay writers is positioned as a debate between writers and editors. But as I discussed in chapter 4, most editors mediate between freelancers and publishers or management, who make business decisions and hold the power to determine how much money is allocated to freelancers. Most editors are given a set budget per month to commission freelance works, which determines the kind of articles they can publish. Budgets range. A *Boing Boing* editor has $1,000 to $2,000 per month to spend (which works out to $250 or $350 for what he deems "journalism" versus fifty dollars for a television recap), while an editor for *Outside*, a long-running magazine owned by a small publishing company, has a budget of $20,000. He spends most of it on writers on contract; the rest is dispersed in small amounts, such as seventy-five dollars for a short Q&A or $1,500 for a feature-length piece. "Over the past year, I've paid as little as nothing and as much as $5,000 for Web work," he writes. "Everything is negotiable" (cited in Sicha et al. 2013).

In an online discussion between writers and editors about what writers should be paid for digital journalism, one writer notes that he makes a living doing freelance digital journalism, which for him consists of "longish pieces that are 'blog posts' but typically involve some research" (ibid.). To do this, he tries to write only for outlets that pay more than $50 to $100 per article and he works ten- to twelve-hour days, seven days a week. Other accounts of writers who are "making it" express similar exhaustion: twelve-hour workdays, dozens of articles per week, unable to take extended breaks for fear of missing out on work, no access to health insurance, and no ability to save for the future. Unsurprisingly, many who share their stories are young. Adler (2012) describes freelancer Paul Tassi's work life: "Tassi writes upwards of 15 posts per day between *Forbes* and other outlets, including his own website ... He also uploads video for one website and serves as managing editor for another. Overall, he makes a good living, but he doesn't get health insurance from any of his gigs, and he doesn't know how much money he will make in a month until the traffic numbers and ad revenue have come in. Tassi is only 24, so for him it seems a manageable workload and lifestyle." Editors often argue that "younger, hungrier kids" happily underprice their labour to kick-start their careers. But an emerging freelancer challenges that excuse: "Working for less is not a matter of willingness, but options. We lack options and thus either take what's available or go do something else. The general secrecy surrounding pay doesn't help our cause much" (cited in Sicha et al. 2013).

More concerning than low rates is performance-based pay for articles. Many writers are paid based on how many people read, click on, or share their work. This practice, which thoroughly injects media work with market logic, is fuelled by the booming analytics industry that supplies media companies with precise measures of what a reader reads, how long they stay on a page, where they place their cursor, how an article travels through social media, geographic location, and other data (Basen 2014). "Tracking how many people view articles, and then rewarding – or shaming – writers based on those results has become increasingly common in old and new media newsrooms," writes Jeremy Peters (2010, B1). The *Christian Science Monitor*, for example, sends staff daily emails listing page views for each article written (B1). Outlets like *Gawker, Forbes, America Online*, and *Bloomberg News* compensate journalists based in whole or part on web traffic to their stories (B1; Carr 2014a, B1). The *Globe and Mail* introduced a paywall along with an incentive strategy to encourage select journalists to produce articles that will attract paid subscribers, a process dictated by predictive analytics (Toughill 2014). To test out potential employees, *Gawker*, a New York City–based gossip and news blog that has turned into a successful digital journalism company, established Recruits, a program that gives aspiring *Gawker* writers blog space and a small stipend with "an aggressive bonus structure that will reward the capturing of uniques" – recruits are paid five dollars extra for every 1,000 unique visitors to their blog (Johnson 2014). As a *Gawker* editor told a reporter, "the program is designed to motivate writers to produce their very 'best work,' while keeping them at ... a 'step between [an] unpaid and full-time employee'" (Fischer 2014). Winners of this work-as-contest experiment get a full-time gig or a freelance contract.

Other writers are paid a portion of the advertising revenue a company can generate overall or from a writer's individual article. Since advertising revenues fluctuate, so does the amount of money available to pay writers. The *Awl*, for example, pays writers 10 per cent of its gross revenue (Sicha et al. 2013), a number undoubtedly always in flux. Web-based publications launch with arrangements to pay writers based on a small set fee and bonuses once they reach certain "traffic targets" (Adler 2012). One journalist recounts being asked to write for a new website that "sought to be 'an edgier *Huffington Post*'" with a payment scheme as follows: "Instead of staff writers, it had contributors who spent roughly ten hours a week blogging and aggregating news on a given topic. In exchange, [contributors] would receive a majority of the revenue generated by ads sold on the pages they created" (ibid.).

These examples demonstrate a shift ushered in with digital journalism, whereby individual articles are expected to act as stand-alone commodities. Online articles are not published on a particular schedule nor at a particular time. They are released in a steady stream, circulated through social media, and decontextualized from a particular media outlet or larger whole. Accordingly, individual articles are expected to act as profit centres, attracting enough eyeballs to sell to advertisers to justify the expense of their commissioning. Freelancers are expected to do the promotional labour necessary to boost an article's readership and, therefore, the company's ad sales. (They are also expected to bring an "audience" with them to every media outlet for which they write.) This arrangement escalates pressure on freelancers to consider the market first and foremost when pitching an idea and constructing a piece, to promote their article (work that is unpaid), and to produce a piece of writing that will, independent of the imprimatur of a publication or association with a media institution, appeal to readers and advertisers. This is a significant shift. In the print era, whole media objects were produced as commodities for consumers to purchase. Each article was part of a larger issue of a magazine or edition of a newspaper and sold either to subscribers for a subscription fee, to advertisers as an issue to be placed in, or for a cover price to a buyer at a newsstand. In the digital age, the single journalistic object is fragmented and decontextualized. Its success is measured in numbers of shares, likes, tweets, and reblogs, by how many people click through, and by whether or not they read the entire article. The individual article is a commodity in and of itself; it must be financially viable from the start. As one editor explains: "Pre-web, we never viewed an article on a page as having had x number of 'reads' and then counted them against the adjoining ads on that page to determine value" (cited in Sicha et al. 2013). Yet digital journalism does just that. One *Gawker* editor determines freelance rates through "idiosyncratic piece-rate calculations that try to account for the capital costs of doing the piece and/or the expected traffic value and/or the writer's market value" (ibid.).

Under such practices, journalism becomes content and journalists become content producers. Content – what Astra Taylor (2014, 15) calls "that horrible, flattening word" – increasingly stands in for what used to be called articles or stories (Cole and Harcup 2010). Whereas "article" or "story" called attention to a unique piece of work, content refers to a mass of undifferentiated material produced by people who are, essentially, interchangeable. "It is as though all our words have become gauzy filler material, the pale fluff inside decorative throw pillows," writes journalist Gene Weingarten (2011). A freelancer named Nicole Dieker (2016) boasts of earning about US$38,000 a year producing content, writing 5,000 words per day for twenty dollars per hour in 2013, increasing her earnings to about US$43,000 in 2014 and US$63,000 in 2015. "I am one of the unsung, invisible hacks of the internet generation," she writes (Dieker 2013). "I help fill blogs and news sites and online stores with the new text those sites need every day. Within an hour I can give you the ten best celebrity wedding dresses, or a thousand words on how to get your kids to eat healthy snacks. I can ghostwrite to match your blog's tone and style, if you need a post in a hurry." Welcome to work in the content factory, where anyone can produce the raw material needed to feed the circuits of online capital accumulation. "It isn't particularly hard to write any of this because it's already obvious how the writing should go," Dieker notes. "This type of writing is like driving a car to the airport; you already know how to get there, you just need to make sure you follow the rules and don't crash along the way."

While named labour has traditionally been essential to many cultural products, particularly bylined journalism, in the brave new world of digital journalism, most of the time it does not really matter who produces content or of what it consists. One journalist notes that on digital media platforms, "journalists ... become easily replaceable cogs in the machine, one byline morphing seamlessly into the next" (Salmon 2015). Kreider (2013) calls the word content "contemptuous coinage" that "is predicated on the assumption that it's the delivery system that matters, relegating what used to be called 'art' – writing, music, film, photography, illustration – to the status of filler, stuff to stick between banner ads." But John Patrick Leary (2014) argues that the problem is not that "content" is distinct from and replacing "art." Rather, the rise of content represents the "privatization of the desires, knowledge, and experiences we gain from the stories we read, watch, and remember." So, the rise of content does trigger concerns about taste or artistic or journalistic standards, but also signifies how emergent digital technologies are being used to extend and deepen the commodification of culture, further transforming journalism into a substance valued solely for its ability to link advertisers to consumers – a continuation in journalism's historical development, but one with deep implications for contemporary media workers.

Contentification puts pressure on media workers' work and livelihoods. Even "success" stories are deflating. One writer reports making a good living by focusing on "one-thought 800-word pieces" (cited in Meyer 2015). Freelancers and editors express concern about the devaluation of journalism. Says an editor: "When your freelance budget gets slashed you feel the higher ups breathing down your neck and are forced to treat the pieces for your publication as content. [Journalism is] a commodity used to get traffic ... and nothing more" (cited in Sicha et al. 2013). So it is no surprise that editors report being challenged to publish reported articles, investigative journalism, or pieces that require extensive research. Personal essays, quick-hit blog-style pieces, and commentary are easier to find. Freelancers experience the commodification of journalism simultaneously as the commodification of the self. They must work hard to promote themselves and their work, position themselves as a brand to associate with, and make their articles both a way to earn a living and a tool for prospective work. After all, at such low rates of pay, at the very least an article must attract some attention. Explains one freelancer: "If you aren't paid for your story, you are doing it solely in the hopes that people will read it and that it will enhance your name recognition. If no one reads it, you've wasted your time. You want to produce something sexy enough that the editors will put it on the homepage and other bloggers will link to it. So freelancers have reason to sex up their content in an effort to attract eyeballs" (Adler 2012). Writers and editors are acutely aware of the way they are yoked to market forces, but many see few alternatives in the new digital journalism landscape.

MAKING FREELANCE LABOUR VISIBLE ONLINE

It seems, in the words of one writer, that "capitalism is kicking journalists' asses" (Wong 2014). Indeed, the story I have told thus far shows a bleak picture for freelancers working in digital media. For most, the Internet has not fulfilled its promise as a land of boundless opportunity and easy money. Rather, digital publishing models that demand much more for much less are the result of media capitalists' strategic use of technology to "[strip] labour costs to the bone" (Ross 2009b). And so digital journalism is marked by low pay, no pay, and deepening commodification, fuelled by a deep power imbalance between individual writers and the companies for which they work. Yet, while media capitalists use the Internet to devalue the work of writing, freelancers use the same tools to publicize, address, and try to improve their conditions. For many, this comes in the form of the first-person accounts of work experiences I've examined in this chapter, individual efforts to make visible payments and treatment by publishers. In one notable experiment, Dieker posts her weekly earnings from freelance writing on her blog for all to see (hello-the-future.tumblr.com). In 2014, she earned US$40,966.48 from freelance writing, producing about twenty articles per week, and in 2015 she increased her earnings to US$63,571.12, which she did by "hustling for more" work when she didn't meet her monthly income target, looking for a higher-paying client every three months, sending out a new pitch every week, and working longer hours (Dieker 2015, 2016). Dieker is positive about her work and publicizes her experiences as a form of knowledge sharing with other freelancers. Making her earnings visible throws into relief the value and devaluing of freelance labour.

Less established writers are not as willing to attach their names to their complaints and so participate in anonymous collective expressions of dissent through blogs, tweets, and tumblrs, including Who Pays Writers? Cobbling together information on publications' often-opaque payment schemes is a way to challenge their power and make use of the Internet's capacity for anonymity and transparency. As Martin notes, secrecy about payment rates only benefits those who sign the cheques (Who Organizes Writers? panel 2014). Another freelancer wants to see this project pushed further, with freelancers scanning and uploading contracts to compare publishers' practices and creating a form of "standards setting." Freelancer Scott Carney launched a similar project, WordRates, as a Google document that anyone could access to input rates paid by US newspapers and magazines. Carney ran a Kickstarter campaign in 2015 to turn the spreadsheet into a stand-alone website to enable freelancers to upload and compare contracts and to rate editors and publications for which they write. "Just comparing rates and contract terms between publications will give writers the power to take control of their financial future instead of just being subject to whatever the whims are of the particular publication they're working with," Carney says. "I hope there's a cultural shift because of this" (cited in Sanders 2015a). Visibility projects such as Who Pays Writers? and WordRates are acts of solidarity and can counter the competitiveness and individualization fostered among freelancers, a form of networked solidarity, or using digital tools for support and solidarity-building among dispersed and isolated workers (Brophy, Cohen, and de Peuter 2015). Carney argues that since unionization and collective bargaining for freelancers is impossible under current labour laws, "the only real option seems to be to organize our negotiating potential" through making rates visible (Sillesen 2015). Martin, in a 2015 personal communication, reports that freelancers are excited about Who Pays Writers?, and many consult it when pitching a project or negotiating payment. "There's also a sort of fun, gossipy quality to it," she says. As for editors, they have mixed feelings:

Editors I've talked to at publications ... are annoyed by it, but can't really express that because they know it's the right thing ... As an editor, we are in sort of a tough spot, because you don't set the budget, generally speaking. And you want better writers and you want to pay more, but you maybe don't have the funds to do it. And so they are kind of annoyed by it, but they are secretly rooting for it. I have heard, through the grapevine, that some editorial folks at very large, corporate publications ... don't like it. (ibid.)

Pay Me Please is another visibility project that attempts to name and shame media companies into paying writers money owed. The site's tagline is "when publishers don't pay up, let the world know" (www.beaconreader.com/pay-me-please). Pay Me Please hosts a running list of payments owed to freelancers, including the media outlet (from small websites and magazines to large media organizations like the Associated Press, the Canadian Broadcasting Corporation, and Fox News), money owed (from tens to thousands of dollars), what the work was for, and the number of days a payment is overdue. Anyone can add a missing payment, and most entries include the writer's name. Freelance journalist Iona Craig launched Pay Me Please after she was owed payment by various BBC outlets (Teicher 2014). According to Craig, many payments are made after being listed on the site; sometimes just the threat of being listed is enough to get a company to pay up (Teicher 2014). When payments are made, the word "settled" appears, but the entry remains online, a standing record of the delayed and missing payments freelancers always chase.

On Twitter, freelancers and other cultural workers use the popular hashtag #dontworkforfree to publicize and deride advertisements for unpaid work, to express anger at being asked to work for free, and to encourage other cultural workers to refuse. A United States–based freelancer anonymously tweets from the handle @crapwritinggigs, broadcasting "grumpy comments and pointed observations" about online postings for freelancers (CMG Freelancers 2015). Sample tweets include "Hilarious. @KEYDifference is looking for 'smart writers' to write 500-word posts for $5" and "make $0.02/word writing for @thebabereport. Or write for a company that actually values your time and skills." "I'd like to let other writers know that $20/post is an insult and they're worth waaaay more," the anonymous tweeter says (cited in CMG Freelancers 2015). In May 2014, a group of Canadian freelancers hijacked a Facebook post by the *Globe and Mail* advertising the twenty-fifth anniversary of Facts and Arguments, a daily column written by *Globe* readers for which the paper does not pay. "Why not pay the writers?" asked freelancer Jacyln Law, prompting dozens of comments by freelancers decrying unpaid writing. The post is public, visible on the newspaper's Facebook page. Freelancer Ann Douglas commented: "I remember hearing an editor from the *Globe and Mail* speak at a writing conference years ago. She noted that the *Globe and Mail* was able to charge premium rates for advertising on the Facts and Arguments' page because the page was so well read. Surely, the writers who have made this page so popular with readers deserve to be compensated for their work" (*Globe and Mail* 2015). While not an organized campaign (there is no evidence of the request to pay writers moving beyond Facebook), the conversation is an example of writers' increasing willingness to make their names and opinions on their working conditions public. Such efforts are a form of counter publicity, whereby media workers create media texts and appropriate communicative technologies to use as tools to broadcast messages about their labour conditions (Brophy, Cohen, and de Peuter 2015). Counter publicity undercuts freelancers' sense of individual frustration and isolation and plays a vital role in developing a collective response to labour pressures.

Social media has also been useful for organizing campaigns or co-ordinated efforts to make freelancers' conditions visible and to push for change. In September 2013, Canadian freelance journalists used social media as part of their campaign to resist restrictive copyright clauses in agreements from TC Media. Initiated by l'Association des journalistes indépendants du Québec and run in coalition with four other journalists' and writers' associations, the campaign used the hashtag #nesignezpas (don't sign) to draw attention to the new contract, which would require freelancers to sign away moral rights "and grant TC Media full copyright across all of its brands, in all languages, on all platforms, for eternity ... applied to all current and yet-to-be invented media forms where writers' works appeared" (Salamon 2016). The campaign pushed TC Media to amend the contract, demonstrating to Canadian freelancers that online tools can help mobilize a disparate group. "Freelancers work in isolation ... but the digital realm allows us to come together in ways that previously were more difficult to do," explained a long-time freelancer (cited in Salamon 2016). The Canadian Media Guild and the Canadian Writers Group launched Story Board, a website that publishes articles about freelance issues and writers' own reports on their working conditions. It was on Story Board that two Canadian freelancers posted critiques of companies they worked for that helped spur public conversations about the state of freelance media work in Canada. In an article called "Why I Am No Longer Writing the Column I Loved for the Toronto Star," Ann Douglas publicly resigned from her column due to the contract imposed on her that allowed the *Toronto Star* to license her writing to third parties without her permission (Douglas 2013). Douglas expresses frustration over the new "freelance agreement" the *Toronto Star* demanded she sign. "The word 'agreement' implies that the two parties have had some sort of discussion and have found some common ground," she writes. "That simply never happened in this situation. The 'freelance agreement' was presented to me as a fait accompli – something to be signed – or not." Another long-time freelancer used Story Board to push issues of copyright and contracts into public conversation, also decrying the contracts large media companies are pushing on freelancers, withholding his labour from one publisher until it changes its contract (Teitel 2013). Big names in Canadian journalism have used digital platforms to draw attention to issues all freelancers face, demonstrating the utility of digital tools for labour organizing among this constituency.

Other digital tools are more ambivalent. Consider crowdfunding platforms, which are promoted as having the potential to liberate freelancers from media institutions. For many, crowdfunding – "using micropayments by large numbers of people to finance creative projects" (Jian and Usher 2014, 156) – holds promise for freelancers to independently and directly fund journalism and writing careers. Sites like Kickstarter, Patreon, or Indiegogo enable freelancers to pitch plans for projects, from ongoing to one-off articles, to current and future readers (the sites, most of which are for-profit companies, take a cut of the funds raised). As incentive to donate, journalists offer donors "rewards" such as postcards from their travels or advanced copies of the work (Hunter 2015), but the ultimate exchange for funds is a finished piece of journalism they can self-publish or sell to a media outlet. Donations range from one-time

gifts of five dollars or hundreds of dollars to monthly donations –
on Beacon, donors can subscribe to individual writers for five dollars per month – gesturing toward a patronage model, one of the
earliest methods of financially supporting artists (Hesmondhalgh
2012). In this spirit, it is not uncommon to see a "donate" or "tip the
writer" button at the end of articles and blog posts. The promise of
crowdfunding is that, unlike investors, funders do not expect a return on their investment. The aim is to have the work out in the
world or to support a journalist's career.

Scholars who study crowdfunding have largely attended to questions of audience participation and what crowdfunding means for
consumers of journalism or for the type of journalism that can be
produced. (The way scholars have defined crowdfunding places
agency on the audience, which finances the project, rather than on
the individual freelancer, whose labour, initiative, promotion, and
pitching is what makes the project happen.) Overall, however, there
is a general consensus that crowdfunding sites foster a shared commitment to journalism's social importance, enabling journalists to
cover stories that are generally neglected or under-resourced by
mainstream news organizations, particularly advocacy and activist
journalism. Crowdfunding provides useful technological infrastructure for workers with no institutional support. The sites make
it straightforward to set up a project, post a video, invite friends via
social media to donate and promote the project, and, critically, get
paid. Because crowdfunding sites have accumulated such a large network of donors, there's a high chance a freelancer's project will be
supported by strangers and people outside of their immediate networks (MacPhee 2012). Crowdfunding holds promise for enabling
journalists to bypass media institutions and self-organize – not to
mention decommodify – the work of journalism.

Yet crowdfunding is a response to precarious media work, declining investments in investigative journalism, shrinking freelance
budgets, and the increased challenges freelancers face (Hunter 2015),
and should be considered in light of the various issues I have outlined in this chapter. Crowdfunding in most cases benefits those
journalists who already have connections, wide networks, and a reputation – all required to promote a project and raise funds. It depends on hours of unpaid work: pitching a project, selling oneself
and ideas, requesting money, and managing the raising of funds, all

part of freelancers' increasingly frenetic pace of work. On crowd-funding sites, the pitch is a drawn-out process. A freelancer is not just pitching a piece to an editor at a media organization, but engaging in an extended campaign of selling, promoting, and convincing. Journalists report finding it difficult and uncomfortable to engage in the sell, noting the stress it puts on personal relationships and their limited ability to continuously request donations (Aitamurto 2011; McPhee 2012). As currently organized, crowdfunding cannot sustain journalism in the long term, as people are more interested in making one-time donations to specific projects (Jian and Shin 2014). The largest crowdfunding sites are privately owned and use algorithms and their own self-interest in promoting certain projects, which gives some projects visibility over others. Ultimately, the entrepreneurial imperatives inherent in crowdfunding could put pressure on journalism itself. As Josh McPhee (2012) writes: "Kick-starting a project demands that we transform ourselves from artists into marketers."

FREELANCERS, JOURNALISM, AND DIGITAL TECHNOLOGY

Freelancers' digital journalism experiences point to the troubled relationship between journalism and technology under capitalist modes of media production. While many anticipate great opportunities for journalism in a digital age, workers' perspectives make the limits to these opportunities clear. Freelance journalists are constrained by the continuing power inequalities between writers and the media institutions for which they work. The power inequality is linked to freelancers' self-employment status. But it also has to do with the way that technologies are used in production, which we can understand through the labour process theory, where journalists' labour is deployed in particular ways to enable the accumulation of profit in digital media outlets. Facing challenges to accumulation strategies, media industries are reorganizing to extract greater surplus value from writers through outsourcing, no pay, low pay, piecework, and the ongoing commodification of journalism itself. Yet technology is a site of struggle. While media corporations use technologies to lower labour costs, freelancers use them to make their labour visible.

By making accounts of their labour experiences public, freelancers demonstrate that journalism is not just a job or a craft, but also a key part of the value creation process in capitalist media production. Freelancers are using digital technologies to challenge assumptions about their work, protect themselves, connect with other freelancers, share information, and build solidarity – critical interventions for a dispersed and often invisible workforce. Freelancers' accounts of their work demonstrate the contradictions they experience while working (Cooley 1981). While they get great satisfaction from their work, they are increasingly dissatisfied with low pay, long hours, and with type of journalism they are increasingly asked to produce. Public expressions of such contradictions serve various purposes. In some ways, they publicly pressure publications to respect writers' rights. In others, they make clear the challenges freelancers face are not just individual struggles, but shared experiences of work. In his op-ed in the *New York Times*, Kreider (2013) offers freelancers a template to use to refuse to write for free: "Thanks very much for your compliments on my [writing/illustration/whatever thing you do]. I'm flattered by your invitation to [do whatever it is they want you to do for nothing]. But [thing you do] is work, it takes time, it's how I make my living, and in this economy I can't afford to do it for free. I'm sorry to decline, but thanks again, sincerely, for your kind words about my work." Here, advice to fellow freelancers serves as a public denunciation of no-pay journalism and an effort to build a collective refutation of writing for free. And while Douglas's (2013) public resignation over a restrictive contract calls for freelance writers to "[stand] firm, shoulder to shoulder" to resist exploitative contracts, the refusal to write for free can be better described as a "mood" rather than a "movement," more specifically, a mood of "antifree" (*n+1* 2014). Antifree, explain the editors of *n+1*, "attracted 25-year-olds who objected to being paid $50 by a corporate website that presumed them lucky to get the experience. It attracted veteran journalists who balked at being asked to write for a large, profitable magazine's website for chump change ... These were individual stories, but they added up."

Although stories add up, a mood alone cannot change labour conditions. As the *n+1* editors note, demanding to be paid is important, but it is only a first step in a much larger struggle, and strategies to improve labour conditions for freelance writers (and all cultural workers) must go further. Their suggestion? To "create and strengthen a union – one that can demand standards for contracts, reprimand institutions for reneging on terms or norms of conduct, and otherwise represent the interests of culture workers before the ultimate bearers of responsibility for the diminishing of salaries and security: media conglomerates, corporate boards, and shareholders" (ibid.). Indeed, even unpaid *Huffington Post* bloggers feel that a union, online organizing, or "withholding contributions" should be used to "[address] digital labour issues in the future" (Fuller et al. 2011, 11). Martin also thinks freelancers need to organize. "There's a greater need for in-person organizing and solidarity among freelancers," she says. "Collecting the information [via Who Pays Writers?] ... is just the preliminary step to that type of thing ... writers need to start coming together and setting informal standards amongst their communities and amongst their markets." And while collective organization is not a major theme of the freelance accounts I reviewed, it does appear in some pieces. A freelancer named Jennifer Mills (2013) writes: "Right now, we have too much flexibility and not enough strength. Too much exposure and not enough light being cast on working conditions. It's time to stop framing this discussion in terms of individual choice and start shoring up our bargaining power." Technology is not the fix freelancers need to improve their conditions of work and life. A better solution, as freelancers and some media unions have begun to discover, is collective organization and policies that can protect against precarity.

6

Unite the Write:
Freelancers and Collective Organization

"The writer, owing to his temperament, his lack of business training, and his frequent isolation from other members of his profession, is especially unfit to drive a good bargain with those who buy his manuscripts."
                    Pamphlet issued by the Author's League of America, 1912
                    (cited in Hepburn 1968, 70)

Despite their individualistic outlook and historical characterizations as "lone wolves" and "mavericks" (Edmonds 1976; Drobot and Tennant 1990), freelancers are, in fact, joiners. Canadian freelance writers belong to a multitude of organizations, groups, and informal networks that range in size, scope, and focus, from national organizations such as the Canadian Association of Journalists and regional groups such as the Saskatchewan Writers Guild to more focused organizations such as the South Asian Journalists Association. There are dozens of other writers' groups in Canada, and established and emergent groups for self-employed writers exist in the United States, the United Kingdom, and Europe.

Freelancers join organizations for many reasons: to access health benefits; to temper endemic isolation; to develop skills and receive training; to meet others; to find work; and to seek advice on careers, contracts, and fees. Although there have been various writer-led initiatives and small successes over the years, and while existing organizations have a history of advocacy, boycotts, lobbying, and winning lawsuits against media companies, freelancers have stopped short of gaining the most powerful tool workers have historically obtained through union membership: collective bargaining for agreements that would, at the very least, guarantee minimum payments and fair contracts. Organizing freelancers is challenging: they are contracted under highly individual terms, work in physical isolation from one another, and generally have different mindsets about how to address work-related challenges.

More critical, however, are legal challenges to organizing. Freelancers inhabit what organizer Joel Dullroy (2013, 3) calls "a grey zone of employment activity, outside the protections of long-established labour regulations" in most Western states. Legally classified as self-employed workers or independent contractors (despite the fact that many are economically dependent on one organization), freelancers are "outside the ambit of labour protection and collective bargaining" and therefore positioned as entrepreneurs or small business owners who do not require legal protection (Fudge 2003, 36–7). Canadian labour law does not typically support the unionization of workers who move between work sites, as labour law is based on the assumption that "individual work sites are 'natural' bargaining units," with the exception of some workers, such as those in construction (Vosko 2000, 264). Under the Canada Labour Code, only two categories of workers can access collective bargaining rights: employees in a standard employment relationship who work for a single employer on a single worksite, continuously, and dependent contractors, which includes workers who do not have employment status but who are deemed to be "in a relationship of considerable economic dependence and subordination" with a single employer (Vosko 2005, 143–4; Cranford et al. 2005, 4).

Freelancers are classified as independent contractors and have therefore remained outside the scope of labour law. Whereas employees are involved in "a contract of service" to their employer, under common law, self-employed workers are considered to contract *for* services, leaving them without access to collective bargaining rights (MacPherson 1999, 355). Collectively organizing to increase rates of pay would, for one, put freelancers at risk of violating Canada's Competition Act, under which self-employed professionals acting together to set prices could be viewed as attempting to influence the market, deemed anticompetitive, and charged with "conspiracy in restraint of trade" (Vosko 2005, 167–80; Canada 2011). Although this law may seem absurd when considering the power of writers vis-à-vis publishers, "concern over anti-competition" remains a major challenge for self-employed cultural workers to collectively bargain (Vosko 2005, 145). In the 1980s, the Writers' Union of Canada (TWUC) tried to negotiate minimum terms via standard contracts with the Association of Canadian Publishers. The association ended negotiations on the grounds that implementing standard contracts would breach the antimonopoly provisions of the Competition Act – it was only willing to sign onto a voluntary code of practice, which TWUC did not endorse (Lorinc 2005, 55).

Some Canadian cultural workers' organizations have been negotiating collective scale agreements with producer associations since the 1940s, including Union des artistes, the Alliance of Canadian Cinema, Television and Radio Artists (ACTRA), the Canadian Actors' Equity Association, and the American Federation of Musicians of the United States and Canada, but these have been "voluntary recognition arrangements," which are not governed by legislation – engagers are "not compelled by law to negotiate" (Vosko 2005, 146, 145). In the United States, the National Labor Relations Act (1935) prevents "any individual having the status of an independent contractor" from unionizing and bargaining collectively. This legal positioning in many ways cements the tendency to consider freelancers as independent contractors selling a service, entrepreneurs, small businesses, and, above all, professionals, further limiting the notion that some form of unionization is possible. And so, freelancers' collective forms of organization have, for the most part, been founded on and limited by a conception of freelancers as professionals rather than as workers who must confront labour-capital relations.

As I outlined in chapter 2, journalistic professionalism has long been tied to a notion of journalistic objectivity, which was promoted by nineteenth-century publishers to sell newspapers to mass publics. Publishers later harnessed a version of professionalism to prevent newsworkers from unionizing, arguing that members of a labour union could not be objective when reporting the news. Journalists adopted this argument, perpetuating the idea that "pressure groups" such as unions could compromise the integrity of reporting (Paris 1978; Fedler and Taylor 1981, 83). As journalist and professor Herbert Brucker wrote in 1949, "the concept of a pressure group like The Guild in charge of reporting and interpreting the news is grotesque" (242, cited in Fedler and Taylor 1981, 83). In such a view, union membership is considered "inappropriate" or "demeaning" (ibid.). Many contemporary freelancers share the view that unions are incompatible with writing for a living. When I asked my survey respondents if they would ever join a labour union, one replied: "Probably not. Writing is a strongly individual and mostly meritocratic business. One writer's work is not equivalent to another's in the way it is with, say, autoworkers. No matter who works on a car, at the end of the line you've got a car. Not so with writing – the difference in quality between the top end and bottom end, in terms of skills, is far too wide to negotiate collectively as a single body re: wages." Another replied: "It seems counterintuitive to join a union if the appeal of freelance work is free-agency and self-control. I would rather not have my work appear 'courtesy of' a union should I wish to write for a small publication" (no existing union for freelancers has such a requirement).

Journalists' views that unions could undermine professionalism and autonomy points to the contradictory class location freelancers occupy: ideological alignment with publishers – immediately represented in many instances by editors – despite freelancers' declining working conditions, power, and control over their work (Wayne 2003; Deuze and Fortunati 2011). As Mike Wayne (2003, 23) notes: "One way in which intellectuals have attempted to explain their social role has been to depoliticize what it means to be elaborators and disseminators of ideas. This involves uncoupling knowledge production from vested social interests, defining professionalism as rising above the social conflict between capital and labour, and instead promoting 'objectivity' and 'rationality' as the very essence of what it is intellectuals do." Journalists have long placed great importance on objectivity, which for many is a signal of professionalism (Hackett and Zhao 1998).

Journalists employed at North American newspapers began collectively organizing in the 1930s and 1940s to regulate pay and working conditions and to improve their occupational status (Leab 1970; Deck 1988), but freelancers have not been part of these unions. Until recently, freelancers have constituted a small component of the media labour force. Freelancing was an exception, not the norm, and organizing this cohort has not been worthwhile for unions. Freelancers are also very difficult to organize. No one knows how many people work as freelancers and it is challenging to locate potential members, let alone organize people who do not work for a single employer, in the same location, or in a physical workplace. Freelancing is fluid: people shift in and out of freelance status, further challenging efforts to organize. Freelancers, who depend on media companies outsourcing work, have long had competing material interests with media unions, which have typically tried to limit outsourced work to protect members' jobs. Finally, because of an inability to access, and in some cases an outright aversion to, union membership, most freelancers have become adept at relying on individual coping strategies to address challenges they face, making unionization seem unnecessary and not worth the effort.

But things are changing. Freelancers and existing media unions are rethinking traditional approaches to effectively organize and represent freelancers, with the aims of gaining power and improving working conditions. Organizing freelancers has occurred in waves, resulting in a mélange of labour-focused, politicized groups and professional associations. While freelancers' most attention-getting strategies have been one-off campaigns and projects aimed at low pay and poor contracts (such as Who Pays Writers? and Pay Me Please, discussed in chapter 5), they have also been experimenting with collective forms of organization, many through affiliation with trade unions. In this chapter, I survey some histories and highlights of freelancer organizing in Canada, the United States, and the United Kingdom, demonstrating that while history shows such organization is possible, there are real challenges involved with effectively mobilizing and representing this constituency. Real promise lies in emergent alt-labour formations, unions' expanding commitment to organizing self-employed workers, policy proposals such as status of the artist acts, and conceptualizing job security beyond employment relationships. Key to all of these efforts, however, will be disrupting the sense of individualism that has been cemented through professional associations and service-based organizations and shifting freelancers' occupational identities from individuals to members of a broader class of working people.

FREELANCE JOURNALIST ORGANIZATIONS

Canada

Typically, writers' organizations in Canada have been professional associations, yet some have taken on duties that would normally fall to a union, such as grievance and contract support. Most were founded by literary writers, but many included journalists and non-fiction writers, as book authors earned extra money by freelancing for magazines (Davey 2007, 105). The Canadian Society of Authors formed in 1899 to address authors' concerns about copyright but faded after ten years (Kelly and Vincent 2007, 123). The Canadian Authors Association formed in 1921, and by 1933 absorbed remaining Canadian Society of Authors members. It assisted established and aspiring writers in developing their writing skills, located publishing markets, and promoted Canadian authors and their books (ibid.; Moore 2007). In the 1940s, Canadian writers went through a period of politicization, lobbying for standardized contracts and income tax averaging and submitting briefs and opinions to government studies and reviews (Kelly and Vincent 2007, 125). A period of intensifying cultural nationalism from the late 1960s throughout the 1980s resulted in increased government funding for the arts, including funding for writers' groups, which rapidly increased in number, especially in small communities. The League of Canadian Poets formed in 1967 and the Saskatchewan Writers Guild in 1969, for example.

The next iteration of large-scale organization was the Writers' Union of Canada (TWUC), founded in 1973 and open to writers who had published at least one trade book. A group of writers established TWUC to give authors a voice in the industry and at government inquiries and royal commissions (Moore 2007). Despite its name, TWUC operates like a professional association, but a sense of urgency and militant spirit led its founders to settle on the word "union" in the name, even though it has never been able to collectively bargain. TWUC's early activities were guided by the political and cultural climate of book publishing in Canada and included promoting Canadian writers, picketing bookstores, and lobbying the government on policy issues. TWUC was integral to the development and 1986 passage of public lending rights legislation, which remunerated authors whose books were borrowed from public libraries (Kelly and Vincent 2007, 125). It developed a model contract, provided advice and grievance services, and developed a system of royalty audits. Although it began with the intent to negotiate standard contracts on behalf of its members, TWUC was dissuaded by publishers' reluctance and a fear of being judged anticompetitive under Canadian competition law.

Early writers' groups in Quebec included the École littéraire de Montréal, established in 1895, and l'Association des journalistes canadiens-français, which existed in from 1903 to 1906 and was dedicated to "professional concerns" such as campaigning against literary piracy, which was rife in Quebec at the time. Focus on such issues raised "writers' awareness of the need to assert their rights" (Kelly and Vincent 2007, 127). In 1921, French authors established a French section of the Canadian Authors Association. This partnership lasted until 1936, when French writers broke away from the English organization. Some writers formed the Société des écrivains canadiens "to provide francophone writers with a credible organization while respecting their desire for cultural autonomy" (128). Rifts among writers in this group led to the creation of the Union des écrivains québécois (129). Today, freelance journalists in Quebec are represented by l'Association des journalistes indépendants du Québec, which actively runs campaigns that address freelance payments and contracts.

One of the most active sites of freelancers' collective activity is through informal channels of communication, such as email lists. Email lists are a low-effort way to break the isolation of working alone and to gain a sense of community. They are also useful for advice on stories, contracts, and careers. For freelancers, email lists can be the virtual equivalent of leaning over an office cubicle wall to ask a coworker a question. But they can also be spaces to develop a collective critique about the condition of freelance writing as an occupation and for recognizing and naming the power relations that structure the industry. One such list, Toronto Freelance Editors and Writers, has almost 900 members and has become a space not only for seeking career advice, but also for mobilizing writers around payment and contract issues and for encouraging one another to join existing freelance organizations.

There are many freelance organizations in Canada, covering a variety of genres and geographical regions, such as the Playwrights Guild of Canada, the Writers' Alliance of Newfoundland and Labrador, and the Manitoba Writers' Guild. One of the most successful is the Writers Guild of Canada, a union for film and television writers that provides screenwriters with minimum scale agreements and strong copyright protection. In the next chapter, I examine in depth four organizations in Canada that currently represent and try to organize freelance journalists: the Professional Writers Association of Canada, the Canadian Freelancers Union, the Canadian Writers Group, and the Canadian Media Guild's freelance branch.

The United States

The Society of Magazine Writers was founded in 1948 to raise magazine writers' professional and economic standing. By 1951 it had sixty-five members, and in 1952 it developed a code of ethics in an effort to standardize writer-editor relationships (Peterson 1964, 125). The society became the American Society of Journalists and Authors, a professional association for "independent nonfiction writers" (American Society of Journalists and Authors 2015). Prior to the society, the Authors League of America was founded in 1912 by book and magazine writers, including some journalists, primarily to improve copyright legislation. In 1921, the league split into two branches, the Dramatists Guild of America for writers of radio and stage drama, and the Authors Guild for novelists and nonfiction writers. The Authors Guild currently has 8,000 members and focuses on legal issues including contract reviews and publishing disputes, offers professional development for authors, and lobbies on issues of copyright and taxation (Authors Guild n.d.). The Great Depression saw the birth of the Unemployed Writers' Group, which became the Writers Union, an activist union with a membership of two hundred aspiring but unemployed writers. The group held weekly meetings and in 1935 organized sit-ins and demonstrations. During a conference for "professional, cultural, and white collar workers," it called for relief programs for writers (Denning 1998, 87).

The Writers Union faded, but by 1981 freelancers were ready to organize again. At the American Writers Congress in New York City that year, a group of freelancers decided to organize a union to address media concentration and the resulting power imbalance between writers and publishers (Friedman 1991, 33). Despite the antiunion climate of the 1980s and the challenge of organizing freelancers, writers formed the National Writers Union (NWU), mandated to improve pay and working conditions for magazine, book, technical, and commercial writers. By 1991, the NWU had 3,000 members in eleven locals across the United States. The union offered a health plan, a job bank, newsletters, seminars, and social events. By the time it was seven years old, it had won over US$250,000 in grievance claims. It negotiated contracts with several independent, mostly progressive magazines (such as *Mother Jones* and *Ms.*), which agreed to minimum wage scales, decent work policies, and recognition of the NWU as a bargaining agent (32–3). Most contracts were renewed every two years, not always under amicable conditions. As Sara Friedman writes: "Most of these contracts ... were negotiated with supposedly friendly politically progressive publications, but their liberal managements when actually confronted with the specter of unionization fought nearly as hard against it as any other employer" (35).

The NWU's biggest struggle came in 1987, when it pursued contracts for freelancers at the *Village Voice*.[1] Writers were frustrated by erratic, arbitrary, and low pay, despite their satisfaction with editorial freedom (35–6). The union spent a year recruiting and collecting authorization for the paper's 200 freelancers, who produced about half of the paper's content each week. Freelancers met in small groups to develop a contract that covered work rules, a pay scale, and union recognition. Early negotiations with the paper in May and June 1988 resulted in an agreement on work rules but a disagreement over pay scales and the question of representation (36). By the end of the 1980s, freelancers at the *Village Voice* remained unorganized, but had won higher pay. This example demonstrates the limits of the legal framework that prevents self-employed journalists from engaging in collective negotiations. Labour law makes no provisions to force companies to recognize freelancers' collective representation and engage in negotiations, and it took enormous, focused effort to get the *Village Voice* to voluntarily negotiate. While Friedman argues that the *Village Voice* effort demonstrated the NWU's potential to challenge a major publication, the NWU did not have the experience needed to win, lacked both financial and human resources (at the time, it was staffed by overworked, underpaid freelancers), and operated under difficult laws. The NWU's membership doubled in the 1980s, enabling the creation of a paid, professional staff. The union debated joining the Newspaper Guild and affiliating with other writers' organizations and eventually settled on the United Auto Workers, which NWU members felt "better reflected th[eir] values and best-served th[eir] needs" (40).

The NWU, which currently has 1,300 members, operates out of an office near Times Square in New York City with one full-time officer, president Larry Goldbetter, and one full-time and one part-time staff. It provides members with grievance services and contract advice. It led a lawsuit against the *New York Times* to defend freelancers' copyrights to electronic rights (*Tasini v. New York Times*) and launched a class-action lawsuit against Google over Google Books. The NWU offers group benefits, engages in advocacy, and has won some important victories for its members, but has yet been unable to collectively bargain. After winning the *New York Times* lawsuit, the NWU's membership peaked at 7,000. Current low membership, however, reflects the difficulty of recruiting and retaining members in such a fluid constituency, and without a bigger membership the union is unable to pressure publishers for change (Goldbetter, personal communication 2010). In April 2002, the NWU helped draft a bill introduced to US Congress called the Freelance Writers and Artists Protection Act, which would have redefined artists as employees for legal purposes, thus enabling freelance writers, artists, and photographers to claim exception under antitrust laws that prevent them from engaging in collective bargaining (Holland 2005–06). The bill was opposed by the Society of Photographers and Artists Representatives, the Illustrators Partnership of America, and the American Society of Media Photographers (D'Agostino 2010, 120). The Society of Photographers and Artists Representatives' members opposed the notion of being classified as employees because it would mean giving up all copyright to their works when "authorship is the only means they have of asserting creative control over their work" (Holland 2005–06, 307). The bill never made it past committee and was forgotten under George W. Bush's two terms (Goldbetter, personal communication 2010). In recent years, the NWU has been able to help members claim hundreds of thousands of dollars from two magazines that withheld pay (what Goldbetter calls "deadbeat publisher[s]") and has explored partnering with Who Pays Writers? (Hasan 2015).

Downtown and over the Brooklyn Bridge, a different kind of union is working to address the needs of American freelancers in a range of industries and sectors. The Freelancers Union, formed in 2003, represents "independent workers." It established itself primarily as a group insurance provider for freelancers (offering "health, dental, and other curated benefits for independent workers" at what it deems affordable rates), which it first sold through its own for-profit Freelancers Insurance Agency and, since the passage of the Affordable Care Act in 2014, now sells through a private insurance company (Freelancers Union 2015).[2] The Freelancers Union positions itself as a mutual aid society, in which individuals combine resources to support one another rather than making demands from employers (in her writings, founder Sara Horowitz references new mutualism and histories of social unionism). It has about 300,000 members and, with free membership, was at one time the fastest-growing union in the United States (Ross 2013). In addition to individual supports and services – a tool for generating a contract, forums for freelancers to connect, corporate discounts, and, more recently, health clinics and yoga classes – the Freelancers Union has lobbied policymakers for laws to better protect freelancers in New York State, including getting tax reform passed so that those who earn under $100,000 do not have to pay business and personal revenue tax (Abrahamian 2012). In December 2015, the Freelancers Union helped introduce the Freelance Isn't Free bill to the New York City Council, which would require engagers to provide signed contracts to all freelancers and specify deadlines for payment. The bill would ensure that the Department of Consumer Affairs would enforce the provision and use of contracts and could penalize companies that break the rules with fines or jail (Goldensohn 2015). The bill is endorsed by a range of organizations, including the National Domestic Workers Alliance and the National Guestworker Alliance. As of March 2016, the bill was still in front of New York City Council.

Perhaps because of its size, media attention, or bold advertising campaign – which included striking posters in the New York subway system with slogans like "Working for the Radical Notion of Fairness" and "There Is an 'I' in Union" – the Freelancers Union has faced criticism from those concerned about meaningful forms of worker representation. Although it identifies as a movement, critics argue that it is essentially a lobby group or service organization that treats "workers as consumers" rather than as people "needing workplace representation" (Paul 2014). Online, the Freelancers Union paints freelance life in a cheery light, embraces market-based solutions to supporting freelancers, and cannot (and does not want to) assist freelancers in negotiating contracts, setting minimum rates of pay, or reclaiming absent payments for individuals (Abrahamian 2012). As Sarah Jaffe (2015) explains: "Rather than winning contracts with employers or negotiating on workers' behalf, the [Freelancers Union] aims to bring freelancers together as more of a political constituency than a bargaining unit." And in some ways, like all professional associations for freelancers, the Freelancers Union can be viewed as enabling employers to offload responsibility for work and social security by cushioning risk for individuals. Argues Ari Paul (2014), the Freelancers Union "fosters a disconnectedness that erodes solidarity, and sustains competition between individual freelancers." Yet it has made itself indispensable to freelancers in the United States because of the acute need for affordable healthcare, and it has been able to get politicians' attention and advocate for legal reform. That insurance profits are funnelled into policy development and advocacy is vital as the freelance workforce grows.

Although under labour law traditional media unions cannot bargain for freelancers, unions are beginning to make inroads in representing and supporting them. The Pacific Media Workers Guild, a division of the NewsGuild (formerly the Newspaper Guild, part of the Communication Workers of America), runs a freelance unit. It represents newspaper, language, and communication workers in California and Hawaii, and was the first NewsGuild local to organize freelancers. The unit advocates for freelancers and provides benefits, services, and training, but does so through a labour lens. In practice, this means linking freelance issues to broader social and political concerns and promoting solidarity. Recently, it contracted with a collection agency to help members claim missing payments. In 2013, inspired by lay-offs of photographers and photojournalists at Sun-Times Media Group, the Chicago Newspaper Guild (also part of the NewsGuild) launched Working Journalists to represent freelance media workers. These experiments in organizing freelancers into unions are in their infancy and none can yet collectively bargain for members, yet many would like to and are in the midst of determining how to build membership and, ultimately, influence.

The United Kingdom and Europe

The first British freelancer organization, the Society of Authors, founded in 1884, "was the culmination of at least a century and a half of organizational efforts to protect authors" (Hepburn 1968, 37). The difficulty writers faced in earning a living in the 1960s and 1970s led a faction called the Writers Action Group to push for unionization, but the society voted against this proposal in 1974 (Heyck 2002, 262). In general, early British freelancers regarded themselves as professionals, not workers, and viewed strikes as an impractical way to improve their conditions (248). The Society of Authors agreed to become a union in 1978 only after learning that it would not have to associate with Trades Union Congress, the United Kingdom's federation of trade unions, but did so with the provision that a closed-shop model would not be implemented. This prompted several prominent writers to resign. The society's limits lay in its lack of power to enforce standards or influence occupational qualifications (262).

The longest-lasting freelance writers' organization in the United Kingdom is the National Union of Journalists (NUJ), which has been open to freelancers since its beginning in 1907 (Gopsill and Neale 2007, 16). In the 1920s, the NUJ negotiated scale rates with the Newspaper Proprietors' Association (53). As labour conditions in the newspaper industry shifted, the NUJ extended membership to freelancers who work in-house on shifts or short contracts, or who are hired for day work (56). The NUJ's London freelance branch was established in 1951, followed by branches in other cities. By 1980, the London branch had 3,000 members. The NUJ's first and only freelance workers' strike occurred in 1981 at IPC Magazines, one of the country's largest magazine publishers. Because IPC staff, many of which were NUJ members, acted in solidarity with freelancers "by refusing to handle freelance material that came in" during the strike, it was effective in raising freelance rates by over 20 per cent (61). A similar victory occurred at Independent Radio News in 1983 when the forty-member chapel (or local, in North American terms) came very close to a strike, which would have shut down the station, and won pay increases (61). From the 1970s on, the NUJ had agreements on freelance rates with most large publishers, the newspaper publishers' associations, and the British Broadcasting Corporation. It adopted a policy that staff collective agreements had to include provisions on freelance rates, which it achieved at the *Manchester Evening News* in 1973. But the attack on the NUJ in the 1990s, which included union derecognition of both editorial and production workers at British magazines and newspapers, meant that hard-won wage agreements were lost and became difficult to win back (61; Gall 1998, 151–2). The NUJ freelance branch is active in advising members on fees, contracts, and copyrights; pursuing late payments; and providing members with a fees guide, listings to attract work, a frequent newsletter, and research services.

Some freelance journalists also belong to the Writers' Guild of Great Britain, a union representing screenwriters, book authors, poets, and writers in animation and video games. The guild negotiates collective agreements for radio, television, theatre, and film writers, and runs campaigns such as Free Is Not an Option, which aimed to stop the growing amount of unpaid work writers are asked to perform – a survey of its membership found that 87 per cent of respondents in film and television were being asked more frequently to do unpaid work (Writers' Guild of Great Britain 2015). In 1999, the Professional Contractors Group formed in the United Kingdom to respond to IR35, a law that aimed to tax any intermediaries that engaged self-employed contractors, including their own limited company or partnership, which increased taxes for freelancers. The group formed as a single-issue campaign to fight IR35 but has grown into a professional association with 67,000 members, including self-employed workers in all sectors. In 2014, it changed its name to the Association of Independent Professionals and the Self-Employed (Dullroy 2013, 51; IPSE 2015).

In 2014, a campaign called the Freelancers' Rights Movement emerged, organized by Berlin-based freelancer and activist Joel Dullroy with backing from the European Forum of Independent Professionals, an umbrella organization of national associations for self-employed professional workers (such as Platform Zelfstandige Ondernemers in the Netherlands, Verband der Gründer und Selbstständigen in Germany, and Associazione Consulenti Terziario Avanzato in Italy). Despite its towering title, the Freelancers' Rights Movement is, for now, a public online campaign centred on illuminating the growing freelance workforce and raising awareness about issues self-employed workers face in all fields. Its demands are expressed clearly and emphatically: "recognise freelancers! give us access! count us! give us a voice! treat us fairly!" In general, it aims to draw attention to the fact that freelancers and self-employed workers are left out of policy, social security, and government representation in the European Union, and to build a network of freelancers whose names can be used collectively to advocate for freelance-friendly policies. As Dullroy (2013, 1) explains, the Freelancers' Rights Movement is "a social and political quest to protect and improve the condition of independent workers. It is a diverse network of groups and campaigns which are marshalling freelancers to reject some aspects of their atomization and pursue collective empowerment." He hopes ultimately to build an activist organization that can be more active politically than traditional professional associations.

ALT-LABOUR FOR FREELANCERS

While traditional labour unions experiment with models of representing freelancers, most of the organizations that advocate for freelancers specifically are examples of "alt-labour," or labour organizations that mobilize and represent workers who under law cannot access trade unions for the purpose of collective bargaining (Eidelson 2013). Alt-labour's history and promise lies in the formation of worker centres, which typically represent noncitizen, racialized, and marginalized workers in low-wage, temporary, and precarious employment who have historically been excluded from trade unions (Fine 2006). Variations of alt-labour include the fast food workers' Fight for $15 campaign; Wal-Mart workers' strikes; groups in the arts and cultural industries such as W.A.G.E. (Working Artists in the Greater Economy), the Model Alliance, and the Dancers' Alliance; and app-based-drivers' associations, for example (de Peuter and Cohen 2015; Kessler 2015). Alt-labour groups step in where there is no employer to provide workers with "expand[ed] social protections" (de Peuter 2014, 268) and to cushion the risk and costs of self-employment. Freelance organizations give individual freelancers a collective voice, access to important services, and sometimes a place to find work. Although alt-labour groups cannot collectively bargain for minimum terms and protections, they have won some important victories. In Canada, as I demonstrate in chapter 7, these include class action lawsuits and improved contracts. Importantly, alt-labour organizations can also provide key social supports for isolated workers. As Dullroy explains in a 2015 personal communication: "[At] the meetings that we host ... a lot of the people come along for ... emotional support and connection."

Rather than collective bargaining, alt-labour organizations focus on collective support, filling in gaps left by a lack of employment relationship and corresponding state support. For freelancers, alt-labour groups have been good at developing various forms of mutual aid, or "bottom-up infrastructures to support independent work" (de Peuter and Cohen 2015). While mutual aid can be broadly conceived as individuals pooling resources for collective benefit, for freelancers it has largely come in the form of group health insurance and benefits organized through a professional association. Access to health insurance spurred the growth of the Freelancers Union in the United States and freelancers' professional associations in Europe. In Canada, the Writers' Coalition Program provides health, dental, drug, life, and travel insurance to any writer who belongs to any of twenty-two participating organizations. Closer to a model of reciprocity, the Netherlands' Broodfonds (bread funds) consists of small groups of people who pay into a "mutual sickness fund ... based on how much they would like to receive if they fall ill" (Dullroy 2015). The Broodfonds has about 4,200 participants organized into small groups to reinforce a sense of community and payments are referred to as "gifts." In addition to building a bottom-up safety net for freelancers, writers' groups focus on advocacy and lobbying, particularly on claiming unpaid fees and tax reform: because freelancers' incomes fluctuate from year to year, organizations argue that their income should be averaged over time to make taxation more fair.

Conceptualizing the challenges of precarious work more broadly, activists, labour organizers, and researchers propose improved and overhauled policy programs to protect all workers in precarious employment. In Canada, former New Democratic Party member of parliament Andrew Cash worked with alt-labour groups (including the Workers' Action Centre and the taxi workers' association) and ACTRA, the actors' union, to develop the Urban Worker Strategy, a private member's bill to address precarious employment in urban centres. The bill proposed expanded access to Employment Insurance for temporary, self-employed, and freelance workers; income tax averaging to address fluctuating annual incomes; access to pensions and health benefits for workers who are not in an employment relationship; and enforcing labour laws for temporary workers, interns, and those misclassified as independent contractors (Cohen and de Peuter 2013). An organizer with the Canadian Media Guild acknowledges the political potential of an initiative such as the Urban Worker Strategy: "It's an essential thing to bring workers together around this issue of precarity and it comes in a moment when people are figuring it out that that is a common problem, whether you're an office cleaner, a fast-food worker, a television producer ... a writer" (personal communication 2014).

The Urban Worker Strategy, though unlikely to become law unless the New Democratic Party is one day elected to federal government, is the first major sign of a political party in Canada acknowledging the limitations of tying social security to employment. The proposed policies are in line with the "beyond employment" model of social protection that Leah Vosko (2010, 219) proposes, which would provide every person, "regardless of their labour force status," with labour and social protections "from birth to death, in periods of training, employment, self-employment, and work outside the labour force, including voluntary work and unpaid caregiving." Such a vision, which delinks social security from job tenure, is shared by freelance activists such as Dullroy:

> My view is that we should ... divorce social benefits from the employment contract and make them independent, make them hinge on the individual, and follow the individual around through the course of their lives. You work, you pay into the system – no matter that work is you do, it pays into the system on some level – and you are entitled to some of the results from it. And then maybe if you have a contract, you have certain extra benefits like security and whatever perks the employer wants to throw at you to keep you around. But those basic sustaining elements of life should not be dependent on employment contracts. (personal communication 2015)

Even more broadly, yet not on the agenda of writers' organizations specifically, is the push for a universal guaranteed basic income, which is gaining global traction. Although the specific form it would take is debated, a proposal for a guaranteed annual income for each citizen regardless of employment status would go a long way to addressing precarity for all workers (Standing 2014). For journalists in particular, a guaranteed annual income would compensate for unpaid work, exploitative contracts, and the time between assignments spent pitching and looking for work (de Peuter 2014).

Proposals like the Urban Worker Strategy and a universal basic income point to the inadequacies of current policy and labour frameworks for addressing the needs of a growing freelance workforce. Labour laws and social policy in countries like Canada and the United States are remnants of the Fordist era's fading gendered model of standard employment and must be overhauled to meet the needs of contemporary workers in precarious employment in growing numbers of occupations and sectors (Lewchuk et al. 2013). Key, also, will be reforming labour laws that prevent self-employed cultural workers from joining together to collectively bargain. Canada does, however, have one promising law on the books that holds the potential to enable freelance journalists and other cultural workers to access collective bargaining rights.

THE STATUS OF THE ARTIST

The Status of the Artist Act is the first federal legislation to recognize the rights of self-employed professional artists to collectively bargain under an expanded scope of collective bargaining law. Enacted in 1995, the Status of the Artist Act addresses the risk of freelancers violating the Competition Act if they join together to demand minimum fees (Vosko 2005). Under the act, workers do not have to prove that they are employees to access labour protections (Cranford et al. 2005, 179–80). Status legislation grew out of UNESCO's (1980) *Recommendation Concerning the Status of the Artist*, which among other things aimed to "improve the social security, labour and tax conditions of the artist, whether employed or self-employed, taking into account the contribution to cultural development which the artist makes."[3] Canada was the first state to enact such legislation, and the implications could be groundbreaking for self-employed cultural workers (Ontario, Quebec, Saskatchewan, and Nova Scotia have also enacted similar legislation).

The broad goal of the federal Status of the Artist Act is to improve working conditions and economic rights of artists in Canada (Cliche 1996). The act evolved out of a long history of activism around artists' precarious conditions, including low incomes despite high education and training; disproportionate participation in part-time or seasonal work compared to other workers; disproportionate self-employment; and a lack of job security and employment-related benefits (MacPherson 1999). In Canada, debate about the act began in 1951, when the Royal Commission on National Development in the Arts, Letters and Sciences acknowledged that Canadian artists could not earn a living wage just from selling their works. Artists' organizations lobbied the government throughout the 1970s. In 1978, the government's *Federal Tax Issues of Concern to the Arts Community in Canada: An Analysis* (known as the Disney report) recommended that artists be accorded dual status under Canadian tax and labour laws: self-employed status for taxation purposes and access to Employment Insurance and the Canada Pension Plan (CAPPRT 2002).

The federal government did not act on the Disney report (Cliche 1999), but did sign the UNESCO's recommendation in 1980 and later established the Federal Cultural Policy Review Committee to review Canadian cultural policy and institutions, including the status of artists. The committee reported that "despite decades of pressure from the arts community ... [artists'] living conditions were virtually unchanged; the income of many if not most of these artists classifies them as highly specialized working poor" (cited in CAPPRT 2002). It was not until the 1986 Siren-Gélinas Task Force on the Status of the Artist – established to investigate artists' labour and living conditions – that concrete actions were taken. Among its recommendations, the report suggested legislation that would recognize organizations representing self-employed "professional artists" as agents for the purpose of collective bargaining (ibid.).

Provincially, Quebec passed status of the artist legislation in 1987 and 1988, the first in Canada to grant collective bargaining rights to groups of artists, including writers (CAPPRT 2002).[4] The acts' primary purpose is to "recognize the unions, guilds and professional associations representing artists, and to regulate or encourage collective bargaining between them and the producers, promoters, and employers [that] engage artists" (Neil 2010, 13). The first act, which

covers artists in sectors with a history of voluntary collective bargaining, like filmmaking, introduced provisions for negotiating a
first contract and for arbitration. The second, which covers those
more likely to work under individual contracts, such as writers, contains requirements for contracts and "provides authority for the
government to establish minimum standards for such contracts
through regulation" (ibid.). It requires producers to form associations and "mandates first-year contract arbitration one year after an
artists' association serves notice of its intent to bargain" (Cranford et
al. 2005, 182–3).

In 1990, the federal government committed to introducing federal status of the artist legislation. Part one of the Status of the Artist
Act was proclaimed in 1992, part two in 1995 (CAPPRT 2002).[5] Part
one established bodies to advance artists' interests under Canadian
Heritage, and part two established a labour relations regime that
recognizes self-employed artists, including writers and editors, as
professionals that can legally engage in collective bargaining at the
federal level (Cliche 1996; Canada 1992). Already, however, the act's
limitations were clear: it only covers artists in the federal jurisdiction, and so effectively excludes private sector companies and engagers, which are the most highly capitalized and powerful players
in Canadian cultural production.[6]

In 1996, the Professional Writers Association of Canada (PWAC)
was certified to have the exclusive right to represent its members in
collective bargaining. In total, twenty-four associations have been
certified in twenty-six sectors (Neil 2010, 12). These associations report that certification has imbued their organizations with a sense
of legitimacy and credibility and that the act has enabled them to
"speak with one voice" and "bring economic pressure to bear" in
dealings with engagers (CAPPRT 2002). Associations also report that
under the act they are "better organized than when the legislation
was first implemented and better able to work on behalf of their
members" (ibid.). However, and perhaps most crucially, the act has
yet to bring about concrete changes in artists' working conditions
(Vosko 2005). One problem is that many associations have not been
able to negotiate their first scale agreement because of a lack of provisions to encourage, let alone enforce, federal producers to form associations for the purpose of collective bargaining or to ensure a
first agreement is reached (MacPherson 1999; Cranford et al. 2005,

183). Many artists' associations have pushed for the act to be revised to include provisions for first contract and negotiations, and to encourage the formation of producer associations (CAPPRT 2002).

A more significant limitation is the Status of the Artist Act's scope. The act covers federal jurisdiction,[7] but the majority of artistic and cultural production – and all private sector production – in Canada occurs under provincial jurisdiction (Neil 2010, 21). Effective status of the artist legislation must be enacted at the provincial level to make collective bargaining possible. Saskatchewan and Nova Scotia have passed versions of the act: Saskatchewan's Arts Professions Act mandates the use of written contracts, which the government can regulate, and Nova Scotia's legislation enables artists' associations to set minimum payments (Nova Scotia 2012).

In Ontario, where the majority of Canadian publishing is concentrated, discussions about a status of the artist act began in 1992 with research reports and community consultations. Following lobbying and pressure from artists and cultural workers' organizations, including the Ontario Federation of Labour's Cultural Industries Working Group,[8] the Status of Ontario's Artists Act was passed in 2007. The act is modest in scope and focuses primarily on promoting the arts and culture. It recognizes the social and economic value of artists' contributions, commits to developing arts and cultural policies to encourage artistic production, and, in a somewhat patronizing gesture, designates an annual "Celebrate the Artist Weekend" (Ontario 2007, s. 6(1)). The act contains no reference to collective bargaining and contains nothing concrete to improve artists' economic conditions. The closest it comes to discussing labour relations is its promise to "strengthen the ability of arts and culture organizations to provide support for artists" (s. 5(g)). The act fails to deliver the possibility for concrete change to artists' working conditions that organizations lobbied for, and many continue to press for meaningful status of the artist legislation in Ontario (TWUC 2010; ACTRA 2011; CARFAC n.d.).[9]

Meaningful status of the artist legislation would go a long way to improve freelance writers' conditions. Status could offer self-employed workers labour market protections without the imposition of a standard employment relationship. The Writers Guild of Canada, which represents film and television writers, demonstrates that an association of self-employed independent writers can achieve labour market protections and enjoy fair remuneration for their labour by negotiating collective agreements with associations of producers, while enabling them to work for multiple engagers and negotiate above minimum scale agreements. Indeed, the organizations I examine in the next chapter are interested in collective bargaining on behalf of their members, and granting them scope to negotiate under provincial labour law is key to increasing the economic security and related power of media and cultural workers in precarious employment. The potential of the provincial act was made clear in 2014, when the Supreme Court of Canada ruled that, under the federal Status of the Artist Act, the National Gallery of Canada must recognize Canadian Artists Representation/le front des artistes Canada[10] as bargaining agent for visual artists, leading to the end of a twelve-year negotiation process and minimum payments to all artists who exhibit in the gallery (Sibley 2015).

An effective status of the artist act in Ontario could be the push freelance writers need to join the unions that are now established to represent them. At the very least, since many forms of cultural work are not location specific, workers in Ontario need access to the provisions provided to cultural workers in Quebec and Saskatchewan, which include enforcement of the use of written contracts and authority to "establish minimum standards for such contracts through regulation" (Neil 2010, 13). Achieving this will, however, take extensive organization, pressure on provincial governments, and mobilization. The emerging freelance writer organizations in Canada that I examine in the next chapter may one day be positioned to take on such a fight.

WRITERS UNITE?

When I asked respondents to my survey if they would join a union, 42 per cent said "yes," 39 per cent said "no," and 19 per cent said "maybe." Other, more recent, surveys show greater interest in unionization. A survey conducted by Contently of 643 freelancers, 82 per cent of whom were writers, found that 68 per cent of freelancers "would be interested in joining an official union for freelancers if it were legal for freelancers to unionize" (Teicher 2015). Project Word (2015, 22) reports that 93 per cent of 250 freelance investigative journalists it surveyed would join "a collective of freelancers for the right cause."

Freelance writers' interest in collective organization reveals the tensions inherent in organizing this constituency, between individual, professional needs and freelancers' collective interests. While freelancers who responded to my survey are interested in the possibility of unionization, they are primarily interested in access to individual services. They would join a union primarily for access to higher pay (78 per cent) and professional development (78 per cent), to connect to other writers (71 per cent), and to access job postings (75 per cent). Many would join for more political reasons: 52 per cent to collectively bargain with publishers, 59 per cent to have a collective voice, and 62 per cent to have some influence over the direction and future of freelance writing as an occupation. So, while freelancers may initially be drawn to collective organizations to access professional tools and individual benefits, organizers may be able to tap into a desire for collective representation. When I asked freelancers how effective a union could be in protecting self-employed writers, 38 per cent said "somewhat effective" and 39 per cent said "not effective" (8 per cent said very effective and 15 per cent had no opinion). Yet when I asked more specifically how effective a union could be assisting writers in negotiating wages and copyright, improving pay and contracts, and providing benefits, professional development, and contacts, the majority selected "somewhat effective" over "very effective," "not effective," and "no opinion" (between 40 and 50 per cent for each). One of these areas, copyright, has been selected by freelancers as an area in which they are willing to support collective bargaining (PWAC 2006, 41).

Many freelancers' responses show a lack of awareness of how a union for freelance writers could work. When asked if they would join a union, one freelancer responded: "I have to say no, because a union normalizes wages and I aim to make as much as I can." Another says: "I would be afraid to jeopardize my freedom to write for whomever I choose if I could only work for union publications (or if certain publishers only hired non-union writers)." In these cases, unionization represents restriction, standardization, and restraints on individual decision-making.

Another major challenge, evident in the case studies I explore in the next chapter, is getting freelancers to meaningfully participate in organizations. Most campaigns and organizations are driven by a small group of individual organizers with broad political vision and dedication to the cause, but building membership and enticing members to do more than pay dues and use services is a challenge. Freelancers often say they do not have time to participate. Manjula Martin, who runs Who Pays Writers?, explains: "Getting that cheque in your hands is a full-time job" (Who Organizes Writers? panel 2014). For others, dues or membership fees are high, or do not seem worth the services they receive in exchange. For the most part, freelancers understand writers' organizations as entities they join to access services; they expect that an organization will have immediate benefits on an individual level. One freelancer I surveyed has not joined a writers' organization because "I'm not sure what the benefit is. I haven't seen any changes in the way people do business or the pay. When that happens I may join. For now I'll do things myself, on my own terms." Another says: "When the freelance union actually achieves or reaches a decent contract for freelancers that is binding on newspaper and magazine publishers, I will join." A long history of professional association models has entrenched a service model as the basis for a freelance writer organization and constrains collective models that require more active participation.

That little has changed for the majority of freelancers over the years despite existing organizations has fuelled a defeatist attitude and a reluctance to put energy into trying new approaches to bringing about change. The prevailing sentiment in my survey is that the situation for writers has not improved and likely never will. A board member of the Professional Writers Association of Canada explains in a 2011 personal communication: "[Freelancers have] an element of skepticism ... and it's understandable given the erosion of rights, the lack of increase in pay rates. I think some folks, especially long-time freelancers, find it hard to imagine that anything is going to change in that area, so they might have a fatalistic view about it." Stagnating wages, restrictive contracts, and a general lack of control have exacerbated freelance writers' aversion to collective organization, intensifying freelancers' experiences of declining individual power, which translates into a sense of declining collective power. As Joanne Kates and Jane Springer (1984, 246) note, "The feeling of marginality is a powerful internalized weapon for keeping people from being active in their own interests."

Yet histories and contemporary examples of freelance media and cultural worker organizing can challenge freelancers' fatalistic views. In the 1980s, the National Writers' Union (NWU) was able to organize those "who saw themselves as hopelessly and ideologically un-organizable" (Friedman 1991, 31). At the union's inception, freelance writers felt they did not need a union, feared they could be easily replaced, and worked in a climate that understood writers as privileged, despite poor material conditions (31). Writes Friedman (32): "American writers had subsisted unorganized on the celebrity status of a few and the mythology of privilege and romance incumbent on garret life." Most of all, freelancers found it "offensive" to identify as workers, preferring instead to view themselves as artists or entrepreneurs (32). Despite this, freelancers' conditions were so poor (low and erratic pay, arbitrary editorial practices, lack of compensation for extra work, copyright grabs, no benefits or access to social protections) that the prospects of a union disrupted the mythologies and provided a concrete way forward.

Surveying the NWU's accomplishments over the years, Friedman argues that because the NWU is a union, it has been the most "aggressive" writers' group "in confronting employers" (33). More recent examples offer inspiration, too: in December 2009, the German Journalists' Association (Deutscher Journalisten-Verband), which also represents freelancers, and the United Services Union negotiated an agreement with the Federation of German Newspaper Publishers on minimum payment and rates for copyrights, including first publication rights, resale of pieces, and posting content electronically; rates are based on newspapers' circulation and the type of article (Story Board 2011f). A report by Impresa Communications (2011, 13), commissioned by the Canadian Media Guild and the Canadian Writers Group to study models of freelance compensation, cites the German examples as useful for demonstrating how freelance unions can successfully negotiate with publishers. The report notes that "German court rulings have struck down or issued injunctions against 'all-rights' contracts" (14), suggesting another possible route for Canadian freelance organizations. In its 2000 staff contract with the Guardian News Group, the National Union of Journalists (2004, 20) achieved some language to protect freelancers' payments and copyright, "which after a period of exclusivity on the papers' websites, reverts to the freelancer and provides for additional compensation for syndication of articles."[11]

As freelancers watch the media industries become more powerful and profitable, they are increasingly aware of the implications of a lack of formalized organizational support. Of freelancers who responded to my survey, 51 per cent attribute publishers' low pay to the fact that writers are not organized collectively. Australian freelancer Jennifer Mills (2013) writes, "What separates precarious arts workers from other workers is not the style of our labour, or the fact that we love what we do, or our special 'creative' egos which are supposed to make us grateful for any attention. It is one thing, and one thing only: the fact that we are not organized." In a recent rallying cry, Jonathan Tasini (2012), a freelance writer and former president of the NWU, attributes the spreading demand on writers to work for free to freelancers' being unorganized: "Ultimately ... this is about power. Actors, news writers, screenwriters and some journalists make a decent living because unions established basic conditions and marshalled power – the 'work for free' virus has spread precisely because millions of creators throughout the world lack collective organization. That isn't inherent in what we do – it's because we've failed to get out of our pyjamas and on to the street."

The metaphoric failure that Tasini refers to is largely due to the structural individualism required of freelancers, which I explored in chapter 4. Freelancers' comments on unions from my survey demonstrate a deeply individualistic outlook. "I don't want to waste time navel-gazing with other writers," says one. "I identify strongly as an entrepreneur and skilled tradesperson/professional and find many 'creative types' obnoxiously self-absorbed and precious. I don't agree with the pay-related aims of many writer's org[aniza-tions] ... and don't want to waste time debating policy when I could be, you know, working. That said, I network informally with writer and editor pals." Another says: "I would be interested in joining a union if I could see some direct and immediate benefits and if the time needed to contribute was not too great." Others are more willing to see what collective organization can offer. As one freelancer explains, "years of frustration with low pay and other exploitative aspects of the status quo in freelance writing" led them to join a freelance writers' organization. Another was motivated by "the same reasons [writers] set it up in the first place ... there needs to be more respect for writers, more money, less interference with our rights."

Potential for freelancers lies in efforts to unionize digital-first newsrooms, which began in the summer of 2015, when *Gawker* unionized. After a very public debate over whether or not to unionize, over one hundred editorial employees voted eighty to twenty-seven to join the Writers Guild of America, East. As *Gawker* senior writer and key organizer Hamilton Nolan (2015) explains: "A union is the only real mechanism that exists to represent the interests of employees in a company. A union is also the only real mechanism that enables employees to join together to bargain collectively, rather than as a bunch of separate, powerless entities. This is useful in good times (which our company enjoys now), and even more in bad times (which will inevitably come)."

Over the next few months, journalists at *Salon* and writers at *Vice*'s American office also joined the Writers Guild of America, East, and editorial workers at the *Guardian US* became members of the News-Guild. Media coverage reported that issues that prompted unionization included fairness and transparency in pay, raises, and promotions; wage scales for minimum salaries; improved workplace communications; having a voice in decision making; and, as Nolan explains, since "the 'new media' industry is almost completely not unionized ... an organized work force is an important part of making sure this industry functions fairly in decades to come" (cited in Warren 2015). In a discourse reminiscent of freelancers, the newly unionized journalists made clear that they love their jobs and "don't feel systematically taken advantage of" (ibid.). While freelancers are not currently part of these unions, there is potential for freelancers' pay and contracts to be included in future negotiations. Nolan told a reporter as much: "There is definitely interest in addressing issues facing contract (non-full-time) employees in the contract" (cited in Thomsen 2015). Indeed, in the summer of 2015 digital journalists launched a campaign to organize digital media workers writ large, on mediaworkersunite.com, which includes a statement on freelance media workers' rights. In December 2015, journalists at *Vice Canada* announced they were organizing with the Canadian Media Guild and included benefits for contract workers in their lists of demands (Canadian Media Guild 2015a).

Freelance writers have tried many times in the past to organize collectively, with varying success, often expanding their activities to include policy proposals, mutual aid, and legal and legislative reforms, all of which are deeply tied to collective mobilization and pressure. They have worked to build institutional structures and protections currently absent from workers' lives, and these efforts reflect the political, economic, and cultural contexts of their time. Today, amid flux in media industries, widespread precarious employment, heightened discussion of freelancers' challenges, and a need for collective organization, freelancers are looking to new organizing experiments. In Canada, four such experiments are underway: a professional association, an agency, and two trade unions.

Packs of Lone Wolves:
Experiments in Organizing Freelancers

Just as the occupation of freelance writing is riddled with tensions, so too are writers' organizations. On the one hand, approaches to freelance organizing in Canada have reinforced individualism, competitiveness, and a narrow conception of professionalism that prevent writers from confronting and challenging asymmetrical power relations between labour and capital in media industries. On the other hand, new and experimental models of organizing freelancers are being tested that build on this history and hold promise as sites of collective representation and action. In this chapter, I examine four case studies of organizations working to represent and mobilize freelancers in Canada: a professional association, an agency, and two established unions.

Considering the challenges freelancers face – including low pay, new online publishing models, restrictive copyright and contract regimes, declining material conditions, and declining control over their work – and the dominant organizational form they have historically preferred – the professional association – what they need is access to some elements of what traditional union structures have historically offered workers: representation, negotiation, and protection of collective agreements, or, at the very least, collective power that can stand up to publishers. Current experiments in freelance organizing have the potential to build collective power and make concrete changes to writers' conditions. Each faces many of the challenges I outlined in the previous chapter, particularly an inability to collectively bargain under current labour law. Yet new efforts are tapping into a desire for change. "I think everyone is aware that there are troubles in publishing," explains Canadian Writers Group (CWG)

founder Derek Finkle, "but on the other hand, people are less toler-
ant of being exploited" (personal communication 2015). A Canadian Media Guild organizer agrees: "There is much more of a sense
now that freelance work isn't going to get better if we don't fight to
change it ... it's because the people doing the work have no power"
(personal communication 2014). Gaining a sense of collective power
through some of the alt-labour initiatives I examined in chapters 4
and 5 or via engagement with the labour movement more broadly
will be critical for improving freelancers' conditions.

THE PROFESSIONAL ASSOCIATION

The largest professional association for writers in Canada is the Professional Writers Association of Canada (PWAC), an organization
with 700 members and twenty-three chapters across the country.
PWAC members write for magazines; newspapers; books; websites;
and corporate, government, and nonprofit clients. PWAC's (2015)
mandate is to "foster an environment where professional non-
fiction writers are respected for their skill and fairly compensated for
their work; provide a collective voice to promote the value of members' work; support and promote members at all stages of their careers; lobby for freedom of the press and freedom of expression in
Canada as a founding principle of PWAC." These activities are typical
for professional associations, which are committed to "establishing,
maintaining, and enhancing professional identity" through actively
promoting a profession; monitoring regulation and advocating for
legislation that protects members; and providing members with information, professional development, and services such as group
benefits (Hurd 2000, 12). In competitive labour markets, they help
members find work by providing employment listings, salary profiles, and career counselling (Hurd and Lakhani 2008, 5–6). Overall,
professional associations focus primarily on serving individuals
(Heckscher 1988, 185).

A major role of professional associations "is to be an information
source for members" (Hurd 2000, 12). To this end, PWAC maintains
an informative website and member email lists, an especially crucial service for freelancers, who work alone and have little face-to-
face contact. Unlike associations of regulated professions such as
medicine or law, PWAC neither sets educational standards and pro-

fessional criteria nor provides licences to control access to the labour market, but over the years its activities have extended beyond professional development and advocacy. PWAC, in Chris Benner's (2002, 134) conception of professional associations, is "both an individual strategy for people to improve their career opportunities and a collective strategy to improve the status of the occupation as a whole."

Although in its current orientation PWAC focuses primarily on servicing members as individuals, it was established to address the needs of writers as a class of workers and change their economic relations with magazine publishers. The organization was founded in 1976 as the Periodical Writers Association of Canada, with seventy-five initial members.[1] PWAC aimed to formalize the casual, individualized nature of freelance writing, to improve writers' abilities to earn decent livings, to provide a professional designation, and to build a collective voice. At PWAC's first meeting, held in Toronto on 1 May 1976, writer Alan Edmonds announced that the goal was to "create a pack of lone wolves." He described freelance writers as nonjoiners and mavericks. "We are ... here," he said, "out of self-interest ... and it so happens that in many cases and places our self-interest coincides" (Edmonds 1976). Two years earlier, a letter in the *Globe and Mail* revealed that *Maclean's* magazine had lowered article payments to $600 from $1,000 and a group of writers met to discuss how to respond. As Edmonds explained: "[The writers] met, decided that an association of writers should be formed, but ... before it actually came into being a letter of protest should be written to *Maclean's*. This letter was published in the *Globe and Mail* and *Maclean's* backed down – and the organization promptly died" (ibid.).

At the May 1976 meeting, other writers raised further issues of concern, including low pay rates, a lack of power to negotiate these rates, the need for kill fees, and a code of ethics to standardize practices and formalize freelancing writing as a profession. More than material gains, writers at the time were concerned with garnering respect for their occupation. Like reporters of the nineteenth and early twentieth centuries, they wanted to be treated as professionals; they wanted writing for a living to be considered real work. So, the group decided to focus on improving freelancers' professional status rather than on building membership, as mobilizing masses of writers may have seemed like a step toward generating adversarial relations with publishers.[2]

Archival records of PWAC's formation reveal a spirit of collectivity and resistance in the early years. A founding member suggested the group be called the Periodical Writers' Union of Canada and early documentation contained union language such as "rank and file." An early press release titled "Why Join?" explained to potential members that, "as an individual, you're powerless to fight exploitation. As a member of the Association you benefit from group support and power" (PWAC 1976a). The release emphasized the context in which freelancers worked: magazines were cutting writers' pay despite increases in circulation and advertising. "Changes," the release stated, "are obviously in order."

As first steps toward change, PWAC developed a code of ethics for writers and editors and a model contract that stipulated what were, at the time, "unheard of protection[s] for writers" (Kates and Springer 1984, 239), including fees for rewrites, kill fees, and payment schedules. The contract stipulated that unresolved disputes would be referred to an arbitration board comprised of one publication representative, one PWAC representative, and one other representative agreed upon by both parties, with a majority rule binding (PWAC 1978, 1). The contract was an improvement on the "gentlemen's agreement[s]" that had previously governed writer-publication relations (Drobot and Tennant 1990, vii). PWAC (1978a) issued a press release after it signed its first contracts, with the *Canadian* and *Content* magazines, and William French, the *Globe and Mail*'s literary critic, covered the agreements for the paper. French (1978) wrote that it took nearly one-and-a-half years to negotiate the contract with the *Canadian* and that, to mark the occasion of its signing, "PWAC executives and *Canadian* editors got together over champagne. Pity all union-management relations aren't so civilized."

Throughout the late 1970s, PWAC negotiated its new contract with nineteen Canadian magazines. PWAC's contracts, negotiated with editors, focused on fostering respectful working relationships between freelancers and editors. In contrast, current contracts deal predominantly with copyrights to works and are drafted in legal departments by corporate executives; editors generally have very little say over the terms. Current contracts are much more economic-focused than their historical predecessors and signal a shift in the nature of magazine and newspaper publishing and industry-labour relations. PWAC aimed to eventually engage in collective bargaining and threatened to strike twice, against *Weekend* and *Chatelaine* (Kates and Springer 1984, 239). Its grievance committee was strong and won most of its challenges against magazines that mistreated writers (ibid.). By 1980, PWAC's original leadership stepped down, largely due to volunteer burnout, but also because of a disagreement with the membership over how political the organization should be (ibid.). PWAC's direction subsequently shifted from worker-focused action toward professional development and providing group insurance. Emphasis on collective bargaining faded. As Joanne Kates and Jane Springer (ibid.) write, "People had wanted better wages and working conditions and the contract that would ensure this, but they did not want to call the organization a union or to be identified with union practices."

PWAC's executive debated the union question several times. At its first meeting in 1976, writers distinguished between "an association sharing interests and a union wielding bargaining power," suggesting that "the word 'union' might alienate potential members" (PWAC 1976c). Some time after that meeting, the executive voted on a motion to request funding from the Canadian Labour Congress (CLC), as PWAC could demonstrate a capacity to lobby collectively for fees and contracts. Votes were split evenly between "for" and "against," and one vote was cast in favour to break the tie. Because the question of affiliation was political, the executive brought the motion to members at a convention. However, in a letter to all members, dated 30 October 1978, PWAC President Erna Paris wrote: "Several members have told the new executive they cannot remain in PWAC if we approach the CLC for money. These people feel that as journalists we would be compromised by an affiliation with the CLC, even by exploratory talks, just as we would be compromised by a corporate affiliation. They also argued that we would be in a conflict of interest situation should any of us ever be assigned to a labour story." The conflict of interest argument echoes publishers' antiunion arguments in the early days of journalist collective organization. In this case, PWAC's executive ultimately decided that the circumstances surrounding the CLC vote were not ideal.[3] Paris wrote that if there was a strong mandate then the executive would reluctantly accept the resignation of a few members, but to avoid the risk of splitting the new organization over a tie-breaking vote, the executive unanimously requested that the motion to explore funding from and affiliation with the CLC be rescinded (Paris 1978). Reluctance to orient toward a labour organization shaped PWAC's future.

In 2005, with a membership of 600, PWAC changed its name to the Professional Writers Association of Canada, acknowledging writers' inability to earn a living solely from periodicals. The first name change motion was raised at an annual general meeting in 1990, when a member suggested that most writers earn a large portion of their income from corporate, newspaper, and other forms of writing (PWAC 1990). PWAC surveyed writers and considered the type of organization that would attract new members: a professional association or a union? As the minutes from the meeting in Charlottetown note, "The consensus was that during a recession, collective bargaining and unionization by self-employed individuals would prove self-destructive" (PWAC 1991, 4). Fifteen years later, the decision to change PWAC's name cemented its direction.

Since then, executive directors, staff, and the board have worked to professionalize PWAC's governance model, moving further from being a grassroots, member-driven organization toward one in which paid staff have autonomy to conduct the organization's business (staff are accountable to an elected national and regional board of directors, while members can participate in volunteer committees). The shift happened around 2003, when then-executive director John Degen and the board wanted to build a more collaborative relationship with publishers. As Degen explains:

> There has been a longstanding tendency in the writing community to take the "trade union versus the boss" stance – despite the fact that there was no trade union for writers – in every possible disagreement. We had this file at PWAC of really angry statements against publishers. How do you expect to run a business with all this rhetoric flying around? It was a different era, a different generation ... The [PWAC] board that hired me was a visionary board and was saying, we can't keep doing this, we can't keep slapping the people that we should be shaking hands with. Instead, we need to find a way to build bridges. (personal communication 2010)

A PWAC staff member says, "We've moved from being antagonistic toward publishers and editors to being an ally and a partner in the industry," a position that entails avoiding "demonizing" publishers or adopting an "adversarial attitude" (personal communication 2010). An executive board member explains PWAC's approach as one that seeks "common ground" and to have dialogue with publishers (personal communication 2011). Under this cooperative vision, PWAC wants to be viewed as a partner in developing industry-wide solutions rather than a confrontational group defending only writers' interests (PWAC 2006). Degen explains this philosophy as taking a "multi-pronged approach to long-range industry change. Evolution as opposed to revolution" (freelance writers' email list, 12 March 2007). So, while PWAC participates in boycotts of publishers' unfair contracts and mediates nonpayment or copyright complaints for individual members, it also cooperates with industry on projects it hopes will improve writers' conditions in the long term.

PWAC has a strong history of advocacy. When rights-grabbing contracts emerged in the 1990s, it negotiated with publishers and won some changes to contracts that placated writers. In tandem – and revealing a more confrontational streak within its ranks – some members created an online Copyright Hall of Shame to try publicly pressure publishers to improve copyright terms. PWAC has participated in consultations and made submissions to the government on copyright reform, promoting the protection of creators' rights in copyright legislation (PWAC 2006, 35). As I discussed in chapter 3, the organization played a central role in assisting Heather Robertson settle two class-action lawsuits against publishers.

In 1985, PWAC founded the PWAC Copyright Collective, which in 1988 became Access Copyright, the Canadian copyright licensing agency, a not-for-profit copyright collection management group that administers copyright licences and distributes royalties among its membership, which includes writers, visual artists, and publishers. Creators register their works with Access Copyright and the agency collects fees from copied and reused works for members. Access Copyright also advocates on behalf of creators and has been a particularly loud voice in debates over Bill C-11, the Copyright Modernization Act, which passed in June 2012 and which some writers' groups argue will negatively affect writers' abilities to be paid for their work under fair dealing clauses.[4] Access Copyright membership can generate extra income for freelance writers who have already been paid for their works, provided that they own the copyright to their pieces. However, the agency is unable to address what has become the major source of tension between freelancers and corporate publishers: owning copyrights to writers' works and fairly compensating writers for multiple uses of their works. Although Access Copyright is an important advocate and body for dealing with use of already-published works, it does not have the capacity to protect writers at the most crucial point of the production process: *before* works are published.

PWAC (2006, 22) reports that its members earn an average of nearly $5,000 more per year than nonmembers, but it has not been successful in raising writers' rates overall. The organization's early model contract is no longer used and it has since tried with little success to enforce a voluntary contract. It has lobbied industry and governments on issues of payments and rights for writers and has produced research on rates and industry best practices (PWAC 2006; Scott 2009). PWAC (2006, 17) has supported industry's efforts to increase government funding for the magazine sector, with hope that publishers' profits will trickle down to writers. Staff members believe that most Canadian magazines struggle financially in the face of decreased revenue from advertisers and rising postal rates, especially publications not owned by large media conglomerates. As one staff member says: "Our industry ... is not getting a particular easy ride now. The economics of magazine publishing are not hugely profitable, except for the larger corporations. The thing that's bad about the magazine industry, what's difficult, is that they depend on advertising dollars to pay for the content. So the business model they've got does not provide any extra money for content" (personal communication 2010). He argues that PWAC should do its best to defend its writers' economic, social, and legal interests, but that writers and their organizations must help develop solutions beyond simply demanding increased pay (ibid.).

The maintenance of "cordial relations" with employers is characteristic of professional associations (Hurd 2000, 13) and has a long history in artistic and cultural production, which Lorraine Farkas (1999) attributes to the fact that artists and their producers (or engagers, clients, or publishers) are both "involved in the creative process and to some extent they can change hats." But an assumption of cordial relations with editors means ignoring the labour-capital relationships structuring cultural production. For freelancers, the acceptance of cordiality and mutual benefit is linked to a historical identification between writers and editors, journalists and owners, who were bound through an assumption of shared goals and commitment to the work itself, the publication, or industry survival (Davis and Scase 2000, 28). Although identification of shared goals has been constructed in many cases to mask power inequities, the consequence has been that friendships and personal loyalties between writers and editors – who mediate between writers and their true employers, publishers – have been considered central to the writing process and cornerstones of industry relations.

The perception of cordial relations has limited how far PWAC can push for writers' rights. Cordial relations do not address power relations and can neutralize the sorts of antagonisms that can lead to action for change. Although PWAC provides important resources to writers and has been a vital voice in copyright debates, it primarily serves writers on an individual basis, often reinforcing freelancing's individualizing tendency. The organization's vision for its future is to focus more sharply on assisting writers in self-promotion and career development. It plans to shift focus "inward" to improve member services "and help PWACers become better entrepreneurs" (PWAC 2009, 6). An executive board member argues that PWAC plays an important role at this historical juncture in publishing, as it can help writers become self-sufficient so that they do not have to be utterly reliant on publishers to earn a living. "The world is changing in a way that can be very advantageous to freelancers," he explains, and PWAC aims to empower writers to embrace new and explore alternative publishing models, such as self-publishing books and writing online (personal communication 2010). It wants to provide more professional development (it has offered, for example, a daylong workshop on negotiating rates and contracts) and has revamped writers.ca, a website to connect writers and publishers, facilitate the buying and selling of work, and provide a showcase for members.

Yet, there is a political challenge in building an organizational model focused predominantly on assisting members in becoming individually competitive, professional, and self-reliant. Professional associations risk following the same logic industry employs under neoliberal capitalism: fostering flexible workers who can adapt to industry whim, who engage in self-improvement to upgrade skills and knowledge, picking up slack from companies and from the state, both of which take increasingly less responsibility for workers. It is possible that professional associations can encourage industry to withdraw entirely from investing in and supporting workers. Thus, this model risks reinscribing neoliberal relations and encouraging workers to cope and adapt, rather than empowering workers to collectively resist publishers' power and envision alternate modes of cultural work and production.

Although professional associations have been integral to promoting freelance writing as a legitimate occupation, for writers' professional development, and for fostering connections among isolated individuals, the model has reinforced the professional status of writing, which has had lasting implications on writers' contemporary experiences with collective organization. The professional association model cannot protect writers as workers. This limitation has become clear as publishers, once considered friends, allies, and partners in the production of Canadian culture, have grown, consolidated, and transformed their practices to increase exploitation of surplus value from writers' labour power. The lack of strong organization among freelancers, particularly in a way that can establish and enforce minimum standards for fees and contracts, is a major reason why they experience low pay and insecurity and a lack of control over rights to their works. As magazine publishing has transformed into a large industry with aggressive practices of exploitation, freelancers have had very little power to shape its direction, especially when it comes to writer' rights and remuneration.

Because PWAC cannot control access to the labour market, it cannot engage in collective bargaining, which is a weakness of the professional association model in general (Hurd 2000; Benner 2003, 203). Degen notes that there has always been a desire for collective bargaining or a similar effort among PWAC's membership, expressed through annual membership surveys. "They all wanted it," he says, "but how could we actually get it done?" (personal correspondence 2010). PWAC's membership is small and experiences high turnover. One critic describes PWAC as providing "little more than handholding services to new writers" who, once established, are no longer members (Wilson 2010). Michael OReilly, a former PWAC member who became the founding president of the Canadian Freelance Union (CFU), relates an example of PWAC's limited power. PWAC has had ongoing discussions with publishers about raising rates and improving contracts, he explains in a 2010 personal communication: "[Publishers] were always willing to talk but in the end they were never willing to do anything." During a meeting with a senior editor at the *Toronto Star*, "we were making progress but he said to me, 'if I sign this and we come to an agreement, there's no way for you to enforce it on your side, you have no ability to tell your members to do anything.' I danced around the subject, but ultimately he was bang on." Experiences like these led OReilly and other PWAC members to conclude that freelancers need a union that could collectively bargain for minimum protections, which eventually led to the foundation of the CFU.

THE FREELANCE UNION

The CFU, established in 2009, was the first trade union for media freelancers in Canada. It aims to improve the economic status of freelancers, or what it calls "independent communications professionals" – mainly writers, but also photographers, editors, and web designers (Canadian Freelance Union 2009). The CFU began as Local 2040 of the Communications, Energy and Paperworkers Union of Canada (CEP), a 150,000-member private-sector union with a large media component that included telecommunications, broadcasting, print, and new media workers. In 2013, the CEP merged with the Canadian Auto Workers to become Unifor, with a promise that the new union would include "workers in precarious, temporary, contract, self-employed, and freelance positions" who have not been able to access a union, as well as unemployed workers, youth, "individual workers in non-union workplaces," and workers who are not in a certified bargaining unit (CAW CEP Proposal Committee 2012, 30). As of 2015, Unifor has two "community chapters": the CFU and Unifaith, which represents ministers and workers at the United Church of Canada.[5] The CFU's goal is long term: to build collective power by organizing all freelance media workers in Canada and to engage in collective bargaining with publishers. Shortly after forming the CFU, OReilly, its first president, told me in a 2010 personal communication that the union is "a model of getting all the workers under one tent and trying to command a little bit of power in the marketplace."

The CFU follows a model of occupational or craft unionism, which many argue is necessary for knowledge workers in "boundaryless" workplaces – or no workplaces at all – and for workers who have a strong occupational identification but who want to remain mobile across labour markets (Cobble and Vosko 2000; Benner 2002; Stone 2004). A freelancer I surveyed emphasizes the importance of the ability to move between engagers: "I would hesitate to join a labour union if I felt there was any risk of losing the flexibility and versatility that makes freelancing appealing." Benner (2003, 182) notes that as flexible and precarious employment relationships proliferate and as private-sector trade union membership declines, workers develop "occupational communities," or groups of workers who share skills and labour market experiences rather than an employer. The CFU would like to eventually collectively negotiate with publishers for minimum rates and working conditions so that members would be encouraged to negotiate beyond that minimum. This form of agreement, called a scale agreement, is common among creative worker unions in the film and television industry. It is useful for raising the floor to protect those most in need of protection and higher pay (Vosko 2005).

The opportunity for freelance journalists to participate in a craft unionism arrived with the establishment of the CFU. The CFU began as a CEP campaign, when some executive members acknowledged the pressing need for media unions to organize the growing freelance labour force. As Peter Murdoch, then the CEP's vice-president, media, explains:

> What [the CEP] saw ... was fairly devastating cuts by newspapers ... At the same time, we realized there was a growing group of people that were freelancers, and that there were fewer jobs generally in the media, and students graduating with ... debt and no jobs were turning to freelancing as a foot in door ... So we thought we had to do something for the freelancers, and at the same time we became aware that these newspaper chains that were kicking people out of newsroom were also forcing freelancers to sign Dickensian contracts that offered little in either payment and in terms of rights. We thought we should start getting involved in this. Not because we thought we'd get lots of members, quite the reverse, but because it's important to ensure that workers in media were getting at least a fair shake, and we

wanted to see what we could do to help them out. (personal communication 2011)

The CFU launched a campaign to gauge interest among writers and recruited 600 charter members (dues were twenty-five dollars). Initially, freelancers were optimistic about a union's potential. Conditions had become so poor that they were ready to go beyond established writers' groups to try a new model (OReilly, personal communication 2010). OReilly (ibid.) believed the CFU was necessary because other attempts at assisting freelancers failed: "There's been a continued attack on periodical writing as a profession in North America ... and nothing has changed, despite numerous attempts over the years to fight back and do things differently. We've failed to change the dynamic, that's why we're trying the union approach." The union was inaugurated on 3 October 2009 at a meeting in Ottawa that was broadcast online to encourage email and web-chat participation. Once the union became official, the elected executive – which includes representatives from across the country – began the difficult task of signing up full-fledged, dues-paying members.[6] As of April 2016, the CFU had recruited just under 250 members.

The CFU's small executive, all working freelancers, recruits through one-on-one discussions, over email, and by speaking at writers' events. It launched without a strategy or budget for organizing, taking an "if the union is built the people will come" approach (Brophy 2006, 635). Most members are directed to the CFU by friends or colleagues or stumble upon its website (OReilly personal communication 2010). The CFU has negotiated discounted joint membership agreements with PWAC and provincial writers' associations, and has used their networks for promotion. In August 2015, the CFU launched its first-ever organizing campaign, and hired organizers to focus recruitment in Vancouver, Toronto, and Halifax (Canadian Freelance Union 2015), increased its social media presence, and began to host social events. Once the union has signed up a large enough membership, it wants to target freelancers at particular publications or who work for specific publishers. It would like to leverage the power of the larger union's established bargaining units: so far two locals have tried to introduce clauses into agreements with newspaper publishers (Torstar in Toronto and the Pacific Press in

Vancouver) stating that all freelance work would be performed by CFU members – effectively creating a closed shop, similar to the arrangement the Canadian Media Guild has at the Canadian Broadcasting Corporation (CBC) – but this strategy has so far been unsuccessful as it requires a larger, more influential membership.

The CFU offers writers benefits and grievance services; press passes (without an employer, it is difficult to obtain media accreditation); contract advising; a web forum for member discussion; and plans to offer online professional development sessions. The CFU advocates on behalf of freelancers as a group. In April 2011, when the *London Free Press* encouraged readers to post material to its website under an initiative called Your Scoop, the CFU issued an open letter decrying the paper's solicitation of unpaid, reader-generated content (Ruscitti 2011; OReilly 2011). In 2013, the CFU worked with freelancers to successfully fight an extremely poor contract at Canada Wide Media (Gamage 2013). Like PWAC's effort, the CFU wants to establish a virtual "hiring hall," which Murdoch feels is key to convincing freelancers to join. "If people start getting work out of [our hiring hall], then the numbers will come along," he says in a 2011 personal communication.

While there is some overlap with PWAC's services, the CFU is more attentive to labour relations and employment issues, and technically has Unifor's strength behind it to engage in advocacy and bargaining. Both PWAC and the CFU envision the organizations working together, although the CFU aims to be more confrontational. OReilly recognizes the power relations that structure freelancers' experiences and links declining rates of pay and rights-grabbing contracts to media concentration and business strategies of profitable publishers. He recognizes that writers have a long history of lobbying for rate increases, predominantly through PWAC, but argues that concrete gains can only be accomplished through collective pressure. He refutes the assumption writers are simply not good at negotiating. Rather, he argues, individual writers do not have the power to negotiate. "It's the standard problem with labour and owners," he says. "They're big, we're small, they squeeze" (personal communication 2010). He wants rates tripled and for contracts to fairly compensate writers for copyrights.

The CFU faces challenges, primarily the difficulty of organizing thousands of writers spread across the country who have varied interests and experiences. Freelancers in Canada are a heterogeneous group in various stages of their careers with different expectations about the kind of work they want to do and different understandings of themselves as workers. Because writers work alone, usually in their homes, it is difficult to locate and contact potential members. Building a mass membership that includes successful and well-known writers will be key to getting publishers to negotiate over wages, contracts, and rights. Under current labour law and due to the provincial jurisdiction of most publishers and freelancers' self-employed status, publishers cannot be legislated to bargain. Thus, the CFU will need to rely on voluntary recognition, which is common among workers who bargain with multiple employers (Arthurs, Carter, and Glasbeek 1984, 205).[7] Under voluntary recognition, and "in lieu of certification, a union may gain the right to act as an exclusive bargaining agent if the employer voluntarily agrees to recognize its status" (ibid., 35).

Unions in the film and television industry and the American Federation of Musicians (of which the Toronto Musicians Association is Local 149) have negotiated agreements with producer associations and engagers that are not protected under labour law (MacPherson 1999, 4; Coles 2012, 53). These unions have been able to do so because, as Larry Haiven (2006, 101) writes, "The unions have made themselves invaluable to the industry in a way seldom seen in 'normal' industrial relations." These unions play a central role in controlling access to and coordinating labour markets and organizing production for film and television, and engagers rely on them for worker training and career building. In short, unions undertake work that industry does not do (Coles 2012; Haiven 2006).[8] In contrast, because of the nature of freelance writing work – highly individualized, less focus on standardized skills, and with no barriers to entry – the CFU will need to provide publishers with incentive to negotiate. While it can make claims to represent skilled and quality writers, unless it can build numbers to wield clout, including all the writers on which particular publishers rely, it will be challenged to convince publishers to engage in voluntary negotiations.

An unexpected challenge is that writers are frustrated with the slow-moving process of organizing a union. Many feel they cannot wait for a long-term strategy and seek a quicker solution to their problems (OReilly, personal communication 2010). Others expect the organization to be able to make concrete changes before they will join. As one survey respondent notes, "When the [CFU] actually achieves ... a decent contract for freelancers that is binding on newspapers and magazine publishers, I will join." This comment demonstrates a lack of understanding of the union-building process, which can be long and difficult but always requires members' active participation. Most freelancers are accustomed to belonging to service organizations that do not require active participation or revolve around collective action, a mindset that must change if they want to establish an effective union. Some freelancers are concerned that the CFU's parent unions, first CEP and then Unifor, have not invested enough resources to build the CFU effectively and to make it powerful enough to take on publishers. A common complaint is that the CFU does not have enough staff to organize a vast and dispersed group of workers. Finally, many are skeptical of being courted by a union that has historically worked to limit the amount of work contracted to freelancers as a strategy to protect full-time jobs. Still, some are willing to be patient. As one freelancer says, "I thought it was important to join the CFU as an experiment to see if collective action and the union movement could do anything to make writers' careers more secure. I will keep supporting their work ... in their first year they have made some good progress." OReilly believes that the CFU is the right vehicle for transforming freelancers' conditions. "Ultimately what a trade union does differently is that it brings real collective power to the table," he says. "An association does that to a certain extent, but ultimately cannot command the kind of solidarity that's required to take on the larger economic issues" (personal communication 2010). But to take on these issues, the CFU needs the strength of thousands of freelancers behind it.

THE LITERARY AGENCY

Those seeking a quicker fix turned to the Canadian Writers Group, the first author agency in Canada to represent freelancers who write for periodicals and newspapers. Launched in May 2009 by Finkle, a freelance journalist and former magazine editor, the CWG is modelled after traditional literary agencies, which emerged in the 1840s in Britain and the United States to fill book authors' needs for "something resembling a trade union" (West 1988, 78). Literary agents first appeared in Canada in 1950 and expanded in the 1970s, but their clients have historically been book authors (Davey 2007, 112). Agents serve as intermediaries between publishers and authors by negotiating contracts and rates. They freed authors from the business aspects of their careers to focus on writing and enhanced their status: "[An agent] indicated to the world that the writer was a professional whose work was significant enough to be managed by another professional" (Gillies 2007, 26). Indeed, part of Finkle's motivation for launching an agency for magazine writers was to enhance the seriousness with which publishers treat freelancers, what he believes is a necessary step toward raising writers' rates.

In an agency, Finkle saw not only a new response to freelancers' payment problems, but also a business opportunity. His recruitment notice, posted in September 2008 on a freelance writer email list, announced that he sought "Canada's most talented, in-demand freelancer writers." By March 2009, he had two hundred applications, from which he selected fifty people to represent. The CWG plans to represent about one hundred writers, with Finkle acting as a kind of one-man hiring hall (albeit one run by a private business owner rather than a union), matching writers to work. He negotiates rates and contract terms for writers he represents, and for an additional fee they receive an online profile with which to promote themselves to potential clients. Finkle chases publishers for late payments and sources work for clients. He is actively involved in contract discussions, which at one time involved negotiating for all the writers he represents at particular magazines. Finkle's meetings with editors have yielded changes to contracts at several magazines for writers he represents. Negotiations with *Reader's Digest*, which had not altered its writers' contracts in years, led to changes because Finkle represents fifty of the publication's writers (Finkle 2010). He wants publishers and editors to move beyond per-word payments to better reflect the time that goes into articles and to promote a stronger understanding of the value of writers' labour time (Wilson 2010).

The CWG raises tensions about the politics of worker representation. Fundamentally, Finkle understands that writer-publisher relationships are built on asymmetrical power relations that favour bottom-line driven corporations (personal communication 2010). He argues that publishers pay writers poorly because they can:

"When [publishers] say they don't have the money ... what they're saying is, 'We've chosen not to spend the money on writers'" (cited in Carraway 2008). Finkle often employs the language of collectivity, which has historically been the domain of unions, and he is not against his writers withholding their services from a publisher to achieve better pay and contracts (Finkle 2010). His early strategy was to represent all the writers at a particular publication, then negotiate CWG-specific contracts with that publication, which mirrors collective bargaining practices and the CFU's goals, and demonstrates how freelancers could entice publishers to voluntarily negotiate.

But, unlike a union, a literary agency is a privately owned, for-profit enterprise. While unions are mandated to bring equity to all members, a literary agency selects a few authors to represent, usually those who can provide the highest return on its investment of time and resources. Whereas a union ideally emphasizes solidarity and a collective understanding of workers' struggles, an agency can reinforce the individualism and competitiveness already entrenched in freelancers' labour experiences. The CWG's roster represents those Finkle calls "top level" freelancers: writers who have experience and a good reputation, and already earn among the highest rates in the industry (personal communication 2010). Such an arrangement has some writers concerned that the agency could cement already-existing inequities, with a few earning well and the majority struggling. A freelancer I surveyed whose application Finkle rejected says, "I found this kind of terrible. It's the [writers] who are starting out who need the most help."

Other freelancers, however, believe that an agency is the ideal solution for solving their problems, as it will have immediate effects: the moment a writer joins, they have someone to actively negotiate on their behalf. Advocates of the agency model argue that "name-brand" freelancers have clout with publishers, and once they begin to command higher rates, other writers – even those not represented by the agency – will feel more empowered to negotiate. This tendency is called the "spillover" effect, which posits that all workers benefit from unions because nonunion employers tend to match unionized competitors' wages or treat their workers well to avoid unionization (Yates 2009, 41). But Finkle is not interested in the possible spillover effects his agency may have. As he explains, "I think it's going to be made pretty clear that we're only negotiating for the people that we represent, because otherwise you have this expectation by everyone, 'Oh, I don't have to do anything. I'll just do my own thing and reap the benefits of that negotiation.' And on some level, maybe that might be possible, but the reality is they won't be reaping any benefits unless there is some ... pretty significant collectivity from the writers themselves" (personal communication 2010).

It is unclear how writers can act collectively under the CWG's model, wherein one person selects and represents a certain small group of writers. Finkle feels no responsibility to represent all freelancers in Canada. He has negotiated contracts at several magazines that are only used for his writers (personal communication 2010). He also negotiated a pay grid for twelve CWG writers who contribute to *Reader's Digest*, based on the writers' experience and the amount of work that goes into a piece, as well as an extra fee to cover the extra rights demanded in the magazine's contract, which include exclusivity and reprint rights in the magazine's foreign editions (Story Board 2012b). Finkle says that although the new agreement was initially only used with CWG writers, the magazine has sent it to other freelancers (ibid.). Yet there is no guarantee that a contract Finkle negotiates will benefit writers he does not represent. In terms of a business model, it is not in the agency's interest to publicize contract negotiation information. Therefore, a privately owned agency model can keep writers in competition with one another rather than removing elements of competition between workers, as unions aim to do.

THE AGENCY-UNION ALLIANCE

The CWG's development took an unprecedented twist in fall 2010, when it partnered with the Canadian Media Guild (CMG), a 6,000-member local of the Communications Workers of America/Syndicat des Communications d'Amérique Canada, the Canadian branch of the 600,000-member Communication Workers of America (CWA Canada n.d.). The CMG represents workers at the CBC[9] and its 600 freelancers – the only freelancers in North America protected by a collective agreement. This unique arrangement is due to a Canada Labour Relations Board decision in May 1982 that examined freelancers' employment status and ruled that since they had to use the broadcaster's equipment on the premises in order to do their work, they were in a position of economic dependence and therefore should be covered by the union representing employees (Canadian Labour Relations Board 1983, decision no. 383). Over the years, the CMG inherited the freelance branch[10] and now negotiates minimum scale agreements for freelancers as part of regular bargaining, enforces the contract, and provides negotiating and legal assistance to freelancers.

Because of labour laws and the Competition Act, the CMG has until now been unable to represent freelancers at other media outlets. Still, in 2010, the union was strategizing on how to renew its efforts to organize freelancers (the CMG had previously been in discussion with OReilly, until he pursued the idea for a freelance union with the CEP, leaving frosty relations between the two unions on the freelance issue). When Lise Lareau, then-president of the CMG, met Finkle and learned about his agency, she realized that partnering with another organization – particularly one that planned to represent the most well-known freelancers in the country – might be the most effective way to reach and represent freelancers. Explains a CMG organizer: "We thought, 'well, let's just partner with this guy, who has been doing that outreach and already has a name among freelance writers and figure out if we can support each other'" (personal communication 2014). At the same time, Finkle decided he could not run his business and undertake advocacy efforts and so saw a benefit in partnering with the CMG. After several months of meetings, the CMG and Finkle formed an alliance and the CMG's parent union, the CWA-Canada, provided investment money to the agency under an initial two-year agreement.

Under the agreement, any freelancer could join the CMG's freelance branch and CWG writers automatically become CMG members. For dues of $150 per year, freelancers could access the CMG's benefit plans and other union resources, but do not receive representation from Finkle. The arrangement gave the CMG access to a growing segment of the media labour force previously beyond its reach and access to the status of the CWG to attract freelancers that the agency does not want to represent. The CWG had access to the resources of a large union: legal counsel on retainer, a strike fund (compensation if writers are in a position to refuse to work), and advocacy power. Together, the CMG and CWG set up Story Board, a website devoted to freelance issues, and commissioned a study of digital rights in cultural industries to strategize about contracts and copyrights (Impresa Communications 2011).

Thanks to the CMG's legal department, the CWG helped a writer win a settlement against Rogers Publishing for third-party syndication of an article (Story Board 2010).[11]

During the alliance, Finkle separated the CMG's advocacy efforts from the website promoting his agency that potential clients visit (Finkle 2010). The only mention of the CMG on the CWG's website is the following: "Canadian Writers Group supports the advocacy of the Canadian Media Guild in its efforts to collectively raise the profile of writers across Canada" (CWG 2010). At the time, Finkle felt that he addressed charges of exclusivity by making it possible for freelancers to join the CMG, but those writers who belong to the agency and those who belong to just the CMG were effectively members of separate and very different organizations – one that provides star writers with individual support and negotiations, and another that operates on union principles and aims to bargain collectively one day, creating competition with the CFU for a small group of workers who are difficult to organize.

In summer 2011, the CWG/CMG alliance began talks with Torstar Corporation about its problematic freelance contracts.[12] Initially the *Toronto Star* refused to acknowledge that Finkle represented and therefore could speak on behalf of a portion of its writers. But the CMG was able to meet with the *Star*'s publisher to discuss the contract, which is in line with the kind of labour negotiations the paper is accustomed to (Lareau, personal communication 2011).[13] The CMG dedicated a percentage of a staff representative's time to organize a campaign around the *Toronto Star*'s contract, primarily by contacting freelancers who write for the paper and mobilizing those affected, most of whom were not yet part of the CMG or the CWG (ibid.).

The campaign was significant, Lareau argues, because *Toronto Star* executives recognized Finkle as a representative of writers and, if the campaign could succeed in changing the terms of the contract, then more freelancers would be motivated to join the CMG's freelance branch. For Lareau, the *Toronto Star* contract was the first issue that enabled the nascent CWG/CMG alliance to demonstrate the benefits of a partnership between an organization that represents a small group of high-profile writers and a large media union with resources to devote to a campaign involving nonmembers (ibid.). Jean Broughton, the freelance branch's staff representative at the time, undertook outreach by contacting freelancers and asking them to sign a letter to the *Toronto Star*, while Finkle negotiated with management. "There were people he had much better access to," Broughton says (personal communication 2012). "[Finkle] has a personal relationship with writers ... He's brought a lot of his people onside." But as the campaign reached the point when it was time to go public, Finkle stepped back. Broughton notes that as a labour organizer, she has a different "theoretical framework" than Finkle, but felt that the two-tiered aspect of the union-agency alliance would work in freelancers' favour: "One thing I like about this campaign is that we're not working on behalf of the most established freelancers, which is who [Finkle] represents. What we're doing is using those people, working with them, to raise [standards] for everyone ... I'm way less interested negotiating exclusive deals for certain people. I'm way more interested in things that raise the floor [for everyone]" (personal communication 2012).

Lareau, who is now vice-president of the CMG, was banking on the high profile of the agency. She argued that if the alliance could sign up the "stars" – those with influence and individual power – then other writers would follow (personal communication 2011). She recognized that partnering with a private agency is unusual for a union, and often had to defend the alliance within her union and in the labour movement. But she argues that innovative, flexible solutions are needed to support and defend freelancers (ibid.). When Lareau first met Finkle he was "fairly dismissive of union traditions," but the two organizations hoped to achieve similar goals: "We speak about the same things, but [Finkle] did it without thinking about unions [and union strategies]. For his business to work, he had to represent a cluster of people at the same time, which is the same thing that unions do. He understood the same power model as unions have: get bargaining power at a particular place. But he would have never used that word" (ibid.).

The official partnership between the CMG and the CWG came to an amicable end in 2014. Finkle says he was tired of fighting with publishers.

During that two year period, I kind of came to the realization as an agent doing my thing that our interests were a little bit at odds, in that, for them [the CMG], what they wanted to do was represent as large a number of people as possible, and I think for a while I got sucked into that a little bit. And I was working way too much for really not much money, and it was unmanageable ... I didn't want to represent 300 people. I want to work with a very specific group of people that I like working with, that fit my way of doing things, that ... are just right for me. (personal communication 2014)

He still supports the CMG and is involved in Story Board, but he is less interested in pushing for change in the journalism industry than in managing a successful roster of writers. His freelancers are shifting away from journalism, as Finkle feels the effort is not worth it for such low fees. More now focus on commercial, ghost, and other nonjournalistic writing. Through his agency Finkle has published successful ebooks, and he will negotiate contracts for individual writers with newspapers and magazines when necessary. His reflections on the alliance make clear the contrasts between organizing models. "I've never been in an union, I don't really understand it," he says. "I mean, I get the basic principle, but there's a lot of politics and bullshit and stuff that goes on and I have no experience with any of it" (personal communication 2014). And so, the CMG is going it alone.

THE MEDIA GUILD

The CMG's freelance branch strategically straddles the line between union and professional association/service provider. datejie green, a freelance media worker and previous national director of human rights and equity at the CMG who was hired on a temporary contract to work full-time as a freelance organizer from 2013 to 2015, says the freelance branch "very overtly stated that we're a union and talked about the union and our track record of working with freelancers at the CBC" (personal communication 2014). On its website, the freelance branch describes itself as providing "direct political representation for freelance members" and a form of "creative unionism," but for now provides similar services as the Canadian Freelancers Union. Any freelancer can join the freelance branch, and its sixty-five non-CBC members include independent writers, journalists, radio workers, graphic designers, academics, librarians, and filmmakers. CMG staff can advise freelancers on contract negotiations and offer access to the union's lawyers if necessary, and members can buy health, dental, and insurance benefits through the ACTRA Fraternal Benefit Society. The freelance branch offers online training and has held workshops and social events in Toronto and Vancouver, attendance at which has grown from about thirty people to around seventy. "It's a real through-the-backdoor set of thinking," says green. "We're figuring out how to get people to think that the union could be helpful to them" (personal communication 2014).

While organizing at the CMG, green focused her efforts on one-on-one meetings with freelancers, cold emailing to recruit, developing advertising and social media strategies, conducting outreach to freelance professional associations, attending literary festivals and public events, organizing workshops, and holding freelance meetups in Toronto, Vancouver, and Hamilton. One major focus was developing internal infrastructure to support freelancers, which mostly involved building a new website that includes a directory. "Freelancers have told me over and over again that getting work for them would be the number one things we could do," she says. "And this is a way of doing it, short of becoming a hiring hall, which would require a lot more staffing and resources" (personal communication 2014). The freelance branch launched an email list for members that helps individuals communicate and can serve as a way for the union to grow its understanding of contracts currently in use, identify problems freelancers face, and determine how best to help them, not to mention building up confidence and motivation to eventually be able to pressure media outlets to voluntarily negotiate contracts.

The CMG has focused collective efforts on restrictive contracts at three media companies. The campaign at the *Toronto Star* did not result in a contract change, but it was the first time the freelance branch was able to mobilize freelancers around a collective goal. The CMG successfully collaborated with the CWG, the CFU, and l'Association des journalistes indépendants du Québec on a campaign against TC Media's restrictive contract (Salamon 2016). Organizers were able to pressure the company to amend its contract. "It was a victory to the extent that it showed the power of collective collaboration and organizing," says green (personal communication 2014). In 2015, with support of CMG staff representative Keith Maskell, the branch worked with a small group of freelancers to challenge a contract from Accessible Media that demanded outright ownership of freelancers' works, "including raw material like the audio interviews and research notes" (Watson 2015). Each of these initiatives strengthens freelancers' understandings of what a collective organization can do for them, and the union's ability to coordinate among a disparate group for an outcome that will benefit all freelancers. green says these examples "create a sense of possibility" for freelancers and reinforce the need to value their labour (personal communication 2014). green also collaborated closely with Karen Wirsig, a staff organizer who focuses on organizing reality television workers, and Katherine Lapointe, who runs the CMG's Associate Members program, which offers free union membership to students and emerging media workers, training in labour rights, and mentoring. green and Lapointe were also involved in monthly phone meetings with freelance organizers also working with the CMG's parent union in San Francisco, Chicago, Washington-Baltimore, St Louis, New York, and Albuquerque.

Taken together, the CMG's freelance efforts demonstrate innovative organizing, a willingness to invest in future media workforces, and a commitment to long-term planning, as few of these initiatives bring in members or money in the short term. But hedging its bets on long-term success is just one challenge the freelance branch faces. It is difficult to locate freelancers. When Broughton was recruiting freelance writers to address the *Toronto Star*'s contract, she went to the reference library and flipped through pages of a month's worth of the paper to identify writers, then contacted those for whom she could find email addresses (personal communication 2012) – a time-consuming task. Even if identified, many freelancers remain reluctant to speak out and risk losing work (green has advised them to say that they consulted lawyers rather than a union). And labour law remains a huge obstacle. "Most of the laws in this country around labour talk about employees, they don't talk about self-employed people. So how to gain traction in that area in terms of any kind of collective advocacy and collective resourcing is still a big question," green says (personal communication 2014). In addition, the CMG and its parent union will need to invest more money, staff time, and resources into freelance organizing over the long term, which is a difficult sell to a union that faces a shrinking membership (its largest source of members comes from Canada's public broadcaster, which has faced an extended period of government cuts and lay-offs). A CMG organizer explains the investment that unions must make to remain relevant to media work forces in the future, an impulse that often runs counter to unions' conservative tendencies:

> Sometimes it takes some convincing for the leadership to recognize it, but you never do organizing for an immediate return on investment. What I tell people around here is that we do this kind of organizing because we need to be relevant in twenty-five years. And if we don't, then we will be completely irrelevant. The old ways of doing things – and when I say old, I mean the mid-twentieth century way that we all grew up with in this movement – it's not the way it works anymore. We had to morph and really think about what people need and how to help them with what they need. (personal communication 2014)

When I interviewed her, green spoke optimistically about the commitment and support of the CMG's parent union, the CWA, but that support is precarious, as many of the union's organizers work on temporary or short-term contracts, with renewal contingent on recruitment. Just under a year and a half into the project, green's third short-term contract was left to expire, leaving the CMG with no full-time freelance organizer. A job posting for her position sought someone to work three days a week for one year, signalling a reduced commitment to organizing freelancers (Canadian Media Guild 2015b).

BUILDING INDIVIDUALS' COLLECTIVE POWER

Initiatives to collectively represent freelancers in Canada overlap yet have distinct features, and each views freelancers through lenses that are often in tension: as professionals and as workers; as individuals and as a group. PWAC, focused on professional development and promoting individuals' work, is limited by its reinforcement of individual competitiveness and cordial industry relations, a commitment to professionalism that comes at the expense of directly addressing power relations. Labour-focused organizations have the potential to challenge power relations and defend writers' rights but are challenged by limited resources, staff, and organizing capacity. As a local of the largest private-sector media union in Canada, the CFU has the potential to wield clout, especially in already-unionized newsrooms. However, to be effective, it will need resources (human and financial) to organize hundreds if not thousands of workers, and until it reaches a critical membership mass, freelancers will likely remain reluctant to join. Thus, the CFU risks becoming another service and benefit provider, competing with other organizations that already do the same.

CMG organizers are grappling with the role that service-model organizing should play in collective representation. "The servicing/benefits provision aspect [of freelance organizing] is fine," past organizer Broughton says, "but the thing that's going to make the change for people – including the blogger at the *Huffington Post* that doesn't get paid – is raising the standards across the board" (personal communication 2012). Notably, writers who signed the letter of protest to the *Toronto Star* were not asked to pay dues and become guild members. The *Toronto Star* campaign brought in no money and did not grow membership, yet Broughton considers it a politically and symbolically important first step in a long-term plan: "[Gaining members] would be nice and it's at the back of my mind, and at some point we'll ask, but to some extent what we [currently] have to offer is our ability to fight, and if we haven't demonstrated that yet, then why would you sign up?" (ibid.). Despite the CMG's stated commitment to organizing freelancers, it currently has no full-time freelance organizer and a history of hiring organizers on short-term, precarious contracts.

The peculiar CWG/CMG experiment – a combination of individual representation and trade union tactics – was built on an idea to harness the status of successful, "name brand" freelancers to secure better contracts and improve conditions for all writers. It failed because an agency is a privately owned business fundamentally structured to maintain divisions among writers by representing a small group of what it considers to be top-tier writers who already command high rates. The agency's success, however, in improving rates for the writers it represents, suggests that freelancers should consider how this model could be more democratic: as a worker owned-cooperative or as union-run agency, for example, based on a mission to bring fair working conditions and equitable representation to all freelancers.

While the CMG has experience and resources to put behind a free-lance initiative, the challenge remains getting a key number of writers to sign on. Another challenge is that there are now three national organizations vying for freelance writers' time, allegiance, and dues, along with dozens of smaller associations and informal networks across the country. Although both the CFU and the CMG's freelance branch aim to collectively bargain with publishers, the two are not currently working together and compete for members. While the current moment represents an unprecedented level of organizing among freelancers, the number of organizations raises challenges. Many writers do not understand why so many organizations exist and are unable to differentiate between them. As one freelancer I surveyed notes: "There are simply too many writers' organizations all doing somewhat the same kind of work. If I were to join them all, I would pay hefty fees and be overwhelmed with information and commitments. I write for periodicals, books, film and some corporate stuff. I would love to see all the writers' organizations come together to negotiate on behalf of all writers." Another says: "I have not seen a direct benefit in joining any of the available organizations. At this point they seem too scattered and disorganized. There needs to be a more unified voice and I will be willing to join an organization when one emerges from the pack. Especially now that I have a greater interest in having benefits, I have taken a greater interest in joining an organization."[14]

One solution is to merge existing writers' organizations to create one big union. This idea is not new. In the 1990s, when the Southern Ontario Newspaper Guild was attempting to break away from its parent union, the Newspaper Guild, many media workers "dream[ed]" of one big media workers' union, representing Canadian media workers across sectors, occupations, and media formats (McKercher 2002, 123–4). In the late 1970s, PWAC was involved in discussions to establish a writers' cooperative, or a "joint writers' secretariat," which would purchase a building in Toronto to house all national writers' organizations and services. In addition to providing office space, the organization would establish a writers' trust to break organizations' dependency on government funding and would serve as an agency to sell writers' works, among other services. This model would have required writers' organizations to work together and was based on a strength-in-numbers model (PWAC 1977, 2). Archived

PWAC (1976c) minutes show that members considered early affiliation with the Writers' Union of Canada and the Alliance of Canadian Cinema, Television and Radio Artists, but did not pursue either. In 1993, Jonathan Tasini, then-president of the National Writers Union, sent PWAC a proposal for a Cultural Workers' Federation. He argued that the global corporate consolidation of media meant that all freelancers face similar challenges, and that a federation with a broad, international scope could unite all writers, provide a reproduction rights agency, and launch strategic and educational campaigns (PWAC n.d.; Reid 1993).

Today's freelancers' organizations could reconsider organizational convergence, especially as corporate media convergence blurs the boundaries between formats of writing. Vincent Mosco and Catherine McKercher (2008, 147) advocate for such a strategy as a way for unions to "bite back," or as a response to corporate convergence and a method of building worker and union power. Indeed, the parent unions of the CFU and the CMG – Unifor and the CWA, respectively – are themselves converged. Although the benefits of union convergence remain "an open question" (ibid., 149), the unique challenges facing freelancers across sectors make the idea worth exploring. As a PWAC staff member says: "Why aren't PWAC and [the Writers' Union of Canada] in the same group? I don't have a strong argument, except for the cultural. There's no reason why we couldn't have an umbrella organization that took those cultural differences into account ... I think we could be a lot stronger. I would favour that, but it's very controversial among our members. There's a reactionary tribalism in PWAC that is preventing that kind of open-minded thinking and exploration" (personal communication 2010).

Potential exists to create a large organization that would be flexible enough to accommodate writers' different needs and large enough to bring in money for organizing and to gain the power to collectively negotiate minimum payments and protections. Freelancers are no longer separated by the type of writing they do and corporate convergence means that most deal with a handful of parent companies that are introducing standardized contracts across media chains. Although it is unclear what one big writers' union would look like and how it would operate – a challenge, to be sure – in today's landscape it is an option worth considering. John Degen says convergence must happen if writers want to gain power in a

rapidly changing digital world: "PWAC and TWUC and the Canadian
Authors Association and the League of Canadian Poets and the Playwrights Guild and the Writers Guild – until they are all under one
roof and acting as a considerable industrial force, whether it's
through a trade union model or just a polite association model, they
don't have the clout" (personal communication 2010).

While unions hold promise for freelancers and established unions
come with resources for organizing, it is important to recognize the
general limitations and challenges of unions as an organizational
model, which go beyond external pressures such as declining membership and density and attacks from employers and the state to
include internal pressures (Yates 2009). For the most part, North
American unions have been challenged to achieve far-reaching social transformation "beyond simply asking for a better deal from
capital and capitalism" (Gindin and Stanford 2003, 422), which is
reflected in the "dual" role unions play: at once trying to advance
workers' rights "while also containing [members'] militancy and activism" (ibid.). Unions have brought great protections and advancement to members' lives, but have also defaulted to "institutional
inertia" (Kumar and Schenk 2009, 44), supported corporatist relationships with industry, engaged in concession bargaining, and been
unable to move beyond traditional organizing models that protect
primarily white, male, single-worksite workers (Gindin and Stanford 2003; Cranford et al. 2006). Labour researchers have criticized
models of business unionism, or service unionism, wherein expert
elected or appointed leaders run the organization primarily in the
"narrowly defined material interests of the membership," and where
members expect the leadership to make decisions and organizations
to provide services (Ross 2008, 139). The freelance organizations I
describe in this chapter risk becoming service organizations. Such a
model, Stephanie Ross argues, "rel[ies] upon and perpetuate[s] a pas-
sive membership whose sense of the union is of an insurance
policy rather than a social movement or agency for collective social
change" (139). In contrast, a model of social unionism or social
movement unionism views workers as both "wage earners and citizens" and focuses on economic and political issues for the purpose
of social change beyond just the workplace (130; Moody 1997). The
push for social unionism comes alongside a call for the broad de-
mocratization of unions so that members have control and partici-

pate in collective bargaining, narrowing the gap between the interests of union leadership and those of rank-and-file members (Kumar and Schenk 2009). Unions have a historical record of deep exclusions, particularly of women, people of colour, immigrants, noncitizens, and youth. Workers of colour have much lower rates of unionization despite wanting to join unions, which Tania Das Gupta (2006, 319) attributes to systemic racism in the labour movement, or "standard and apparently neutral policies, procedures, and practices that disadvantage people of colour" and that are "reproduced over time through written policies and laws." Workers of colour, feminists, and activists attribute race- and gender-based exclusions in the labour movement to unions' unwillingness or inability to organize the unorganized, including workers in precarious forms of employment, who are difficult to organize but who are most in need of union protections (319; Yates 2009). Indeed, demands for decent work and improved legal and social protections for low-wage, racialized, and noncitizen workers and workers in precarious employment increasingly come from outside of organized labour, including from worker centres and other alt-labour groups (Cranford et al. 2006; Cohen and de Peuter 2013). As I noted above in the context of freelance organizing, to organize workers in precarious employment requires long-term strategies, accepting a slow pace, engaging in experimental and innovative outreach and community building, and investing the time and money required to support and sustain this type of organizing (Das Gupta 2006, 332). Some of these challenges are evident in the fluctuating commitments both Unifor and the CMG have made to freelancers, and freelancers themselves will need to play a greater role in organizing and building unions, as well as building alliances between freelancers' campaigns, alt-labour initiatives, and existing union efforts.

Although freelance writers are a diverse group with a range of perspectives on their work and challenges, it is possible to identify some shared aspects of an occupational identity that will need to be transformed for meaningful change to be made, either through campaigns, collective organizing into alt-labour groups or unions, or lobbying for changes to labour laws that prevent self-employed workers from unionizing for collective bargaining. The term "free lance" originally described professional soldiers who sold their services to any army that would hire them and who maintained "no per-

manent connections or professional obligations" (Rogers 1931, 246).
Contemporary freelancers have traded the lance for the keyboard,
yet the notion of independence associated with freelancing persists.
That writers have heralded a literary agency model as the most effective solution (Wilson 2010), and that a professional association
has historically been writers' preferred model for collective activity,
underscores an occupational identity shaped by notions of professionalism and artistic labour and influenced by a neoliberal ideal-
ization of the individual, entrepreneurial worker, undermining the
very notions of solidarity and struggle upon which collective organizing and action are based.

Because of their positions on the margins of the media labour
force, freelancers have worked to adopt a badge of professionalism
to attain legitimacy and to separate themselves from amateurs or
hobbyists. Yet these efforts to position themselves as professionals
as a way to improve their social and occupational standing and to
achieve higher pay have had contradictory effects. Because freelancers are independent contractors, they experience their exchange
of labour for money in terms of meeting a publication in the marketplace as an independent contractor selling services rather than
as a worker exchanging labour power for wages. Thus, most freelancers more closely identify with their editors and publishers, a
strategy of cordiality that follows from freelancers' contradictory
class location. Most do not view themselves as workers who may
have opposing interests to publishers, but rather as small businesses with a stake in the industry who maintain control over their work
and who independently negotiate their position within the industry. Their aim, ultimately, is self-improvement, better marketing, and
attracting more work to leverage that position.

To build the collective power needed to change freelancers' circumstances, freelancers in Canada and their organizations will need
to mobilize on a broader basis and encourage a shift away from an
individualized view of writers as professionals or entrepreneurs toward a more collective, solidaristic view. In Marxist terms, this requires freelancers to transform from a class in itself – a group of
workers who sell their labour power for a wage – to a class for itself,
which "exists only when it asserts its autonomy as a class through
its unity in struggle against its role as labour power" (Cleaver 2000,
83). The development of class consciousness among freelancers de-

pends on challenging their notions that they work only for themselves and illuminating the hard-to-see power relations that structure freelance writing as a form of labour. The most effective approaches to organizing freelancers will be those that can break down the individualism and structural competition that characterize freelance media work and foster an understanding of freelance workers *as workers*, whose precarious employment status is critical to the business strategies of media firms. Although a challenge, the costs of not acting will be high. The pace of collective organizing, campaigning, and lobbying for change is diametrically opposed to the rapid change in media industries, particularly the pace of change in digital-first journalism. Collective resistance, opposition, and building worker power can be painstakingly slow. Yet freelance collective organization in Canada has come a long way in recent years, and the next chapter of freelance labour organizing remains to be written.

Journalism's Precarity Penalty

As a field of research and an intervention, critical political economy of communication examines how ownership structures, regulatory regimes, and capitalist business practices shape the ideas in and expressions of media content, which contribute to and sustain dominant ideologies (Garnham 1990; Murdock and Golding 2005; McChesney 2008; Mosco 2009). Political economists are concerned with how structures of media organization and production enable or constrain media's ability to serve as watchdogs of powerful political and corporate interests and its democratic role of providing diverse perspectives to inform citizens (Curran 2005; Skinner, Compton, and Gasher 2005). Investigating the experiences of freelancers, a precariously employed yet growing segment of the media labour force, demonstrates the importance of considering the organization of labour and the conditions in which journalists work for understanding contemporary media and journalism, conditions that flow from the unequal power relations between labour and capital. It is not only capitalist media's profit motive or the constraints imposed by advertisers, regulators, work routines, or publishers' political and economic interests that shape content, but also workers' employment status, security or precarity, and overall material conditions. In this book, I have emphasized the value of considering the labour process involved in freelancing, or the "activity of labour and the social relations that shape, direct, and manage it" (Weeks 2011, 6). Paying attention to the labour process emphasizes the processes that constitute labour relations, or the power and class relations at the core of media production, wherein workers must sell their labour power for a wage, producing a surplus that they do not control (Örnebring 2010). For freelance journalists, such processes involve media companies trying to extract as much value from their unpaid labour time as possible – as fees are low or nonexistent and the vast amount of work required to produce journalism on a freelance basis is not accounted for – and imposing restrictive contracts that demand increased copyrights for no extra pay. The concentration of media companies and the development of new technologies that enable anyone to become a writer and encourage publishers to outsource production have shifted the power relations of freelancing. What has long been a strategy for individual writers to gain control over their labour process and autonomy in their work is now also a powerful strategy for publishers to offload the risks of production onto those individuals. This is perhaps the greatest contradiction of freelance cultural work: it is precisely by relinquishing control over employees, precisely by workers themselves seeking to work outside of a standard employment relationship, that capital is able to increase the extraction of surplus value from workers. Attending to the labour process makes clear that work conflicts and labour antagonisms do not disappear when workers exit an employment relationship, but rather deepen and intensify – not because of the inevitability of writing as inherently low-paid, insecure work, but because of the way media work is organized under contemporary capitalism. The labour processes and work practices implemented in the production of journalism play a key role in the political economy of media; in the case of freelancers, such practices include treating workers as independent contractors who must negotiate the supposed market value of their work and, in the processes, perpetually undervalue their labour.

Critics of political economy emphasize the relative autonomy that cultural workers enjoy in the production process and the resulting room to negotiate and potentially resist within the organizations for which they work. As Timothy Havens, Amanda Lotz, and Serra Tinic (2009, 247) argue, for example, research that examines media industry structures must acknowledge how "cultural workers seem to negotiate, and at times perhaps subvert, the constraints imposed by institutional interests to their own purposes." Here, the relative autonomy media and cultural workers enjoy is productive, and grants them agency within structural constraints. But what happens to that relative autonomy when media and cultural work occurs outside of the relative security of an employment relationship, or when freelancers must live by continuously selling single pieces of work for very little compensation? The organization of freelance work inserts individuals into fiercely competitive and unequal social relations and infuses their work and lives with insecurity. This, in turn, pressures workers to produce particular kinds of works: not just works that can be sold, but works that can be produced quickly, making the small fees paid per word, per article, or per hour worth a freelancer's time. Such working conditions raise important questions for political economists of media, particularly for those concerned with creating democratic, socially just media: What kind of media can a labour force made precarious produce? And, pressingly, who can afford to become a media worker under conditions of precarity?

In their 2015 study of precarious employment in southern Ontario, Wayne Lewchuk et al. argue that precarious employment has collective, cumulative implications for communities, families, and social life – what they call a precarity penalty. People in precarious employment face low-income, intermittent, and insecure work; do not have access to benefits, training, and childcare; and face stress, social isolation, and risk of mental health issues. Such stresses shape people's participation in and withdrawal from family and community life, and precarity becomes a burden borne by wide swaths of society. Borrowing the concept of a precarity penalty as a way to indicate the broad social implications of precarious employment is helpful for outlining journalism's precarity penalty: the consequences for robust journalism when the work of producing it is made precarious, limiting what type of journalism can be produced and who can access work in media.

Since the birth of publishing industries, capitalist business practices have shaped what writers could write about and what publishers would print (Mills 1956, 143; Hardt 1996, 21; Hamilton 2008, 52). Writers have historically depended on the market to bring works to readers, consenting to and legitimizing capitalist conditions of cultural production, including the exploitative copyright system (Williams 1989, 82; D'Agostino 2010, 246). Such continuities, however, are marked by change, as contemporary freelancers feel unprecedented pressure to write what they can sell to publications, not just what they feel is worth writing. As PWAC (2006, 16) reports, "Market forces often determine [writers'] work." Even relative autonomy, already limited, is contested and tenuous. The space, time, and resources allotted to pursue challenging, critical, or investigative and research-heavy work is shrinking. Unlike staff writers, who enjoy the protection of an employment relationship and steady salaries – and yet who also face immense pressure to do much more with much less – freelance status can prevent writers from taking risks on large, difficult, or time-consuming articles. The lack of the privileges afforded only to staff journalists limits freelancers' work. As one freelancer I surveyed says: "Unless they are very well known, freelancers are at a disadvantage when calling potential subjects. They do not have the backup of a news organization either for clout or for protection from legal consequences." Indeed, publishers' contracts in Canada and the United Kingdom have begun to demand indemnity for publishers in case of lawsuits, further downloading the risk and costs associated with journalism onto individual workers and further discouraging freelancers from pursuing important investigative journalism (National Union of Journalists, personal communication 2010; Broughton, personal communication 2012; Story Board 2012c).

Neoliberal economic and state policy, which privileges free markets above all, precipitated the "growing intrusion of commercial considerations" into cultural production and art (Bourdieu 1998, 102). Under contemporary capitalism, media have become more intensely commodified, commercialized, and fuelled by neoliberal discourse. Media outlets are less willing to produce expensive investigative journalism and are more market-oriented: more dependent on public relations firms as sources, service journalism, celebrity coverage, and producing "commercial content," particularly today, when sponsored content and clickbait reign (Murdock 2003; Hesmondhalgh 2007; Couldry 2010; Spangler 2010; Winseck 2011). New digital publishing models are explicitly designed to maximize profits by monetizing content online using strategies such as assigning stories according to software algorithms or compensating writers based on the number of page views their articles receive, prioritizing fast to produce, easy to digest, shareable content.

The pressure on writers to produce work that fits commercialized media models intensifies as publishers seek raw material to repackage and resell, or to syndicate across multiple platforms, while rates continue to decline. The low rates writers receive and the need to work faster and longer to produce more work places pressure on the kind of writing they can undertake. A freelancer I surveyed says: "Publishers aren't covering research expenses, meaning [research expenses] come out of our pay. And that pay is dropping ... I can't spend a month searching through archives, filing [freedom of information] requests, reading research, and trying to get to know the people in a story when I'm only being paid for one or two days of work on a feature story." Another acknowledges the difficulty in producing high-quality work in such a context: "To pump out stories for twenty to forty cents a word, I can't do any real background investigative work – just dribble if I'm going to make a living." Under these conditions, PWAC (2006, 4) is worried about the viability of freelance writing as an occupation in Canada, and writers and editors express concern about the quality of work in Canadian magazines and newspapers (Scott 2009). The casualization of media labour on a broad scale has important implications for media and culture and will continue to orient increasing amounts of cultural production to the commodity form, binding media and cultural workers even more tightly to market relations (Gunster 2004).

While even the most creative aspects of cultural work must conform to routines, genres, and practices standard to a particular cultural form or industry (Smith and McKinlay 2009b, 32), precarity adds extra pressure to "play it safe" (Bourdieu 1998, 99), including pressure toward the self-discipline – what Brian Holmes (2002, 3) calls "internalized self monitoring" – necessary for navigating precarious work conditions. Freelance and contract cultural workers depend on personal contacts, their record of previous work, and their reputations for future work. The temporal and financial pressure to produce more work, faster discourages writers from taking creative risks or pursuing difficult projects. It limits the time writers can spend researching, writing, and challenging and confirming facts – tenets of quality journalism. "Increasingly dire conditions seemed to be forcing many freelancers to abandon public-interest stories," finds Project Word (2015, 2). According to its survey, over the past five years freelance journalists have curbed investigative reporting because it is too expensive to undertake, as they must pay all the upfront costs and are generally not reimbursed by media outlets (13). The consequences are worth considering in detail:

The public is losing valuable stories. In the past five years, 81% of respondents reported having to forfeit stories due to "resource constraints" – more than half gave up at least five stories (55%), and another one-quarter abandoned more than five stories. Nor were these puff pieces ... Based on comments and interviews with respondents, such aborted stories covered a range of topics, from how the Pentagon handles the health of soldiers and the US role in mass killings in an ally country, to global reproductive rights, an investor's plan to bundle and sell minority-owned broadcaster companies on the public spectrum, and "blatant corruption" in Florida. (13)

Another survey, of journalists in "atypical work arrangements" internationally, also shows a decline in investigative and critical journalism because freelancers are not "adequately remunerated for intense research and/or because of the time pressures on those in insecure employment" (Walters, Warren, and Dobbie 2006, 5). The survey asks a key question: "Does the nature of the employment relationship impact on editorial content?," to which 75.6 per cent of respondents answered yes, either "a lot" or "somewhat" (4). Journalists who are precariously employed feel that precarity results in "timid reporting" (4).

The freelancers I surveyed reported more mixed results. "Though I'm not rich," says one, "I have the freedom to accept or decline work based on whether or not it seems like fun." Another says that the most enjoyable aspect of freelancing is choosing what stories to work on, "versus being a staff reporter, when I had to do a lot of stuff I thought was stupid/boring/irrelevant/actually harmful to the public good." But discrepancy exists between the kind of writing freelancers want to do and the kind of writing they actually do. Just over half of those I surveyed would most like to write long-form narrative features, creative nonfiction, essays, and investigative journalism, primarily for magazines and books. Explains one writer: "[I'd like to do] bigger investigative stories. The stories that peel back the superficial layers and get to the heart of the matter, thus allowing us to see the world differently." The kind of writing most freelancers most often do, however, is for corporate clients, consumer magazines, and trade magazines. While 36 per cent of the freelancers I surveyed say they are writing what they would like to write, others gave the reasons they are not: it does not pay enough to be worthwhile (27 per cent), a lack of contacts at the publications they would like to write for (21 per cent), and no time to pursue that type of writing (15 per cent). Only 5 per cent report that publications do not publish the kind of writing they would like to do, which indicates that the predominant reason for not pursuing long-form features is because of the low pay and the (unpaid) time required to produce them. In a survey conducted by Story Board (2011c), 42.9 per cent of freelancers are writing less for magazines because of increased corporate or other writing, and 42.9 per cent are writing less for magazines because of the rights demanded in contracts.[1]

PWAC's report (2006, 15) also reveals a discrepancy between the type of writing freelancers most want to pursue – for periodicals, books, and American magazines, which have bigger markets and often higher rates of pay – and the type of writing most do – for corporate clients, and shorter magazine pieces that are faster to produce. As one writer says, "I used to earn 100 per cent of my income from magazine writing. Now I earn less than $10,000 per year writing for magazines, but upwards of $50,000 per year doing corporate work" (Scott 2009, 8). Another notes that he has built his career on service journalism (shorter, consumer-oriented articles): "[Service journalism] has paid my bills and helped establish my reputation and skills, but I would like to do more meaningful, issues-related writing. I do some, but there are probably three or four bill-payers for every piece I'm truly proud of." While such challenges are expressed in individual terms, more concerning than individual satisfaction and pride are the social implications of journalism's precarity penalty.

Angela McRobbie (2002b, 2004) makes clear the relationship between precarious labour and cultural production. The intensification of individualized work practices and precarious employment in Britain's arts and culture sectors has led to a blurred distinction between artists' independent and commercial work, a pressure toward commercialization, and a decline in numbers of independent cultural producers. Under neoliberalism and creative industry policies, emerging cultural workers do not have opportunities to develop artistic or cultural practices outside of the commercial realm: "They are instead multi-tasking, de-spacialized cultural entrepreneurs (or entrepreneurs of the self) for whom an even more aggressively free market cultural environment now shapes the opportunities and possibilities for how they work" (McRobbie 2004, 191). Consider the links between fashion journalists' freelance status and the content they produce: the need to foster contacts and sources in the industry prevents them from investigating difficult topics such as sweatshop labour or straying from conventional, uncritical, "broadly promotional" copy (McRobbie 2000, 265). The capitalist social relations that give form to media and cultural production are fundamental to understanding contemporary media production, how production is organized and work experienced, and the kind of content produced. The commodification of labour power and of culture are intimately linked. Both are products of the relentless pressure from media and cultural industry corporations seeking to offload the risks and costs of production.

GENDER, RACE, AND CLASS IN MEDIA WORK

Journalism's precarity penalty extends beyond what type of content it is possible to produce under precarious working conditions. Researchers, activists, and writers have long been concerned about the class composition of media work and the equitable participation of women and people of colour, as those who make media have a say in whose stories are told, and how. Studies of mainstream, corporate media in Canada, the United States, and the United Kingdom continue to show that the media workforce is dominated by white, middle-class men, particularly at senior levels where hiring decisions are made. Women, people of colour, aboriginal people, and working-class people are drastically underrepresented in mainstream media, not just in newsrooms but also in media content: on screens and in newspapers, as subjects of stories and as sources and quoted experts. Portrayals that do exist are often stereotypical, inaccurate, or negative (see, for example, Ungerleider 1991; Joynt 1995; Fleras 1995; Bielby and Bielby 1992; Henry and Tator 2000; Ross 2002; Cavanagh 2004; Miller 2006; Weaver et al. 2007; Doyle 2011; Jones 2011; Pugh Yi and Dearfield 2012).

While research shows that more women than men work as freelance writers, research also shows that men still dominate the pages of the most prestigious, high-paying magazines, that men's books are reviewed more often, and that men are nominated for more journalism awards (VIDA 2012; Madison 2012; CWILA 2013). Research also shows that many women pursue freelance journalism because they disproportionately balance household labour with paid work, and that women freelancers earn less than men, reaffirming the precarious nature of freelancing rather than highlighting this type of work as opportunity for gender equity in journalism (McKercher 2009; PWAC 2006; Morini 2007; Massey and Elmore 2011). As Mark Banks, Rosalind Gill, and Stephanie Taylor (2013, 2) argue, "The cultural and creative industries are ... less inclusive, equal and egalitarian than many of the traditional industries they purported to supplant and surpass." This is particularly the case when it comes to race. As I have noted, 93 per cent of the freelancers I surveyed identify as white. The American Society of News Editors (2015) reports that of 32,900 full-time journalists at daily newspapers in the United States, only 12.76 identify as "racial minorities," a decrease of .58 per cent from the previous year. A report by the National Council for the Training of Journalists finds that 95 per cent of journalists in the United Kingdom are white (Spilsbury 2013).

In Canada, a hugely diverse country, recent statistics on racial diversity in journalism are lacking, despite the issue regularly being debated in media itself. In 1998, David Pritchard and Florian Sauvageau found that 97.3 per cent of Canadian journalists are white. In 2004, only 3.4 per cent of news journalists at thirty-seven Canadian newspapers identified as nonwhite, up from 2.6 per cent in 1999 (Miller 2006). Journalists and educators insist that there is racial diversity in journalism schools and among the ranks of journalists at independent, ethnic, and alternative media outlets, but astute observers note that precarious labour conditions, unpaid internships, and low rates of pay mean that it is more difficult for racialized workers to break into mainstream, corporate media outlets (Rowe 2015; Clarke 2015). "Journalism schools are pumping out so many visible minorities and plenty of women, and they do not get jobs the way white kids do," says journalist Scaachi Koul (cited in Clarke 2015), speaking to the rigid power structures that are so difficult for many to penetrate. Research by Alex T. Williams (2015) confirms Koul's point. Williams found that only 49 per cent of people of colour who graduate from journalism programs in the United States (those who focused on print or broadcast journalism) land full-time jobs, versus 66 per cent of white graduates. "The number of minorities graduating from journalism programs and applying for jobs doesn't seem to be the problem after all," he writes. "The problem is that these candidates are not being hired" (ibid.). A major challenge that many point to is that hiring decisions are made by people in powerful positions in media organizations, positions largely occupied by white males, and that people tend to hire from their networks, which consist of people who often occupy a shared social location (Gill 2002).

An already exclusive sphere in terms of access to employment, the more precarious media and cultural work become, and the more difficult it is for a diverse range of people to participate. As media and cultural work becomes more competitive more reliant on personal contacts and informal networks to navigate entry to jobs, and – critically – based on unpaid labour, fewer people can afford to pursue media work, further limiting diverse portrayals of gender, race, and class experiences. Particularly disconcerting is the spread and normalization of unpaid work as a requirement for entry in the media and cultural industries, as an employee or as a freelancer. Unpaid work in media ranges from the increasing requirement to work for free, either by producing articles "for exposure" or undertaking a low-paid or unpaid internship. A young freelancer explains that she had to turn down a big break on a "major TV show" because the position was unpaid: "I mean, I'm sure some people can afford that," she says. "When I was just getting out of school, I got an internship. It's like a news show. And I was so pumped about it, but then they were like, 'You have to work for free,' and of course I couldn't do it unless I had a family to live with. I didn't have family in Toronto. Only people who are in that privileged position could do those jobs" (cited in Lewchuk et al. 2015, 37). Another freelancer explains that many young journalists view freelancing as "a perpetual tryout for a staff job" and that it is "becoming the industry's new version of the unpaid internship, throwing up a similar barrier to entry for those trying to get into the profession without a parental subsidy" (Meyer 2015). After earning a living writing about poverty and class in America, established journalist Barbara Ehrenreich (2015) watched her "fees at one major news outlet drop to one third of their value between 2004 and 2009" and saw young journalists around her struggling. She was determined to "carry on writing about poverty and inequality" even if it meant she had to pay for her work out of pocket, but soon realized the deep structural problems with such an approach:

I realized that there was something wrong with an arrangement whereby a relatively affluent person such as I had become could afford to write about minimum wage jobs, squirrels as an urban food source or the penalties for sleeping in parks, while the people who were actually experiencing these sorts of things, or were in danger of experiencing them, could not ... There are many thousands of ... gifted journalists who want to address serious social issues but cannot afford to do so in a media environment that thrives by refusing to pay, or anywhere near adequately pay, its "content providers." (ibid.)

Ehrenreich argues that "the impoverishment of journalists impoverishes journalism" (ibid.), pointing to a lack of coverage of poverty in American journalism, or skewed coverage because commentators often have not experienced poverty themselves and are unable to understand its multiple complexities. Little research exists on the relationship between economic class, unpaid labour, and journalism – and virtually none in Canada – but a British study on fair access to professions found that less than 10 per cent of new entrants to journalism in Britain come from working-class backgrounds (Panel on Fair Access to the Professions 2009, 101). The report states, "Between the 1958 and the 1970 birth cohorts, the biggest decline in social mobility occurred in the professions of journalism and accountancy ... Journalists and broadcasters born in 1958 typically grew up in families with an income of around 5.5 per cent above that of the average family; but this rose to 42.4 per cent for the generation of journalists and broadcasters born in 1970" (19). A 2012 follow-up report confirms that journalism is becoming "one of the most socially exclusive of professions" in Britain, as entrance increasingly requires a university degree and the completion of an (often unpaid) internship (Independent Reviewer on Social Mobility and Child Poverty 2012, 54). Research on inequality and access to media work is needed in Canada. Freelancing and other forms of contract work are becoming the norm, either as the form a career takes, as an entry point, or as a stopgap while looking for more secure work. Yet declining wages, increased competition, and restrictive contracts are also becoming the norm. As it becomes riskier and more expensive to freelance for a living, writing will be transformed into work even fewer people can afford to do. As Kate Oakley (2013,

56) writes, "Who gets to make culture ... matters, because it is how we understand ourselves as a society." And so it matters, then, that journalism's precarity penalty means that social location deeply shapes the way that the risks of media production are offloaded onto individual workers.

ALTERNATIVE IMAGINARIES AND INFRASTRUCTURES

The precarious state of media work requires us to envision alternative ways to organize journalism and work. Experiments have long been underway to develop and sustain alternative strategies for producing and funding media, including nonprofit, activist, or community models (Hamilton 2008; McChesney and Nichols 2010; Kozolanka, Mazepa, and Skinner 2010; Pickard 2011). Developing worker- or member-owned cooperatives to forge new relationships between journalists and audiences holds promise, as the cooperative model foregrounds worker autonomy and control and could privilege journalists' normative commitment to the democratic ideals of journalism and integrity of their craft, rather than putting profit first (Boyle 2012). These examples will be increasingly instructive as we move deeper into the digital age and face the pressing need to produce journalism outside of commodified, capitalist models.

Closer to the discussion at hand, however, are alternative imaginaries of work and labour, or envisioning ways to sustainably support independent work outside of an employment relationship. These debates extend well beyond the bounds of media and cultural work and rarely intersect with research on journalists and journalistic labour. But the issues I have examined in this book are not isolated – precarity affects millions of workers in different ways. Debates about precarity and its implications for journalism must link up to ongoing, broader debates about how to address transformations in work, technology, and capitalism more generally. Current scholarly and popular media discussions of how to improve freelancers' conditions tend toward a narrow view on technological fixes (Creech and Mendelson 2015; Siegelbaum and Thomas 2015). Many, including freelancers, labour unions, and industry, advocate for the creation of (more and better) technological platforms to distribute freelance work, or to serve as a marketplace for buyers and sellers of labour to meet. The *Washington Post,* for example, launched Talent

Network – essentially a website to connect freelancers with editors – with great fanfare, including an in-depth video detailing how the idea came about (Baker 2015). The network is a platform for managing freelance pitches and assignments, replete with profiles of freelancers, a tool to pitch editors, assignment posting, and location tracking so that editors can assign stories to freelancers in particular locations. Its developer calls the site UberLancer, a nod to the controversial rideshare app (ibid.). Talent Network is like many that have come before (usually with snappier, Silicon-Valley-esque names like Contently, Newzulu, and Storyhunter), including the websites and directories developed by the unions I discussed in chapter 7. Most emphasize how technology can enable editors to better reach more freelancers and can give freelancers access to more work, but none speak of how it might raise fees or improve contracts. While providing freelancers with assignments and equipping them with the skills and strategies to navigate freelance work is useful in the short-term, we must envision and develop longer-term strategies that can sustainably address precarity rather than just professionalization.

Such visions would begin from the fact that freelance work is here to stay. While many journalists would prefer full-time employment, many recognize the great personal benefits to freelancing and do not want to be in an employment relationship (Smith 2013). While it is critical to foreground the factors that make freelancing precarious, including low pay, lack of access to benefits, and an inability to unionize, it is equally important to understand freelance work as a potential model of labour autonomy, one that could, ultimately, benefit workers and journalism. Here, autonomy is a politicized concept that moves beyond the individual, creative autonomy sought by media and cultural workers in a bid for fulfilling work and toward a notion of autonomy as control over how one's labour is engaged and the terms under which it is commodified in contemporary capitalism (de Peuter and Cohen 2015). Labour autonomy means that all workers, regardless of employment status, would have control over their time, access to decent work, the ability to work less, and access to social security (Vosko 2010). Such a vision of autonomy is linked to the autonomist Marxist concept of the "refusal of work," which is a "theoretical frame and a political agenda" that challenges Marxism's traditional "productivist tendencies," or arguments for more work for everyone (Weeks 2011, 92). As

Kathi Weeks writes, "The refusal of work is not ... a rejection of activity and creativity in general or of production in particular. It is not a renunciation of labour *tout court*, but rather a refusal of the ideology of work as the highest calling and moral duty, a refusal of work as the necessary centre of social life and means of access to the rights and claims of citizenship, and a refusal of the necessity of capitalist control of production" (99). Lives centred around work would shift to lives centred around other aspects of potentially cooperative social life.

Weeks notes that demands that stop at improving the conditions or qualities of work risk being absorbed and neutralized by capital. Such tendencies are clear in media and cultural work, where media industries capitalize on freelancers' desires for flexible working hours and freedom from various constraints. Freelance work can be viewed as a nod toward a refusal of work. As I examined in the preceding chapters, freelancers speak of their work as not work but "freedom," as a chance to pursue a passion for writing and to engage in meaningful activity. Freelancers' inclinations toward refusal are not as politicized as Weeks's vision: none speak of abolishing work or rescuing work from capitalist control, for example. As McRobbie (2007) notes, cultural workers are more likely to engage in a "refusal of *mundane* work" (emphasis added). Yet because of the way work and media production is organized under contemporary capitalism, media and cultural workers' refusal of an employment relationship means ultimately embracing more work, working all the time, and subsuming all of life into working hours (Shukaitis 2014, 199). As it currently stands, in Canada, self-employment means being denied the social protections that could make self-employment sustainable, such as unemployment insurance, pensions, parental leaves, and health benefits. As a vision for how work could be organized, then, the refusal of work is not only an effort to reduce work hours, but to envision ways that people can live and flourish outside of a dependence on work, via expanded social protections delinked from employment.

I use the concept of refusal of work here as "a provocation" (194), for the contradiction in my argument requires freelancers to at once recognize that they are workers and simultaneously embrace an antiwork ethos that could one day be realized through freelance status. But freelancing is riddled with contradictions. It is a form of work

that carries great potential to reclaim for workers time and autonomy, but under capitalist media production the power balance tilts in
favour of capital, making freelance status primarily a viable way for
companies to reduce labour costs and offload the risks and costs of
production onto individuals. The push from below for autonomy
and control collides with capital's compulsion for profit. Pursuing a
model of independent journalism produced by independent workers will require attending to the broader conditions in which all work
occurs and a push for collective responses and transformations in
policy that could unlink social security from standard employment.
Decommodifying journalism will require decommodifying labour.

A critical struggle for freelancers, other workers outside of standard employment, and all workers in precarious employment is over-
hauling legal regimes that prevent them from unionizing and
engaging in collective bargaining. Every organizer I interviewed mentioned this struggle as the major obstacle to mobilizing and representing freelance media workers. Any alternative imaginaries of work
and labour must involve the broad transformation of a labour relations system that "fav[ours] workplace-by-workplace organizing and
bargaining" (Kumar and Schenk 2009, 43). Currently, self-employed
workers who are not deemed to be dependent contractors (determined by a worker's degree of economic dependence on one company) risk violating provisions in Canada's Competition Act, which
prohibits self-employed professionals from coming together to set
prices. Such activity can be considered anticompetitive and workers'
groups can be charged with "conspiracy in restraint of trade" (Vosko
2005, 145). While freelance and self-employed cultural workers could
potentially get companies or associations of companies to voluntarily negotiate, such as in the film and television industries, the current legal framework is a huge challenge to freelance writers'
organizing efforts and will need to change for the power balance between freelancers and publishers to shift. Over the years, some have
advocated for changes to the law that would classify self-employed
workers as employees for the purposes of collective bargaining (Holland 2006). But freelance media and cultural workers want to be able
to negotiate minimum standard agreements that can be enforced by
law without having to be legally classified as employees so that they
can retain ownership over their copyrights, rights that employees
must surrender to their employers. Changing working conditions,

including the spread of freelance, contract, part-time, flexible, and seasonal work, requires changing laws and the current labour relations system.

A meaningful and strong provincial status of the artist could assist in facilitating the contract negotiation and collective bargaining process for freelancers, as it has for visual artists in Canada. Other policy proposals on the table include variants of the Urban Worker Strategy forwarded by the New Democratic Party that would enable workers in precarious employment, regardless of sector, to access social protections such as pensions, unemployment insurance, and better workplace protections (Cohen and de Peuter 2013). A much broader vision would push for a universal guaranteed annual income, or a basic income, which is "an income paid unconditionally to individuals regardless of their family or household relationships, regardless of other income, and regardless of their past, present, or future employment status" (Weeks 2011, 138, citing van Parijs 1992, 3). The notion of some form of basic income has been in circulation since the 1960s and versions of it have been tested in a variety of places. But the call for a basic income has resurged in recent years, proposed by actors from across the political spectrum and motivated by increasing inequality between the rich and poor, intensified automation in workplaces, soaring social assistance costs, and spreading precarity (Wright 2010; Mason 2015). A basic income would provide a floor for all workers (most basic income arguments do not argue for the abolishment of work) that would mean less dependence on wages for survival, would give workers choice about what type of work to do, and would empower them to negotiate the terms under which they work (Weeks 2011, 138–9). If all of life is work, as critics of the social factory have pointed out, then we should all be paid for all of it (ibid.).

A basic income would have particular benefits for freelancers and other media and cultural workers, as Greig de Peuter (2014) argues. A guaranteed annual income could compensate freelancers for intermittent work and unpaid work between gigs (272). It could also account for "contributions to the creative economy – from maintaining the social networks that undergird flexible labour pools, to feeding content to social-media firms, to lending cachet to gentrifying neighbourhoods – that generate financial value but are currently unremunerated" (273). And, finally, a basic income could begin to chip away at class barriers that prevent people from accessing media work (273). Arguments for a basic universal income are linked to feminist struggles for recognition of the importance of social reproduction in capitalism and the unequal way reproductive labour is organized (Weeks 2011). Feminists were among the first to identify the conditions of the social factory, or the fact that "the time of production reaches beyond the discrete workplace, and the relations of production extend beyond the specific employment relation" (142). A basic income would compensate workers for all of the unpaid labour required to sustain life. For freelance media and cultural workers in particular, a basic income would recognize the dependence work has on social life that extends far beyond the actual work of writing and would enable them to refuse poorly paid work and pursue the work in which they are most interested.

If made more secure, freelance status could be an enabler of autonomous journalism (Uzelman 2012), or journalism independent of employers' control and free from commercial impulses, and journalism that journalists themselves believe to be important and worth pursuing. While freelancers will always need to sell articles to media outlets, some security would give them the time and space needed to investigate, ruminate, examine, or advocate without sacrificing the need to be paid to survive. Better supporting self-employment could temper exploitation and ensure freelancers could do the kind of work they want to do. Writing in a different context, Mark Andrejevic (2011, 284) reminds us, "Exploitation is not simply about a loss of monetary value, but also a loss of control over one's productive and creative spirit." To restore that control requires self-employment to be feasible, enabling workers meaningful compensation and social security instead of plunging them into precarity.

"The solution to the failures of journalism," writes Astra Taylor (2014, 78), "is more and better journalism." Producing better journalism will require infrastructures of support, including alternative production models, expanded social protections, and, critically, collective organization in unions or self-organized alt-worker groups. Collective organizing is a challenge, particularly under current labour relations frameworks, but is vital for securing other forms of social protections. And so, it will be important to frame freelance collective organizing efforts as more than an end goal, as a way to ultimately negotiate with publishers for better rates, but as part of a broader struggle for democratic media. Collective representation and organizational support will also be important for equity and accessibility in journalism, and for addressing how race, gender, and class shape media production. In her role as freelance organizer for the Canadian Media Guild, datejie green pushed for a better understanding of racialization and marginalization in media industries and how people of colour, aboriginal people, and working-class people, for example, experience freelance work in different ways. green's vision was to make freelancing inclusive and accessible by providing workers who are otherwise marginalized access to social capital and tacit knowledge needed to get into media organizations and fairly compete (personal communication 2014). If media unions want to engage in meaningful long-term change for workers, they will need to broadly integrate this type of antioppression framework into organizing and staffing, along with matching resources to tackle the long-term challenge of organizing freelancers, as convincing freelancers to join existing organizations remains difficult. "[As a freelancer] you lose confidence, you lose perspective on your own power and your own agency," says green. "You can also lose perspective on life, in the sense that work never goes away. It's a twenty-four-hour experience, you never turn it off. You're dreaming about work, you have nightmares about work, you're working until all hours, you're getting up at all hours ... you lose perspective on making fun time for yourself and down time for yourself, health time for yourself ... So, we're also up against the way in which all of those pressures leave freelancers skeptical of other kinds of supports being available for them" (ibid.).

As I demonstrated in chapter 6, skepticism and reluctance toward collective organizations and supports is not unusual. As Andrew Ross (2000, 28) recounts, "Historically, noncommercial mental workers have found it too challenging, and professionally limiting, to see themselves as workers." Theorizing writers' character through a feminist lens, Valerie Miner (1985, 46) observes the "broad social denial about the labour involved in the making of art" and argues that writers must understand themselves as workers rather than as artists or professionals, as writing is work that is mired in capitalist social and power relations. She writes: "Writers have a lot to learn from coal miners and steel workers whose unionism erases any false notion of privilege about the rights to be paid or to be treated decently for work" (49). Rather than "confron[t] publishers about change," Miner notes that writers instead compete with one another for limited work, money, and attention. She acknowledges that writers' unions in various countries attempt to address writers' challenges, but "until we recognize ourselves as part of a larger scheme of workers, we will be organizing in a vacuum" (49). Concern about inequality and inaccessibility makes a strong case for the urgency of collective organization among freelance media workers, not just to improve freelancers' conditions, but also to ensure that cultural work is accessible and diverse.

The past few decades have been difficult for freelance journalists, who face stagnant fees and demanding contracts and who feel undervalued, overworked, and insecure. Yet media unions and alt-labour groups are engaged in experiments in representing and supporting precarious media workers, and freelancers are increasingly speaking out about their working conditions and developing public modes of holding employers to account (or at least to getting them to pay up). More broadly, workers in a range of media, cultural, and communication industries are pushing back against unpaid and exploitative work, including media interns, reality television workers, models, dancers, digital pieceworkers, and more. A growing number of journalists at digital-first media outlets have voted to join existing unions and are working to negotiate their first contracts. The effects of these activities have yet to play out, but they are making space for the notion that freelance journalism and the privileges it could bring should be open to everyone, not just to those who can afford to gamble on precarity.

Notes

1 I have also chosen the term culture/al over the term creative (as in creative industries), because of its critical edge. The term conjures the critical spirit of Theodor Adorno and Max Horkheimer (2002), who introduced the term "culture industry" in 1944 as a critique of the degradation of art and culture under a rationalized system of capitalist mass production. Adorno and Horkheimer were concerned with the "general shift to the commodification of cultural products and the alienation of the cultural producer as a wage labourer within increasingly concentrated large-scale corporations" (Garnham 2005, 17), processes that are intensified today and that continue to shape freelance writers' experiences. Pluralizing industries acknowledges the heterogeneous nature – what Bernard Miège (1989) calls the logics – of different forms of cultural production while retaining the tensions that arise from the marriage of culture and commerce. The term cultural industries remains resistant to the ideological slant of creative industry discourse, which arose amid two decades of state policies that view the cultural sector as a site of economic investment and urban stimulus, pressuring the transformation of cultural industries into commercial sectors and accelerating the commodification of culture (Garnham 2005).

CHAPTER ONE

1 Some recent examples include Banks (2007), Hesmondhalgh and Baker (2011), Forkert (2013), de Peuter (2014), Oakley and O'Connor (2015), and Maxwell (2015).

2 As with other terminology, the descriptors Fordism and post-Fordism are contested, particularly because of the way they attempt to define a hegemonic form of work that all workers were and are subject to during a particular historical period. For example, certain features of Fordism, including assembly line production, labour control, rationalization of the labour process, and deskilling persist in the post-Fordist period, and many workers experienced flexible, precarious work under the Fordist era. While the term "post-Fordism" indicates a break with the past, it is useful in many cases to indicate specific historical changes that, while still underway, have shaped the political economic context in which freelance journalists work.

3 The content of work matters, for example, in deciding how production can be organized (Ryan 1992; Hesmondhalgh 2007), and sometimes for legal reasons (Vosko 2005).

4 Autonomists make a similar claim without wholly dismissing Marx (Weeks 2011, 93; Cleaver 2000).

5 For sustained attention to cultural workers and alienation, see Stahl (2010, 2013a).

6 Gill (2014a, 13) argues that research on cultural work has not paid attention to exploitation as a structural part of all work under capitalism and that the term is only used to highlight "extreme" cases such as unpaid internships.

7 Marx ([1867] 1990, 129) defines socially necessary labour time as "the labour-time required to produce any use-value under the conditions of production normal for a given society and with the average degree of skill and intensity of labour prevalent in that society."

8 Marx ([1867] 1990, 126) defines use value as something that satisfies a human need or want.

9 Marx ([1867] 1990, 279) distinguishes between labour, or the activity of work, and labour power, or the capacity to work: "The aggregate of those mental and physical capabilities existing in the physical form, the living personality, of a human being, capabilities which he sets in motion whenever he produced a use-value of any kind."

10 This is despite the fact that Braverman extended his analysis into the office and applied his insights to the rationalization of life in general under capitalism. Some scholarship extends to the service sector. For example, the edited collection by Smith, Knights, and Willmott (1991) applies labour process theory to non-manual work, including essays on medical and hospital workers, public service workers, academics, engineers, and

insurance sales workers. Apart from journalists (Murphy 1991), however, the book does not include media or cultural workers.

11 Even models of production that require "named labour" are being transformed. Consider Alloy Entertainment, a company that conceptualizes book projects for publishers, pumping out thirty book projects per year targeted to teen girls. What is unusual about this "book factory" (Semuels 2008) is not the formulaic plots and generic tropes it relies on for mass-market appeal, but the way labour is organized in the production of each book: ideas are brainstormed at a meeting, an editor composes a story, and a writer is hired on spec to draft a chapter. The writer works closely with editors to develop the plot and produce more chapters. Alloy pitches the chapters, a book synopsis, and a cover image to publishers, retaining all rights to the intellectual property. Often, company-owned pseudonyms are used instead of real writers' names, and some names stand in for a team of ghostwriters (Mead 2009). Perhaps an extreme example of the rationalization of literary production, Alloy offers an example of how capital can find ways around the need to grant creative workers relative autonomy if and when it is required for profitable production. Under Alloy's model, it does not matter who writes a particular book. Authors, historically assured the privilege of being named labour, are interchangeable and often not credited for their work.

12 Even when granted relative autonomy in the sense of being free from monitoring and other traditional forms of control, cultural work is performed within the confines of routines, or having to work "within a particular genre or style that the individual does not create, but which is there as a template or recipe for the individual to 'follow' or work within" (Smith and McKinlay 2009b, 32). This is evident in most forms of industrialized cultural production, such as television, films, newspapers, and magazines.

13 Indeed, work under capitalism is constantly reorganized to suit capitalism's needs for valorization and ceding control over the labour process to certain workers is exactly in line with some needs of accumulation. This can range from empowerment strategies on the factory floor (Moody 1997) to injections of "fun" and lax control in cultural and informational workplaces. Ross (2003, 19) documents the myriad ways that playful, permissive new media offices are designed to tap into workers' creative and emotional potential and harness their "freest thoughts and impulses" for productivity. Such practices are present in high-tech workplaces, entertainment firms, and video game companies, where open-concept offices,

nonhierarchical management styles, and philosophies of self-regulation translate into overwork, self-discipline and self-blame, high stress, and emotional exhaustion (ibid.; Dyer-Witheford and de Peuter 2009). The strategy of loosening control can be viewed as a descendent of capitalists' age-old strategy of lengthening the working day. In offices replete with catered meals, on-site laundry, and recreation facilities, Ross (2001, 78) notes, "Who would ever want to go home?"

14 Indeed, some note that this sector has been a model of employment transformation for other sectors (Ross 2000; Cottle 2003b, 3).

15 In *Capital*, Marx ([1867] 1990, 784) identifies capital's need to create a "disposable industrial reserve army." Increased productivity requires fewer workers for production, thus creating a group of workers who are "always ready for exploitation by capital." The existence of the reserve army places pressure on employed workers, forcing them "to submit to over-work and subjects them to the dictates of capital" lest they become part of the industrial reserve. This arrangement benefits capital at all workers' expense (789).

16 As I explain in chapter 3, employees do not own copyright to works they produce. This is part of the trade-off for the security of employment. "Moral rights" typically means that someone who has been assigned economic ownership of copyright cannot alter or modify the work without the author's consent.

CHAPTER TWO

1 Magazines and newspapers are undoubtedly different. Yet journalism is the occupational legacy of freelance writing and most print journalists have historically been employed by newspapers. A lack of magazine history from a labour perspective has encouraged me to draw on the experiences of newspaper workers to learn about writers' working conditions and to understand why journalists would want to become freelancers.

2 Three decades later, writers' guides offered similar advice: "If you decide to depend mostly or entirely on income from freelance work, you have a head start if you have a spouse or a live-in companion who will cover the rent during the months when your pickin's [*sic*] are poor. Another wise precaution is to see whether your bank manager will allow you overdraft privileges" (Drobot and Tennant 1990, 7).

3 For a full discussion of magazine policies, see Audley (1983), Dubinsky (1996), Azzi (1999), McKercher (2001), and Dornan (2012).

4 For Harrison's study, 1,304 surveys were completed, but this includes writers of all media forms, including film, novels, and television.

5 The unionization of journalists in North America began in 1891, when the International Typographers Union began to issue charters for unions of editors and reporters, primarily as an attempt to prevent editorial workers from scabbing, or collaborating with management to produce papers during a strike (Brennen 2008; Leab 1970). Most locals disbanded. Successive pushes to organize were challenged by publishers, but also by the "romance of newspapering," an occupational ideology that stressed individual action and reinforced the notion that hard work and good luck would lead to fame, or at least middle-class professionalism and career mobility (Leab 1970; Salcetti 1995; Brennen 2004). It was not until 1933, with the National Industrial Recovery Act, that journalists began forming the media unions that exist today. The act was designed to decrease unemployment by requiring businesses to reduce work hours and the length of the workweek to spread available work, and its proposed regulations included hour and wage provisions for editorial workers. In resistance to the act, publishers lobbied for reporters to be classified as professionals because the act exempted professionals from regulated working hours (Broun 1935; Leab 1970). Journalists' outrage and organizing led to the formation of the American Newspaper Guild, which began to organize journalists in Canada in the 1940s, and changed its name to the Newspaper Guild. Later, the Communication Workers of Canada was formed, eventually merging into the Communication, Energy and Paperworkers Union of Canada, which merged with the Canadian Auto Workers to become Unifor in 2013. The Newspaper Guild is part of Communication Workers of America.

CHAPTER THREE

1 One report states: "The Ontario magazine industry contributes around 9,000 jobs and nearly $1 billion in economic activity annually to the Ontario economy" and describes the province's magazine industry as being in "a relatively strong financial situation" (TCI Management Consultants 2008, 1, i).

2 PWAC (2006) surveyed 858 freelance writers, most of whom are full-time writers, meaning that writing is their sole source of income.

3 The survey included 459 freelancers, writers, editors, staff, photographers, publishers, and CEOs. Of the total, freelancers comprised 60 per cent of

survey respondents. Only 3 per cent selected "very well," 39 per cent selected "not very well," and 14 per cent selected "not at all well" (Scott 2009, 25).

4 The sample of women freelance journalists in this study was young (between thirty-four and thirty-nine years old) and only 39.4 per cent had children (Massey and Elmore 2011). Suzanne Franks (2013) found that women in many Western countries leave their jobs in news journalism because of sexism, such as being unable to advance their careers and a wide gender pay gap.

5 Transcontinental, now TC Media, published over thirty magazines, owns community newspapers, educational, interactive, and printing arms, and in 2014 purchased Sun Media Corporation's weekly newspapers in Quebec. Its media sector revenues were $688 million in 2014, of which magazines and books bring in $341 million (TC Transcontinental 2014, 8, 10). In 2014 it sold fifteen consumer magazines to TVA Group Inc.

6 Drobot and Tennant (1990, 91) briefly mention this practice in the Canadian context but do not provide specific examples.

7 A similar suit was won against the *New York Times* in 2001. For discussion of this suit and a more comprehensive treatment of legal issues, see D'Agostino (2007, 2010).

8 Ardvisson, Malossi, and Naro (2010) make a similar argument about workers in Milan's fashion industry.

CHAPTER FOUR

1 I posed this as an open-ended question to survey respondents. In 204 responses, the word "freedom" appears one hundred times.

2 Since 2009, all workers in the publishing industries in Canada (including writers, editors, agents, translators, and administrative workers) have been able to access benefits under a plan designed by the Writers' Union of Canada and ACTRA Fraternal. PWAC members can access benefits through this fund. Other freelancers can access benefits through memberships in the Canadian Freelance Union and the Canada Media Guild's freelance branch (see Neil 2010 for an overview of cultural workers' access to social benefits).

3 This example points to a common strategy among employers to lower labour costs: misclassifying employees as freelancers or contractors.

4 Of course, as Lorey (2009, 195) and feminist scholars note, women have never experienced utter separation between work and life, as the home

has historically been a site of reproductive labour disproportionately undertaken by women.

5 Although as Neff, Wissinger, and Zukin (2005, 312) note, the time and sacrifice necessary to pursue careers in modelling or new media, for example, "creates a structural disincentive to exist these industries, even in a difficult economic situation." Similarly, many freelancers feel they have invested too much time and effort in their careers to abandon them outright.

CHAPTER FIVE

1 Journalist Rachel Sanders (2013) compiled an online list of articles by freelancers speaking out, titled "2013: The Year of the Angry Freelancer."

2 Other advertising strategies include sponsored or branded content, where advertisers pay for articles that are produced by sponsors and the media outlet and are often only subtly marked as such. This is a growth area for digital journalism companies and many journalists have been hired to produce sponsored or branded content for sites like *Buzzfeed* and the *Huffington Post*. The practice is contentious among journalists and was a major reason why those at the *Globe and Mail* almost went on strike in 2014.

3 I asked Hansen this question after he spoke about *Medium* at the What Is Journalism? conference, held 9–11 April in Portland, Oregon. Hansen's quotes in this chapter come from his talk at the conference.

4 Who Pays Writers? moved from tumblr in 2013 to become part of *Scratch*. When *Scratch* ceased publishing, Martin committed to maintaining Who Pays Writers? as long as there was a demand for it. The original site exists at whopays.tumblr.com, and Who Pays Writers? is now at whopayswriters.com (including a complete archive).

CHAPTER SIX

1 The paper's staff unionized in the late 1970s, when media mogul Rupert Murdoch purchased the *Village Voice* (Willis 1998, 263).

2 The Freelancers Union grew out of the nonprofit organization Working Today, founded by lawyer Sara Horowitz in 1995 to address the emergent freelance labour force, which had no access to benefits and insurance in the United States.

3 UNESCO is the United Nations Educational, Scientific and Cultural Or-

ganization. The organization met in Belgrade in 1980 to recognize the vital role of artists and to encourage member states to improve and protect artists' social security, labour, and taxation conditions (UNESCO 1980).

4 The act is titled Loi sur le statut professionnel et les conditions d'engagement des artistes de la scène, du disque et du cinéma (An act respecting the professional status and conditions of engagement of performing, recording and film artists).

5 Part one established the Canadian Council on the Status of the Artist, which would be under the jurisdiction of Canadian Heritage and would advise the minister on supporting and promoting "the professional status of artists in Canada" (CAPPRT 2002). Ultimately, the council was never established, which is part of why the act has not been effective.

6 Federal jurisdiction includes "broadcasting undertakings under the jurisdiction of the Canadian Radio-television and Telecommunications Commission, federal government departments, and the majority of federal government agencies and Crown corporations" (CAPPRT 2002).

7 This applies to the CBC, whose employees and freelancers are unionized, and broadcasters, which only covers in-house production: only 22.2 per cent of total production relies on journalists employed by broadcasters. The rest is contracted to independent producers (Neil 2010, 21).

8 The Ontario Federation of Labour Cultural Industries Working Group includes the American Federation of Musicians, Toronto Musicians' Association, the Writers' Union of Canada, Writers Guild of Canada, Directors Guild of Canada, ACTRA, Canadian Artists' Representation/le Front des artistes canadien, Canadian Actors' Equity Association, Ontario Public Service Employees Union, the International Alliance of Theatrical and Stage Employees, and the Communications, Energy and Paper Workers Union (OFL n.d.).

9 In October 2012 the Ontario New Democratic Party proposed a private member's bill, the Tabuns bill, Labour Relations in the Industries of Film, Television, Radio and New Media Act, 2012, which could enable workers in media industries in Ontario to be represented by a workers' association that can serve as a designated bargaining agent and that could negotiate scale agreements. This would address lengthy jurisdictional court challenges as disputes could be resolved by the Ontario Labour Relations Board. The bill is supported by ACTRA Toronto, the Directors Guild of Canada-Ontario, Nabet CEP Local 700M, and the Toronto Musicians' Association (Ontario New Democratic Party 2012).

10 CARFAC, or Canadian Artists Representation/le front des artistes Canada, represents 20,000 visual artists in Canada.

11 The union has unsuccessfully tried to introduce this at other newspapers.

CHAPTER SEVEN

1 Although there is no record of this in PWAC's archives, Valerie Miner (1985, 49) attributes PWAC's origins to a small collective of feminist writers who came together to discuss their mistreatment by editors.

2 Membership criteria at the time was intended to be exclusive, limited to writers who had published at least five articles in Canadian general interest magazines or ten features in Canadian metropolitan daily newspapers within the past three years. This excluded freelancers who wrote for trade magazines and those who did corporate or more specialized writing (PWAC 1976b).

3 Although important, the vote occurred at the end of a meeting, when people were in a hurry to leave, with no recount of tie votes and little time to discuss the implications, which members believed had potential to shape the future direction of PWAC.

4 Under the Canadian Copyright Act, fair dealing permits limited use of copying for research or private study, criticism or review, or news reporting (Canadian Heritage 2009). The Copyright Modernization Act expands fair dealing into the realm of education, which freelancers fear will limit the royalty payments they receive from universities and other educational institutions.

5 Unifor (2015) describes community chapters as "a new way that workers can have some of the benefits of a union, even if you don't work somewhere that has a union or can form one." The chapters are geared toward organizing self-employed and other workers in non-standard employment and offer dental and health plans, group home and auto insurance, political representation, and other benefits of being affiliated with the largest private-sector union in Canada.

6 Annual CFU dues are $125.

7 Historically, voluntarism has been most successful with craft worker unions "who occupied strategic or 'respectable' positions in industry, such as typographical workers and locomotive engineers," and when unions' demands were "reasonable" (Tucker and Mucalov 2010, 218, citing Fudge and Tucker 2001). This need for being reasonable raises questions about cordial relations with publishers that the CFU explicitly seeks

to challenge. Coles (2012, 56–7) notes that the Directors Guild of Canada and International Alliance of Theatrical Stage Employees take a "partners in production" approach to "provid[e] a measure of stability and predictability in a volatile industry," which means they do not usually resort to strikes and are limited in gains they can make for members.

8 Another crucial reason film and television workers have been able to negotiate voluntary agreements is because they work together on set and have the power to go on strike and shut down production, whereas freelance journalists do not.

9 The CMG does not represent workers at the CBC in Moncton or Quebec.

10 The CMG is an example of what Mosco and McKercher (2008, 17) call a converged union: over the years it inherited several other union's members at the CBC, including CUPE, ACTRA, and CEP members, by consolidating bargaining units (43). Currently, a total of thirteen unions and associations represent workers at the CBC and its French language arm, Radio-Canada (CBC 2011).

11 Freelancer Patricia Pearson won compensation from Rogers Publishing after an article she wrote for *Chatelaine* appeared on third-party websites without her consent and was live on *Chatelaine*'s website for twice as long as her contract stipulated (Story Board 2010).

12 As I explained in chapter 3, the contract "grants to the Publisher and to each of its affiliates, an irrevocable, perpetual, worldwide, royalty-free non-exclusive license" without specifying who or what these affiliates are; it demands use of the work for "marketing purposes," which writers fear could mean worldwide syndication under the guise of "promotion"; and requires some freelancers to permit the *Toronto Star* to sell their work to third parties. The terms do not include additional payments to writers (Story Board 2011d).

13 Interestingly, and perhaps problematically for relations between freelance writers' unions, the *Toronto Star*'s newsroom is represented by the Southern Ontario Newsmedia Guild, a local of what was then CEP (and is now Unifor). The CEP was aware of the CMG's campaign to improve the contract for freelancers, but due to its obligations to represent staff could not get involved (Jean Broughton, personal communication 2012).

14 Fees were one of the most predominant complaints about writers' organizations in my survey, revealing freelancers' service mentality toward collective organization. CFU dues are $125 per year, PWAC

membership is $240 per year, and CMG freelance branch membership is $150 per year. Often the organizations will offer promotional discounts.

CONCLUSION

1 The survey, conducted online, does not indicate the number of free-lancers surveyed.

References

Abrahamian, Atossa Araxia. 2012. "The 'I' in Union." *Dissent*, winter. http://www.dissentmagazine.org/article/the-i-in-union.

ACTRA. 2011. "Provincial Election Backgrounder." http://www.actratoronto.com/downloads/member/2011/election_soa.pdf.

Adler, Ben. 2012. "Piecemeal Existence: For Today's Young Freelancers, What Will Traffic Bear?" *Columbia Journalism Review* July/August. http://www.cjr.org/feature/piecemeal_existence.php.

Adorno, Theodor W., and Max Horkheimer. 2002. "The Culture Industry: Enlightenment as Mass Deception." In *Dialectic of Enlightenment: Philosophical Fragments*, edited by Gunzelin Schmid Noerr, translated by Edmund Jephcott, 94–136. Stanford, CA: Stanford University Press.

The Agenda. 2014. "Canadian Magazines Anyone?" *The Agenda with Steve Paiken*, TVO, 4 December. http://tvo.org/video/209274/canadian-magazines-anyone.

Aitamurto, Tanja. 2011. "The Impact of Crowdfunding on Journalism: Case Study of Spot.Us, a Platform for Community-Funded Reporting." *Journalism Practice* 5 (4): 429–45.

Aldridge, Meryl. 1998. "The Tentative Hell-Raisers: Identity and Mythology in Contemporary UK Press Journalism." *Media, Culture & Society* 20 (1): 109–27.

Aldridge, Meryl, and J. Evetts. 2003. "Rethinking the Concept of Professionalism: The Case of Journalism." *British Journal of Sociology* 54 (4): 547–64.

Alexander, Donnell. 2015. "Down and Out in Portland: Lean Seasons Had Always Been Part of My Writing Life, but This Time I Was Dead Broke." *Salon*, 15 May.

http://www.salon.com/2015/05/15/down_and_out_in_portland_lean
_seasons_had_always_been_part_of_my_writing_life_but_this_time_i
_was_dead_broke.

Allan, Stuart. 1999. *News Culture*. Philadelphia: Open University Press.

American Society of Journalists and Authors. 2015. "ASJA Basics."
http://www.asja.org/about/basics.

American Society of News Editors. 2015. "2015 Census." http://asne.org
/content.asp?pl=121&sl=415&contentid=415.

Amin, Ash. 1994. "Post-Fordism: Models, Fantasies and Phantoms of
Transition." In *Post-Fordism: A Reader*, edited by Ash Amin, 1–39. Oxford: Blackwell.

Anderson, Chris, Emily Bell, and Clay Shirky. 2012. *Post-industrial Journalism: Adapting to the Present*. Tow Center for Digital Journalism.
http://towcenter.org/wp-content/uploads/2012/11/TOWCenter-Post
_Industrial_Journalism.pdf.

Andrejevic, Mark. 2011. "Surveillance and Alienation in the Online
Economy." *Surveillance & Society* 8 (3): 288–309.

Antcliff, Valerie, Richard Saundry, and Mark Stuart. 2005. *Freelance Worker Networks in Audio-Visual Industries*. Lancashire Business School
Working Papers. University of Central Lancashire, May.

Arthur, Michael B., and Denise M. Rousseau, eds. 1996. *The Boundaryless
Career: A New Employment Principle for a New Organizational Era*. New
York: Oxford University Press.

Arthurs, Harry William, Donald D. Carter, and Harry J. Glasbeek. 1984.
Labour Law and Industrial Relations in Canada. 2nd ed. Toronto:
Butterworths.

Artz, Lee. 2006. "On the Material and the Dialectic: Toward a Class
Analysis of Communication." In *Marxism and Communication Studies:
The Point Is to Change It*, edited by Lee Artz, Steve Macek, and Dana L.
Cloud, 5–51. New York: Peter Lang.

Arvidsson, Adam, Giannino Malossi, and Serpica Naro. 2010. "Passionate
Work? Labour Conditions in the Milan Fashion Industry." *Journal for
Cultural Research* 14 (3): 295–309.

Ashcraft, Karen Lee. 2007. "Appreciating the 'Work' of Discourse: Occupational Identity and Difference as Organizing Mechanisms in the Case
of Commercial Airline Pilots." *Discourse & Communication* 1 (1): 9–36.

Audley, Paul. 1983. *Canada's Cultural Industries: Broadcasting, Publishing,
Records and Film*. Toronto: James Lorimer & Company.

Authors Guild. n.d. "History." http://www.authorsguild.org/about/history
.html.

Authors' Licensing and Collecting Society. 2014. *A Free for All? Findings from a Survey of Freelance Newspaper and Magazine Journalists.* London. http://www.alcs.co.uk/Documents/a-free-for-all.aspx.

Azzi, Stephen. 1999. "Magazines and the Canadian Dream: The Struggle to Protect Canadian Periodicals, 1955–1965." *International Journal* 54 (3): 502–23.

Bach, Jim. 2014. "Reporters' Pay Falls below U.S. Average Wage." *American Journalism Review*, 5 May. http://ajr.org/2014/05/05/reporter-pay-falls-u-s-average-wage.

Bad Writing Contracts. n.d. "The Contract." http://www.badwritingcontracts.ca.

Baer, Drake. 2013. "Why Everybody's Going Freelance." *Fast Company*, 12 September. http://www.fastcompany.com/3017222/leadership-ow/why-everybodys-going-freelance.

Bain, Alison. 2005. "Constructing an Artistic Identity." *Work, Employment & Society* 19 (1): 25–46.

Baines, Sue, and Liz Robson. 2001. "Being Self-Employed or Being Enterprising? The Case of Creative Work for the Media Industries." *Journal of Small Business and Enterprise Development* 8 (4): 349–62.

Baker, Dilon. 2015. "Will Washington Post's New Talent Network Become the Uber of Freelancing?" *Mediashift*, 25 August. http://mediashift.org/2015/08/will-washington-posts-talent-network-become-the-uber-of-freelancing.

Banks, Mark. 2007. *The Politics of Cultural Work.* London: Palgrave Macmillan.

— 2010. "Autonomy Guaranteed? Cultural Work and the 'Art-Commerce Relation.'" *Journal for Cultural Research* 14 (3): 251–69.

Banks, Mark, Rosalind Gill, and Stephanie Taylor, eds. 2013. *Theorizing Cultural Work: Labour, Continuity and Change in the Cultural and Creative Industries.* London: Routledge.

Banks, Miranda J. 2010. "The Picket Line Online: Creative Labor, Digital Activism, and the 2007–2008 Writers Guild of America Strike." *Popular Communication* 8 (1): 20–33.

Barbour, Noel Robert. 1982. *Those Amazing People! The Story of the Canadian Magazine Industry 1778–1967.* Toronto: Crucible Press.

Barbrook, Richard. 2006. *The Class of the New.* London: Openmute.

Barker, Kathleen, and Kathleen Christensen. 1998. "Controversy and Challenges Raised by Contingent Work Arrangements." In *Contingent Work: American Employment Relations in Transition*, edited by Kathleen Barker and Kathleen Christensen, 1–18. Ithaca: Cornell University Press.

Basen, Ira. 2011. "Age of the Algorithm." *Maisonneuve*, 9 May.
http://maisonneuve.org/pressroom/article/2011/may/9/age-algorithm/.

– 2014. "What's the Impact of All This Data Mining on the Quality of
Journalism?" *J-Source.ca*, 21 May. j-source.ca/article/what's-impact-all-
data-mining-quality-journalism.

Baumol, William J., and William G. Bowen. 1966. *Performing Arts: The
Economic Dilemma*. New York: The Twentieth Century Fund.

Beck, Andrew. 2003a. "Introduction: Cultural Work, Cultural Workplace
– Looking at the Cultural Industries." In Beck, *Cultural Work*, 1–6. London: Routledge.

—, ed. 2003b. *Cultural Work: Understanding the Cultural Work Industries*.
London: Routledge.

Beck, Ulrich. 2000. *The Brave New World of Work*. Cambridge, UK: Polity
Press. First published 1999.

Bell, Daniel. 1976. *The Coming of the Post-Industrial Society: A Venture in
Social Forecasting*. New York: Basic Books.

Benner, Chris. 2002. *Work in the New Economy: Flexible Labor Markets in
Silicon Valley*. Malden, MA: Blackwell.

— 2003. "'Computers in the Wild': Guilds and Next-Generation Union-
ism in the Information Revolution." In *Uncovering Labour Relations in
Information Revolutions, 1750–2000*, edited by Aad Blok and Greg
Downey, 181–204. Cambridge, UK: Cambridge University Press.

Bennett, Andrea. 2015. "The Year in Work." *Hazlitt*, 9 December.
http://hazlitt.net/feature/year-work.

Bennett, Lance W. 2009. *News: The Politics of Illusion*. 8th ed. New York:
Pearson Longman.

Benton, Joshua. 2012. "13 Ways of Looking at Medium, the New Blog-
ging/Sharing/Discovery Platform from @ev and Obvious." NiemanLab,
15 August. http://www.niemanlab.org/2012/08/13-ways-of-looking-at-
medium-the-new-bloggingsharingdiscovery-platform-from-ev-and-
obvious.

Berardi, Franco. 2009. *The Soul at Work: From Alienation to Autonomy*.
Cambridge, MA: MIT Press.

Berman, Dennis K. 2015. "Is the Huffington Post Worth $1 Billion?" *Wall
Street Journal*, 13 June, B3.

Bettig, Ronald V. 1996. *Copyrighting Culture: The Political Economy of Intellectual Property*. Boulder, CO: Westview Press.

Biba, Erin. 2014. "Your Newfangled Media Algorithms Are Bullshit."
Medium, 29 May. https://medium.com/@erinbiba/your-newfangled-
media-algorithms-are-bullshit-493c9597bb55.

Bielby, William T., and Denise D. Bielby. 1992. "Cumulative versus Continuous Disadvantage in an Unstructured Labor Market." *Work and Occupations* 19 (4): 366–86.

Birkhead, Douglas. 1986. "News Media Ethics and Management of Professionals." *Journal of Mass Media Ethics* 1 (2): 37–46.

Boltanski, Luc, and Eve Chiapello. 2007. *The New Spirit of Capitalism*. London: Verso.

Borden, Sandra L. 2007. *Journalism as Practice: MacIntyre, Virtue Ethics and the Press*. Burlington, VT: Ashgate.

The Born Freelancer. 2015. "The Born Freelancer Applies for a Line of Credit, Part 1." Story Board, 22 May. http://www.thestoryboard.ca /the-born-freelancer-applies-for-a-line-of-credit.

Bottomore, Tom, Laurence Harris, V.G. Kiernan, and Ralph Miliband, eds. *A Dictionary of Marxist Thought*. Cambridge, MA: Harvard University Press.

Bourdieu, Pierre. 1998. *Acts of Resistance: Against the Tyranny of the Market*. Translated by R. Nice. New York: The New Press.

Boyle, Dave. 2012. *Good News: A Co-operative Solution to the Media Crisis*. Manchester: Co-operatives UK. http://www.uk.coop/sites/storage /public/downloads/good_news_-_fresh _ideas_2.pdf.

Braverman, Harry. 1974. *Labor and Monopoly Capitalism: The Degradation of Work in the Twentieth Century*. New York: Monthly Review Press.

Brennen, Bonnie. 2004. "The Emergence of Class Consciousness in the American Newspaper Guild." In *Class and News*, edited by Don Heider, 233–47. Lanham, MD: Rowman & Littlefield.

– 2008. "Work in Progress: Labor and the Press in 1908." In Houchin Winfield, *Journalism 1908*, 147–61.

Brophy, Enda. 2006. "System Error: Labour Precarity and Collective Organizing at Microsoft." *Canadian Journal of Communication* 31 (3): 619–38.

Brophy, Enda, and Greig de Peuter. 2007. "Immaterial Labor, Precarity and Recomposition." In McKercher and Mosco, *Knowledge Workers in the Information Society*, 191–207.

Brophy, Enda, Nicole S. Cohen, and Greig de Peuter. 2015. "Labour Messaging: Practices of Autonomous Communication." In Maxwell, *The Routledge Companion to Labor and Media*, 315–26.

Brouillette, Sarah. 2014. *Literature and the Creative Economy*. Stanford, CA: Stanford University Press.

Broun, Heywood. 1935. *It Seems to Me, 1925–1935*. New York: Harcourt, Brace and Company.

Brown, Jesse. 2011. "How that Disposable Pamphlet of Infotainment That's an Inescapable Part of Our Daily Commute – a.k.a. Metro – Is Now the Most-Read Paper in the Country." *Toronto Life*, 27 July. http://www.torontolife.com/daily/informer/from-print-edition-informer/2011/07/27/newsprints-last-hurrah.

Brucker, Herbert. 1949. *Freedom of Information*. New York: The MacMillan Company.

Burawoy, Michael. 1979. *Manufacturing Consent: Changes in the Labor Process under Monopoly Capitalism*. Chicago: University of Chicago Press.

Bureau of Labor Statistics. 2015. Unpublished tabulations from the Current Population Survey.

Byerly, Carolyn M., and Karen Ross. 2006. *Women and Media: A Critical Introduction*. Malden, MA: Blackwell.

Cagle, Susie. 2014. "Eight Years of Solitude: On Freelance Labor, Journalism, and Survival." *Medium*, 15 March. https://medium.com/@susie_c/eight-years-of-solitude-110ee3276edf.

Canada. 1985. Copyright Act, R.S.C., c. C-42. http://laws-lois.justice.gc.ca/eng/acts/C-42.

– 1992. Status of the Artist Act, S.C. 1992, C-33. http://laws-lois.justice.gc.ca/eng/acts/S-19.6.

– 2011. Competition Act, R.S.C., c. C-34. http://laws-lois.justice.gc.ca/eng/acts/C-34.

Canada Revenue Agency. 2015. "Employee or Self-Employed." Canada Revenue Agency. http://www.cra-arc.gc.ca/E/pub/tg/rc4110/rc4110-e.html#factors.

Canadian Freelance Union (CFU). 2009. "Canadian Freelance Union Holds Inaugural Meeting Online across the Country." 30 September. http://www.newswire.ca/en/releases/archive/September2009/30/c2272.html.

– 2015. "Canadian Freelance Union Launches First Ever Organizing Drive." 18 August. http://canadianfreelanceunion.ca/index.php/site/full-story/119.

Canadian Heritage. 2009. "Fair Dealing in Canada." http://www.pch.gc.ca/pc-ch/org/sectr/ac-ca/pda-cpb/publctn/cch-2007/102-eng.cfm.

– 2010. "Canada Periodical Fund." http://www.pch.gc.ca/eng/1268240166828.

Canadian Labour Relations Board. 1983. "Societe Radio-Canada." Decision no. 383. In *Canadian Labour Relations Board Reports*. Toronto: Butterworth and Co.

Canadian Media Guild. 2015a. "Why We Are Unionizing at Vice Canada."
15 December. http://www.cmg.ca/en/2015/12/15/why-we-are-union
izing-at-vice-canada.

– 2015b. "Union Seeking Freelance Organizer." 23 March. http://www.cmg
.ca/en/2015/03/23/union-seeking-freelance-organizer-2.

Canadian Press. 2011. "Torstar to Offer Buyouts to 1,050 Star Employees."
CBC News, 10 November. http://www.cbc.ca/news/business/story/2011
/11/10/torstar-layoff-buyout.html.

CAPPRT (Canadian Artists and Producers Professional Relations Tribu-
nal). 2002. *Evaluation of the Provisions and Operations of the Status of the
Artist Act*. Canadian Heritage. http://www.publications.gc.ca/site/eng
/303283/publication.html.

Carey, James W. 1963. "The Communications Revolution and the Professional Communicator." In *The Sociology of Mass Media Communications*,
edited by P. Halmos, 23–38. The Sociological Review Monograph 13.
Keele: University of Keele.

CARFAC. n.d. "Status of Ontario's Artists – Advocacy Letter." http://www
.carfacontario.ca/~carfacon/advocacy/status_ontarios_artists_advocacy
_letter.

Carlozo, Lou. 2013. "Journatic Regroups after 2012 Debacle." *Net-
NewsCheck*, 21 August. http://www.netnewscheck.com/article/28278
/journatic-regroups-after-2012-debacle.

Carr, David. 2014a. "Risks Abound as Reporters Play in Traffic." *New York
Times*, 23 March, B1.

– 2014b. "A Platform for Writers to Help Them Shine." *New York Times*,
25 May, B1.

Carraway, Kate. 2008. "Freelancers' Union Due." *Eye Weekly*, 28 October.

Castells, Manuel. 2000. *The Rise of the Network Society*. Vol. 2. Oxford:
Blackwell. First published 1996.

Cavanaugh, Richard. 2004. *Reflecting Canadian: Best Practices for Cultural
Diversity in Private Television*. Task Force for Cultural Diversity on Television. http://www.cab-acr.ca/english/social/diversity/taskforce/report
/cdtf_report_jul04.pdf.

Caves, Richard E. 2000. *Creative Industries: Contracts between Art and Commerce*. Cambridge, MA: Harvard University Press.

CAW CEP Proposal Committee. 2012. *Towards a New Union*. August.
http://www.newunionproject.ca/caw-cep-proposal-committee-final-
report.

CBC. 2011. "Unions and Associations." http://www.cbc.radio-canada.ca
/about/unions.shtml.

Chanan, Michael. 1976. *Labour Power in the British Film Industry*. London: British Film Institute.

– 1983. "Labour Power and Aesthetic Labour in Film and Television in Britain." In *Communication and Class Struggle: Liberation, Socialism*, edited by Armand Mattelart and Seth Siegelaub, 317–32. New York: International General.

Charbonneau, Léo. 2013. "While the Journalism Industry Contracts, Journalism Programs Continue to Expand." *University Affairs*, 27 June. http://www.universityaffairs.ca/opinion/margin-notes/while-the-journalism-industry-contracts-journalism-programs-continue-to-expand.

Cherry, Miriam A. 2013. "Cyber-Commodification." *Md. L. Rev* 381.

Christian, Harry. 1980. "Journalists' Occupational Ideologies and Press Commercialisation." In *The Sociology of Journalism and the Press*, edited by Harry Christian, 259–306. Sociological Review Monograph 29. University of Keele, Staffordshire.

Christie, Adam. 2004. *The 'Wellbeing Initiative' – Freelance Journalists, Health and Trade Union Support.* London: The National Union of Journalists Freelance Industrial Council. http://media.gn.apc.org/wellness/wbrprt09.pdf.

Christopherson, Susan. 2009. "Working in the Creative Economy: Risk, Adaptation, and the Persistence of Exclusionary Networks." In McKinlay and Smith, *Creative Labour*, 72–90.

Chukhrov, Keti. "Towards the Space of the General: On Labor beyond Materiality and Immateriality." *E-flux*. http://www.e-flux.com/journal/towards-the-space-of-the-general-on-labor-beyond-materiality-and-immateriality.

Clark, Sandra. 1983. *The Elizabethan Pamphleteers: Popular Moralistic Pamphlets 1580–1640*. East Brunswick, NJ: Fairleigh Dickinson University Press.

Clarke, Shannon. 2015. "Is Canadian Journalism Experiencing a Generational War?" *J-Source.ca*, 23 March. http://j-source.ca/article/canadian-journalism-experiencing-generational-war.

Cleaver, Harry. 2000. *Reading Capital Politically*. Leeds: Anti/Theses and AK Press.

Clement, Wallace, and Leah F. Vosko, eds. 2003a. *Changing Canada: Political Economy as Transformation*. Montreal: McGill-Queen's University Press.

– 2003b. "Introduction." In Clement and Vosko, *Changing Canada*, xi–xxxii.

Cliche, Daniel. 1996. "Status of the Artist or of Arts Organizations?: A Brief Discussion on the Canadian Status of the Artist Act." *Canadian Journal of Communication* 21 (2): 197–210.

CMG Freelancers. 2015. "@crapwritinggigs Twitter Account Mocks Low-Paying Jobs for Writers." 18 June. http://cmgfreelance.ca/en/crapwriting gigs-twitter-account-mocks-low-paying-jobs-for-writers.

Cobble, Dorothy Sue. 1991. *Dishing It Out: Waitresses and Their Unions in the Twentieth Century.* Champagne: University of Illinois Press.

Cobble, Dorothy Sue, and Leah F. Vosko. 2000. "Historical Perspectives on Representing Nonstandard Workers." In *Nonstandard Work: The Nature and Challenges of Changing Employment Relationships*, edited by Francoise Carré, Marianne A. Ferber, L. Golden, and Stephen A. Herzenberg, 291–312. Champagne: Industrial Relations Research Association.

Cohen, Nicole S. 2015a. "Entrepreneurial Journalism and the Precarious State of Media Work." *South Atlantic Quarterly* 114 (3): 513–33.

– 2015b. "From Pink Slips to Pink Slime: Transforming Media Labor in a Digital Age." *Communication Review* 18 (2): 98–122.

Cohen, Nicole, Edward Comor, James Compton, and Brendan Watts. 2014. "Journalistic Labour and Digital Transformation: A Survey of Working Conditions." Paper presented at the Canadian Association of Work and Labour Studies Conference, Brock University, St Catharines, 30 May.

Cohen, Nicole, and Greig de Peuter. 2013. "The Politics of Precarity." *Briarpatch*, 1 November. http://briarpatchmagazine.com/articles/view /urban-worker-strategy-andrew-cash.

Cohen, Sheila. 1987. "A Labour Process to Nowhere?" *New Left Review* 165 (October): 34–50.

Cole, Peter, and Tony Harcup. 2010. *Newspaper Journalism*. London: Sage.

Coles, Amanda. 2012. "Counting Canucks: Cultural Labour and Canadian Cultural Policy." PhD diss., McMaster University.

Committee to Protect Journalists. 2011. "Imprisonments Jump Worldwide, and Iran Is Worst." http://cpj.org/reports/2011/12/journalist-imprisonments-jump-worldwide-and-iran-i.php.

Compton, James. 2010. "Newspapers, Labor and the Flux of Economic Uncertainty." In *The Routledge Companion to News and Journalism*, edited by Stuart Allen, 591–601. New York: Routledge.

Compton, James R., and Paul Benedetti. 2010. "Labour, New Media and the Institutional Restructuring of Journalism." *Journalism Studies* 11 (4): 487–99.

Conor, Bridget. 2010. "'Everybody's a Writer' Theorizing Screenwriting as Creative Labour." *Journal of Screenwriting* 1 (1): 27–43.

Cooley, Mike. 1981. "The Taylorisation of Intellectual Work." In *Science Technology and the Labour Process: Marxist Studies*, vol. 1, edited by Les Levidow and Bob Young, 46–65. London: CSE Books.

Coscarelli, Joe. 2013. "Nate Thayer vs. *The Atlantic*: 'Exposure Doesn't Feed My F*cking Children!'" *Daily Intelligencer*, 5 March. http://nymag.com/daily/intelligencer/2013/03/nate-thayer-vs-the-atlantic-writing-for-free.html.

Cottle, Simon, ed. 2003a. *Media Organization and Production*. London: Sage.

– 2003b. "Media Organization and Production: Mapping the Field." In Cottle, *Media Organization and Production*, 3–24.

Couldry, Nick. 2010. *Why Voice Matters: Culture and Politics after Neoliberalism*. London: Sage.

Cranford, Cynthia J., Judy Fudge, Eric Tucker, and Leah F. Vosko. 2005. *Self-Employed Workers Organize: Law, Policy, and Unions*. Montreal: McGill-Queen's University Press.

Cranford, Cynthia J., and Leah F. Vosko. 2006. "Conceptualizing Precarious Employment: Mapping Wage Work across Social Location and Occupational Context." In Vosko, *Precarious Employment*, 43–66.

Creech, Brian, and Andrew L. Mendelson. 2015. "Imagining the Journalist of the Future: Technological Visions of Journalism Education and Newswork." *Communication Review* 18: 142–65.

Crysler, Julie. 2005. "Unite the Write?" *This Magazine* 39 (3): 56–57.

Cunningham, Guy Patrick. 2015. "Don't Settle: The Journalist in the Shadow of the Commercial Web." *Los Angeles Review of Books*, 16 August. https://lareviewofbooks.org/essay/dont-settle-the-journalist-in-the-shadow-of-the-commercial-web.

Curran, James. 2005. "Mediations of Democracy." In Curran and Gurevitch, *Mass Media and Society*, 4th ed., 122–49.

Curran, James, and Michael Gurevitch, eds. 2000. *Mass Media and Society*, 3rd ed. London: Arnold.

– 2005. *Mass Media and Society*, 4th ed. London: Arnold.

CWA Canada. n.d. "The Union." http://cmgfreelance.ca/en/cwa-canada/.

CWG (Canadian Writers Group). 2010. "Team." http://www.canadianwritersgroup.com/index.php/team.

CWILA (Canadian Women in the Literary Arts). 2013. "2013 CWILA Numbers." http://cwila.com/2013-cwila-numbers.

D'Agostino, Giuseppina. 2004. "Should Freelancers Keep Their Copyrights in the Digital Era?" *Copyright & New Media Law Newsletter* 8 (4): 6–8.

– 2005. "Freelance Authors for Free: Globalisation of Publishing, Convergence of Copyright Contracts and Divergence of Judicial Reasoning." In *New Directions in Copyright Law*, vol. 1, edited by Fiona Macmillan, 166. Northampton, MA: Edward Elgar.

– 2007. *Canada's Robertson Ruling: Any Practical Significance for Copyright Treatment of Freelance Authors?* Law Research Institute Research Paper Series. Toronto: Osgoode Hall Law School.

– 2010. *Copyright, Contracts, Creators: New Media, New Rules.* Cheltenham, UK: Edward Elgar.

Dalla Costa, Maria, and Selma James. 1972. *The Power of Women and the Subversion of the Community.* Bristol: The Falling Wall Press.

Das, Jahanabi. 2007. "Sydney Freelance Journalists and the Notion of Professionalism." *Pacific Journalism Review* 13 (1): 142–60.

Das Gupta, Tania. 2006. "Racism/Anti-racism, Precarious Employment, and Unions." In Vosko, *Precarious Employment*, 318–34.

Davey, Frank. 2007. "Economics and the Writer." In Gerson and Michon, *History of the Book in Canada, 1918–1980*, 103–16.

Davies, Nick. 2008. *Flat Earth News: An Award-Winning Reporter Exposes Falsehood, Distortion and Propaganda in the Global Media.* New York: Vintage.

Davis, Anthony. 1988. *Magazine Journalism Today.* London: Heinemann.

Davis, Howard, and Richard Scase. 2000. *Managing Creativity: The Dynamics of Work and Organization.* Philadelphia: Open University Press.

Davis, Noah. 2013. "I Was Paid $12.50 an Hour to Write This Story." *Awl*, 20 June. http://www.theawl.com/2013/06/dox-dox-dox.

– 2015. "Noah Davis Talks to Scott Carney about the Difficulty of Making a Living as a Freelance Journalist, the Art of Negotiation, and the Evil of Condé Nast." *Pacific Standard.* http://www.psmag.com/business-economics/you-dont.

Day, Wan-Wen. 2007. "Commodification of Creativity: Reskilling Computer Animation Labor in Taiwan." In McKercher and Mosco, *Knowledge Workers in the Information Society*, 85–99.

de Peuter, Greig. 2014. "Beyond the Model Worker: Surveying a Creative Precariat." *Culture Unbound* 6: 263–84.

de Peuter, Greig, and Nicole S. Cohen. 2015. "Emerging Labour Politics in Creative Industries." In Oakley and O'Connor, *Routledge Companion to the Cultural Industries*, 305–18.

Deck, Cecilia. 1988. "History of the Newspaper Guild in Canada 1936–
1986." In *Essays in Journalism*, edited by Heather Hiscox, 15–34. London: University of Western Ontario.

Del Re, Alisa. 2005. "Feminism and Autonomy: Itinerary of Struggle."
Translated by A. Bove. In *The Philosophy of Antonio Negri*, vol. 1, edited
by Timothy S. Murphy and Abdul-Karim Mustapha, 48–72. London:
Pluto.

Denning, Michael. 1998. *The Cultural Front: The Laboring of American Culture in the Twentieth Century*. London: Verso.

Derber, Charles, ed. 1982a. *Professionals as Workers: Mental Labour in Advanced Capitalism*. Boston: GK Hall and Co.

– 1982b. "The Proletarianization of the Professional: A Review Essay." In
Derber, *Professionals as Workers*, 13–34.

– 1982c. "Managing Professionals: Ideological Proletarianization and
Mental Labour." In Derber, *Professionals as Workers*, 167–90.

Desbarats, Peter. 1991. "The Special Role of Magazines in the History of
Canadian Mass Media and National Development." In *Communications
in Canadian Society*, edited by Benjamin D. Singer, 50–66. Scarbor-
ough: Nelson.

Deuze, Mark. 2007. *Media Work*. London: Polity.

– ed. 2011. *Managing Media Work*. London: Sage.

Deuze, Mark, and Leopoldina Fortunati. 2011. "Atypical Newswork,
Atypical Media Management." In Deuze, *Managing Media Work*,
111–20.

Deuze, Mark, and Brian Steward. 2011. "Managing Media Work." In
Deuze, *Managing Media Work*, 1–10.

Deuze, Mark, Phoebe Elefante, and Brian Steward. 2010. "Media Work
and the Recession." *Popular Communication* 8 (3): 226–31.

De Weese, Truman A. 1898. "Journalism: Its Rewards and Opportunities."
Forum 26 (December): 441–51.

Diamond, A. 1996. "The Year of the Rat." *Canadian Forum*, October.

Dieker, Nicole. 2013. "I'm a Hack Writer Who Writes 5000 Words/Day for
$20/Hour." *Billfold*, 15 November. http://thebillfold.com/2013/11/im-a-
hack-writer-who-writes-5000-wordsday-for-20hour.

– 2014. "How Writers (Actually) Get Paid." *Scratch*, Q4. http://scratchmag
.net/article/554bfc8eada6e20454b98515/how_writers_(actually)_get
_paid.

– 2015. "Tracking Freelance Earnings." *The Write Life*, 12 January.
http://thewritelife.com/tracking-freelance-earnings.

– 2016. "Tracking Freelance Earnings: December Income Report from Nicole Dieker." *The Write Life*, 19 January. http://thewritelife.com /tracking-freelance-earnings-december-income-report-from-nicole-dieker/.

Dobby, Christine. 2014. "CBC Slashes 650 Full-Time Jobs and Gives up on Professional Sports to Fill $130M Shortfall." *Financial Post*, 10 April. http://business.financialpost.com/fp-tech-desk/cbc-job-cuts-sports.

Dornan, Christopher. 2012. "Newspapers and Magazines: Of Crows and Finches." In *Cultural Industries.ca: Making Sense of Canadian Media in the Digital Age*, edited by Ira Wagman and Peter Urquhart, 55–76. Toronto: James Lorimer.

Douglas, Ann. 2013. "Why I Am No Longer Writing the Column I Love for the Toronto Star." Story Board, 26 Februrary. http://www .thestoryboard.ca/why-i-am-no-longer-writing-the-column-i-loved-for-the-toronto-star.

Doyle, John. 2011. "Forget Female Empowerment. How about Female Employment?" *Globe and Mail*, 24 August. http://www .theglobeandmail.com/news/arts/television/john-doyle/forget-female-empowerment-how-about-female-employment/article2139336/.

Drahos, Peter. 1996. *A Philosophy of Intellectual Property*. Aldershot: Dartmouth Publishing Company.

Dreier, Peter. 1978. "Newsroom Democracy and the Media Monopoly: The Dilemmas of Workplace Reform among Professional Journalists." *Insurgent Sociologist* 8 (2 & 3): 70–86.

Drobot, Eve, and Hal Tennant. 1990. *Words for Sale*. 3rd ed. Toronto: The Periodical Writers Association of Canada and Macmillan of Canada.

Dubinsky, Lon. 1996. "Periodical Publishing." In *The Cultural Industries in Canada: Problems, Policies, and Prospects*, edited by Michael Dorland, 35–59. Toronto: James Lorimer.

Dullroy, Joel. 2013. "Introducing the Freelancers' Rights Movement." In *Independents Unite! Inside the Freelancers' Rights Movement*, preview edition, by Joel Dullroy and Anna Cashman, 1–6. Berlin: Freelancers Movement.

– 2014. "How Digital Workers Are Getting Organized." Digital Labor Working Group, 14 January. http://digitallabor.commons.gc.cuny .edu/2014/01/14/guest-post-how-digital-workers-are-getting-organized.

– 2015. "Freelancers Unite to Get Sickness and Other Employment Benefits." *Guardian*, 14 January. http://www.theguardian.com/money/2015 /jan/14/freelance-payment-sickness-leave.

Dyer-Witheford, Nick. 1999. *Cyber-Marx: Cycles and Circuits of Struggle in High-Technology Capitalism*. Urbana: University of Illinois Press.

– 2001. "Empire, Immaterial Labor, the New Combinations, and the Global Worker." *Rethinking Marxism* 13 (3/4): 70–80.

Dyer-Witheford, Nick, and Greig de Peuter. 2009. *Games of Empire: Global Capitalism and Video Games*. Minneapolis: University of Minnesota Press.

Eagleton, Terry. 2005. *The Function of Criticism*. London: Verso. First published 1984.

Edmonds, Alan. 1976. Introductory remarks. Minutes of the Writers' Meeting. 1 May, Toronto. PWAC archives, folder 5-1, executive minutes, 1976–1977. Box R 11523, #5.

Edmonds, Rick. 2015. "Newspaper Industry Lost 3,800 Full-Time Editorial Professionals in 2014." *Poynter*, 28 July. http://www.poynter.org/news /mediawire/360633/newspaper-industry-lost-3800-full-time-editorial-professionals-in-2014/.

Edstrom, Maria, and Martina Ladendorf. 2012. "Freelance Journalists as a Flexible Workforce in Media Industries." *Journalism Practice* 6 (3): 1–11.

Ehrenreich, Barbara. 2015. "In America, Only the Rich Can Afford to Write about Poverty." *Guardian*, 6 August. http://www.theguardian.com /commentisfree/2015/aug/06/america-rich-write-about-poverty.

Eidelson, Josh. 2013. "Alt-Labor." *American Prospect*, 29 January. http://prospect.org/article/alt-labor.

Ekinsmyth, Carol. 1999. "Professional Workers in a Risk Society." *Transactions of the Institute of British Geographers* 24 (3): 353–66.

– 2002. "Project Organization, Embeddedness and Risk in Magazine Publishing." *Regional Studies* 36 (3): 229–43.

Elk, Mike. 2011a. "Labor-Funded Progressive Leaders Cross Huffington Post Picket Line." *In These Times*, 13 June. http://inthesetimes.com/working/entry/11520/labor_funded _progressive_leaders_cross_picket_line_write_unpaid_for_hu.

– 2011b. "Huffington's Bogus Defense of Unpaid Bloggers." *In These Times*, 2 August. http://www.inthesetimes.com/working/entry/11771 /huffingtons_bogus_defense_of_unpaid_bloggers/.

Elliott, Philip. 1978. "Professional Ideology and Organisational Change: The Journalist Since 1800." In *Newspaper History from the Seventeenth Century to the Present Day*, edited by George Boyce, James Curran, and Pauline Wingate, 172–91. Beverly Hills: Sage.

European Federation of Journalists. n.d. Freelance. http://european journalists.org/policy/freelance.

Farkas, Lorraine. 1999. "Self-employed Workers and Collective Bargaining." *Workplace Gazette* 2 (2). http://www.execulink.com/~psharpe /cmesa/selfemployedworkers.html.

Fedler, Fred, and Phillip Taylor. 1981. "Reporters and the Newspaper Guild: Membership Attitudes and Salaries." *Journalism Quarterly* (Spring): 83–88.

Fine, Janice. 2006. *Worker Centers: Organizing Communities at the Edge of a Dream*. Ithaca: IRL Press.

Finkle, Derek. 2010. Remarks at Canadian Writers Group Launch Party. Toronto, Gladstone Hotel, 17 December.

Fischer, Mary Clare. 2014. "The Pay-per-Visit Debate: Is Chasing Viral Traffic Hurting Journalism?" *American Journalism Review*, 27 March. http://ajr.org/2014/03/27/pay-per-visit-debate-chasing-viral-traffic-hurting-journalism.

Fisk, Catherine L. 2009. *Working Knowledge: Employee Innovation and the Rise of Corporate Intellectual Property 1800–1930*. Chapel Hill: University of North Carolina Press.

Fleras, Augie. 1995. "Please Adjust Your Set: Media and Minorities in a Multicultural Society." In *Communications in Canadian Society*, 4th ed., edited by Benjamin Singer, 406–31. Toronto: Nelson Canada.

Florida, Richard L. 2002. *The Rise of the Creative Class: And How It's Transforming Work, Leisure, Community and Everyday Life*. New York: Basic Books.

– 2012. *The Rise of the Creative Class, Revisited.* New York: Basic Books.

Forkert, Kirsten. 2013. *Artistic Lives: A Study of Creativity in Two European Cities*. Surrey: Ashgate.

Foucault, Michel. 1988. "Technologies of the Self." In *Technologies of the Self*, edited by Luther Martin Huck Gutman and Patrick Hutton, 16–49. London: Tavistock.

Franks, Suzanne. 2013. *Women and Journalism*. Oxford: Reuters Institute for the Study of Journalism.

Franzen, Jonathan. 2013. *The Kraus Project*. New York: Farrar, Straus and Giroux.

Freelancers Union. 2015. "Benefits." https://www.freelancersunion.org /benefits.

French, William. 1978. "Obscene Poetry Thrives in Hastings." *Globe and Mail*, 2 May.

Friedman, Jane, and Manjula Martin. 2013. "Who Pays Writers? We Asked the Editors." *Scratch* Q4.

Friedman, Sara. 1991. "Uniting Freelance Writers: The National Writers

Union." In *With Just Cause: Unionization of the American Journalist*, edited by Walter M. Brasch, 31–40. Lanham, MD: University Press of America.

Fudge, J., and E. Tucker. 2001. *Labour before the Law: The Regulation of Workers' Collective Action in Canada, 1900–1948*. Toronto: Oxford University Press Canada.

Fudge, Judy. 2003. "Labour Protection for Self-employed Workers." *Just Labour* 3 (Fall): 36–45.

Fudge, Judy, Eric Tucker, and Leah F. Vosko. 2002. *The Legal Concept of Employment: Marginalizing Workers*. Ottawa: Law Commission of Canada.

Fulford, Robert. 1981. "A Sort of Reckless Courage: The Philosophy of the Press in English Canada." In *The Journalists*, by R. Fulford, L. Gagnon, F. Sauvageau, G. Bain, W. Stewart, G. Leblanc, D. Clift, T. Sloan, P.I. Laroche, and J. Cloutier. Research Studies on the Newspaper Industry, Vol. 2, Royal Commission on Newspapers. Ottawa: Minister of Supply and Services Canada, 3–17.

Fuller, Ryan, Ethan Tussey, Michael Curtin, and Joshua Green. 2011. *Huff-Po Bloggers Raise Status and Pay Concerns: Responses to the AOL-Huffington Post Merger*. Carsey-Wolf Center Media Industries Project. Santa Barbara: University of California.

Gall, Gregor. 1998. "The Changing Relations of Production: Union Derecognition in the UK Magazine Industry." *Industrial Relations Journal* 29 (2): 151–62.

– 2000. "New Technology, the Labour Process and Employment Relations in the Provincial Newspaper Industry." *New Technology, Work and Employment* 15 (2): 94–107.

Gamage, Michelle. 2013. "Freelancers Fight Back." *Langara Journalism Review*, 3 July. http://www.ljr.ca/2013/07/03/freelancers-fight-back.

Gardiola, Christal. 2009. "Writers and Editors Weigh in on the CWG." *Masthead Online*. http://www.mastheadonline.com/news/2009/20090529655.shtml.

Garnham, Nicholas. 1997. "Concepts of Culture – Public Policy and the Cultural Industries." In *Studying Culture*, 2nd ed., edited by Ann Gray and Jim McGuigan, 54–61. London: Arnold.

– 1990. *Capitalism and Communication: Global Culture and the Economics of Information*. London: Sage.

– 2005. "From Cultural to Creative Industries: An Analysis of the Implications of the 'Creative Industries' Approach to Arts and Media Policy

Making in the United Kingdom." *International Journal of Cultural Policy* 11 (1): 15–29.

Gasher, Mike. 2007. *Crisis? What Crisis? A Report on the Restructuring of the Daily Newspaper Industry in Canada*. Unpublished report prepared for the law firm Trudeau, Morissette & St Pierre.

Gehl, Robert W. 2011. "Ladders, Samurai, and Blue Collars: Personal Branding in Web 2.0." *First Monday* 16 (9).

Gerson, Carole, and Jacques Michon, eds. 2007. *History of the Book in Canada, 1918–1980*. Vol. 3. Toronto: University of Toronto Press.

Gibb, Camilla. 2014. "The More You Write, the Less You Make." *Globe and Mail*, 3 November. http://www.theglobeandmail.com/globe-debate /the-more-you-write-the-less-you-make/article21422784.

Gill, Rosalind. 2002. "Cool, Creative and Egalitarian? Exploring Gender in Project-Based New Media Work in Europe." *Information, Communication and Society* 5 (1): 70–89.

– 2011. "'Life Is a Pitch': Managing the Self in New Media Work." In Deuze, *Managing Media Work*, 249–62.

– 2014a. "Academics, Cultural Workers and Critical Labour Studies." *Journal of Cultural Economy* (7) 1: 12–30.

– 2014b. "Unspeakable Inequalities: Post Feminism, Entrepreneurial Subjectivity, and the Repudiation of Sexism among Cultural Workers." *Social Politics*: 1–20.

Gill, Rosalind, and Andy Pratt. 2008. "In The Social Factory? Immaterial Labour, Precariousness and Cultural Work." *Theory, Culture and Society* 25 (7–8): 1–30.

Gillies, Mary Ann. 2007. *The Professional Literary Agent in Britain, 1880–1920*. Toronto: University of Toronto Press.

Gindin, Sam, and Jim Stanford. 2003. "Canadian Labour and the Political Economy of Transformation." In Clement and Vosko, *Changing Canada*, 422–42.

Globe and Mail. 2011. "Quebecor's Sun Media Cutting 400 Jobs: Union." *Globe and Mail*, 28 November. http://www.theglobeandmail.com /globe-investor/quebecors-sun-media-cutting-400-jobs-union /article2252657/.

– 2015. Facebook post, 5 May. https://www.facebook.com/theglobe andmail/posts/10153214193583904?comment_id=10153214454618904 &notif_t=like&pnref=story.

Goldensohn, Rosa. 2015. "Wage-Theft Bill Threatens Employers with Jail, Requires Contracts for Freelancers." *Crain's New York*, 7 December.

http://www.crainsnewyork.com/article/20151207/BLOGS04/151209907
/wage-theft-bill-threatens-employers-with-jail-requires-contracts-for-
freelancers.

Gollmitzer, Mirjam. 2014. "Precariously Employed Watchdogs? Perceptions of Working Conditions among Freelancers and Interns." *Journalism Practice* 8 (6): 826–41.

Gopsill, Tim, and Greg Neale. 2007. *Journalists: 100 Years of the NUJ*. Lon-
. don: Profile Books.

Gorz, Andre. 2010. *The Immaterial*. Translated by C. Turner. London:
Seagull.

Gregg, Melissa. 2008. "The Normalization of Flexible Female Labour in
the Information Economy." *Feminist Media Studies* 8 (3): 285–99.

– 2011. *Work's Intimacy*. London: Polity.

Gunster, Shane. 2004. *Capitalizing on Culture: Critical Theory for Cultural
Studies*. Toronto: University of Toronto Press.

Gustin, Sam. 2011. "Unpaid Blogger Hits 'Slave Owner' Huffington with
$105M Class Action Lawsuit." *Wired*, 12 April. http://www.wired.com
/2011/04/tasini-sues-arianna.

Gynnild, Astrid. 2005. "Winner Takes It All: Freelance Journalism on the
Global Communication Market." *Nordicom Review* 26 (1): 111–20.

Hackett, Robert A., and Steve Anderson. 2010. *Revitalizing a Media Reform Movement in Canada*. Vancouver: Creative Commons.

Hackett, Robert A., and Yuezhi Zhao. 1998. *Sustaining Democracy? Journalism and the Politics of Objectivity*. Toronto: Garamond Press.

Haiven, Larry. 2006. "Expanding the Union Zone: Union Renewal
through Alternative Worker Organizations." *Labor Studies Journal* 31
(3): 85–116.

Hamilton, James F. 2008. *Democratic Communications: Formations, Projects,
Possibilities*. Lanham, MD: Lexington Books.

Hannis, Grant. 2008. "New Zealand Print Freelancers: Who They Are,
What They Earn, Where and What They Publish." *Pacific Journalism Review* 14 (1): 79–92.

Hardt, Hanno. 1990. "Newsworkers, Technology, and Journalism History."
Critical Studies in Mass Communication 7 (4): 346–65.

– 1995. "Without the Rank and File: Journalism History, Media Workers,
and Problems of Representation." In Hardt and Brennan, *Newsworkers*,
1–29.

– 1996. "The End of Journalism: Media and Newswork in the United
States." *Javnost/The Public* 3 (3): 21–41.

– 2005. "Conditions of Work and Life of Journalists. International Labor Organization. Excerpts from an International Survey 1925/26." *The Public* 12 (1): 5–14.

Hardt, Hanno, and Bonnie Brennen, eds. 1995a. *Newsworkers: Toward a History of the Rank and File*. Minneapolis: University of Minnesota Press.

– 1995b. "Introduction." In Hardt and Brennen, *Newsworkers*, vi–xiii.

Hardt, Michael, and Antonio Negri. 2000. *Empire*. Cambridge, MA: Harvard University Press.

Harrison, Brian R. 1982. *Canadian Freelance Writers: Characteristics and Issues*. Ottawa: Department of Communications.

Harvey, David. 1990. *The Condition of Postmodernity*. Malden, MA: Blackwell.

– 1996. *Justice, Nature and the Geography of Difference*. Malden, MA: Blackwell.

– 2005. *A Brief History of Neoliberalism*. Oxford: Oxford University Press.

– 2006. *The Limits to Capital*. London: Verso.

– 2010. *A Companion to Marx's Capital*. London: Verso.

Hasan, Shafaq. 2015. "No 'Free' in Freelancer: Nonprofits Take on Problems of the Emerging Workforce." *Non-profit Quarterly*, June 23. http://nonprofit-quarterly.org/2015/06/23/no-free-in-freelancer-nonprofits-take-on-problems-of-the-emerging-workforce.

Havens, Timothy, Amanda D. Lotz, and Serra Tinic. 2009. "Critical Media Industry Studies: A Research Approach." *Communication, Culture & Critique* 2: 234–53.

Hearn, Alison. 2010. "Structuring Feeling: Web 2.0, Online Ranking and Rating, and the Digital 'Reputation' Economy." *Ephemera* 10 (3/4): 421–38.

Heckscher, Charles C. 1988. *The New Unionism: Employee Involvement in the Changing Corporation*. New York: Basic Books.

Heinrich, Jeff. 2012. "Huffington Post Quebec Loses High-Profile Contributors." *Gazette*, 1 February. http://www.montrealgazette.com/news/Huffington+Post+Quebec+loses+contributors/6078768/story.html.

Henry, Frances, and Carol Tator. 2002. *Discourses of Domination: Racial Bias in the Canadian English-Language Press*. Toronto: University of Toronto Press.

Hepburn, James. 1968. *The Author's Empty Purse and the Rise of the Literary Agent*. London: Oxford University Press.

Hermes, Jeffrey P., John Wihbey, Reynol Junco, and Osman Tolga Aricak.

2014. *Who Gets a Press Pass? Media Credentialing Practices in the United States*. Berkman Center Research Publication No. 2014-11, 5 June. http://ssrn.com/abstract=2451239.

Hesmondhalgh, David. 2007. *The Cultural Industries*. 2nd ed. London: Sage.

– 2012. *The Cultural Industries*. 3rd ed. London: Sage.

Hesmondhalgh, David, and Sarah Baker. 2011. *Creative Labour: Media Work in Three Cultural Industries*. London: Routledge.

Heyck, Thomas William. 2002. "Freelance Writers and the Changing Terrain of Intellectual Life in Britain, 1880–1980." *Albion* 34 (2): 232–67.

Hill, Kelly. 2014. *A Statistical Profile of Artists and Cultural Workers in Canada*. October. ttp://www.hillstrategies.com/sites/default/files/Artists_CW_Canada2011.pdf.

Himmelwit, S. 1983a. "Exploitation." In Bottomore, Harris, Kiernan, and Miliband, *A Dictionary of Marxist Thought*, 157–58.

– 1983b. "Surplus Value." In Bottomore, Harris, Kiernan, and Miliband, *A Dictionary of Marxist Thought*, 472–5.

Holland, Brad. 2005–2006. "First Things about Secondary Rights." *Columbia Journal of Law & The Arts* 29: 295–324.

Holmes, Brian. 2002. "The Flexible Personality: For a New Cultural Critique." European Institute for Progressive Cultural Policies. http://eipcp.net/transversal/1106/holmes/en/base_edit.

Houchin Winfield, Betty. 2008. "1908: A Very Political Year for the Press." In Houchin Winfield, *Journalism 1908*, 17–31.

– ed. 2008. *Journalism 1908: Birth of a Profession*. Columbia, MI: University of Missouri Press.

Huffington, Arianna. 2011. "About That Lawsuit ..." *Huffington Post*, 13 April. http://www.huffingtonpost.com/arianna-huffington/huffington-post-lawsuit_b_848942.html.

Hunter, Andrea. 2015. "Crowdfunding Independent and Freelance Journalism: Negotiating Journalistic Norms of Autonomy and Objectivity." *New Media & Society* 17 (2) 272–88.

Hurd, Richard W. 2000. Professional Workers, Unions and Associations: Affinities and Antipathies. Albert Shanker Institute Seminar on Unions Organizing Professionals. http://www.ashankerinst.org/Downloadshurd.doc.

Hurd, Richard W., and Tashlin Lakhani. 2008. *Unions, Associations and Twenty-First Century Professionals*. Nyon, Switzerland: Union Network

International. http://www.uniglobalunion.org/apps/UNINews.nsf/...
/UNI_Associations-en.pdf.

Hutchins, Corey. 2014. "The New Media Contract Provision: Respond to
All E-mails within 48 Hours." *Medium*, 8 November. https://medium.com
/alt-ledes/the-new-media-contract-provision-respond-to-all-e-mails-
within-48-hours-38ec8f9fba11.

Huws, Ursula. 2003. *The Making of a Cybertariat: Virtual Work in a Real
World*. New York: Monthly Review Press.

– 2014. *Labor in the Global Digital Economy*. New York: Monthly Review
Books.

Iddamsetty, Anshuman. 2014. "Perpetual Dissatisfaction." *The Arcade*,
episode 28. Hazlitt. http://penguinrandomhouse.ca/hazlitt/podcast/ar-
cade-episode-28-perpetual-dissatisfaction.

ILO [International Labor Office]. 2000. *Symposium on Information Technologies in the Media and Entertainment Industries: Their Impact on Employment, Working Conditions and Labour-Management Relations*.
Geneva: ILO, 28 March. http://www.ilo.org/public/english/dialogue/sec-
tor/techmeet/smeioo/smeir.htm.

Im, Yung-Ho. 1997. "Towards a Labour-Process History of Newsworkers."
Javnost/The Public 4 (1): 31–48.

Impresa Communications. 2011. "Methods and Models for Freelance
Compensation." Draft report prepared for the Canadian Writers
Group and the Canadian Media Guild. February.

Independent Reviewer on Social Mobility and Child Poverty. 2012. *Fair
Access to Professional Careers*. London: Cabinet Office. http://www.cabi-
netoffice.gov.uk/resource-library/fair-access-professional-careers-
progress-report.

Ingram, Matthew. 2010. "On Your Mark, Get Set: Demand Media Files for
an IPO." *Gigaom*. 6 August. http://gigaom.com/2010/08/06/on-your-
mark-get-set-demand-media-files-for-an-ipo.

IPSE (The Association of Independent Professionals and the Self-Employed). 2015. "History." https://www.ipse.co.uk.

Isaac, Mike. 2014. "Medium, Evan Williams's Post-Twitter Media Startup,
Raises $25 Million Round." *Recode*, 28 January. http://recode.net/2014
/01/28/medium-evan-williams-post-twitter-media-startup-raises-25-
million-round.

Jaffe, Sarah. 2015. "Where's Our WGA? The Union Situation for Freelancers." *Scratch*, Q1.

Jian, Lian, and Jieun Shin. 2014. "Motivations behind Donors' Contributions to Crowdfunded Journalism." *Mass Communication and Society* 18 (2): 165–85.

Jian, Lian, and Nikki Usher. 2014. "Crowd-Funded Journalism." *Journal of Computer-Mediated Communication* 19 (2): 155–70.

Johnson, Joel. 2014. "Introducing Recruits." *Joel Johnson*, 10 February. http://joel.kinja.com/introducing-recruits-1520191540.

Jones, Owen. 2011. *Chavs: The Demonization of the Working Class*. London: Verso.

Journalist. 1888. "Working on Space." 31 March, 8.

Joynt, Leslie. 1995. "Too White." *Ryerson Review of Journalism* (Spring). http://www.journalism.ryerson.ca/m6046/.

Jung, E. Alex. 2014. "Wages for Facebook." *Dissent* (Spring): 47–50.

Jurkowitz, Mark. 2014. "The Growth in Digital Reporting: What it Means for Journalism and News Consumers." *State of the Media*. Pew Research Center, 26 March. http://www.journalism.org/2014/03/26/the-growth-in-digital-reporting.

Kates, Joanne, and Jane Springer. 1984. "Organizing Freelancers in the Arts." In *Union Sisters: Women in the Labour Movement*, edited by Linda Briskin and Lynda Yanz, 238–55. Toronto: The Women's Press.

Kaul, Arthur J. 1986. "The Proletarian Journalist: A Critique of Professionalism." *Journal of Mass Media Ethics* 1 (2): 47–55.

Keller, Bill. 2013. "It's the Golden Age of News." *New York Times*, 3 November. http://www.nytimes.com/2013/11/04/opinion/keller-its-the-golden-age-of-news.html.

Kelly, Peggy Lynn, and José Vincent. 2007. "Writers' Networks and Associations." In Gerson and Michon, *History of the Book in Canada, 1918–1980*, 122–30.

Kessler, Sarah. 2015. "What Does a Union Look Like in the Gig Economy?" Fast Company, 19 February. http://www.fastcompany.com/3042081/what-does-a-union-look-like-in-the-gig-economy.

Kesterton, Wilfred H. 1967. *A History of Journalism in Canada*. Toronto: McLelland and Stewart.

Kielbowicz, Richard B. 1989. "The Media and Reform, 1900–1917." In Sloan and Stovall, *The Media in America*, 263–79.

Kingston, Paul William, and Jonathan R. Cole. 1986. *The Wages of Writing: Per Word, per Piece, or Perhaps*. New York: Columbia University Press.

Koenig, Sarah. 2012. "Forgive Us Our Press Passes." *This American Life*, episode 468, "Switcheroo." 29 June. http://www.thisamericanlife.org/radio-archives/episode/468/switcheroo?act=2.

Kozolanka, Kirsten, Patricia Mazepa, and David Skinner, eds. 2012. *Alternative Media in Canada*. Vancouver: UBC Press.

Kperogi, Farooq A. 2011. "Cooperation with the Corporation? CNN and the Hegemonic Cooptation of Citizen Journalism through iReport." *New Media & Society* 13 (2): 314–29.

Krasovec, Primož, and Igor Z. Zagar. 2009. "Divisions and Struggles of the Slovenian Journalistic Guild: A Case Study of Contemporary European Journalism." *Journalism Studies* 10 (1): 85–89.

Kreider, Tim. 2013. "Slaves of the Internet, Unite!" *New York Times*, 26 October, SR1.

Kuehn, Kathleen. 2014. "Why Are So Many Journalists Willing to Write for Free?" *J-Source.ca*, 3 February. http://j-source.ca/article/why-are-so-many-journalists-willing-write-free.

Kuehn, Kathleen, and Thomas F. Corrigan. 2013. "Hope Labor: The Role of Employment Prospects in Online Social Production." *The Political Economy of Communication* 1 (1): 9–25.

Kumar, Deepa. 2007. *Outside the Box: Corporate Media, Globalization, and the UPS Strike*. Urbana: University of Illinois Press.

Kumar, Pradeep, and Christopher Schenk. 2009. "Union Renewal and Organizational Change: A Review of the Literature." In *Paths to Union Renewal: Canadian Experiences*, edited by Pradeep Kumar and Christopher Schenk, 29–60. Toronto: University of Toronto Press and Garamond.

LaFrance, Adrienne. 2014. "Why Venture Capitalists Are Suddenly Investing in News." *Quartz*, 12 March. http://qz.com/186492/why-venture-capitalists-are-suddenly-investing-in-news.

Lane, Carrie M. 2011. *A Company of One: Insecurity, Independence, and the New World of White-Collar Unemployment*. Ithaca: Cornell University Press.

Lapointe, Kirk. 1996. "Freelancers Must Negotiate." *Media* 3 (3): 10.

Lasarow, Bill. 2011. "On Strike from the Huffington Post." Visual Art Source, 28 February. http://www.visualartsource.com/index.php?page=editorial&com=news&pcID=21&aID=774.

Laskow, Sarah. 2013. "Copyright for Copy Writers: Work-for-Hire Contracts in a Digital Age." *Columbia Journalism Review*, 10 July. http://www.cjr.org/cloud_control/work_for_hire_digital_copyrigh.php?page=all.

Lazzarato, Maurizio. 1996. "Immaterial Labor." In *Radical Thought in Italy*, edited by Paolo Virno and Michael Hardt, 133–47. Minneapolis: University of Minnesota Press.

– 2004. "From Capital-Labour to Capital-Life." *Ephemera: Theory and Politics in Organization* 4 (3): 187–208.

Leab, Daniel J. 1970. *A Union of Individuals: The Formation of the American Newspaper Guild, 1933–1939*. New York: Columbia University Press.

Leadbeater, Charles. 1999. *Living on Thin Air: The New Economy*. London: Viking.

Leary, John Patrick. 2014. "Keywords for the Age of Austerity 9: Content." 15 July. https://theageofausterity.wordpress.com/2014/07/15/keywords-for-the-age-of-austerity-9-content.

Lewchuk, Wayne, et al. 2013. *It's More Than Poverty: Employment Precarity and Household Well-Being*. Poverty and Employment Precarity in Southern Ontario. http://www.unitedwaytyr.com/document.doc?id=91.

– 2014. "Is Precarious Employment Low Income Employment? The Changing Labour Market in Southern Ontario." *Just Labour* 22: 51–73. http://www.justlabour.yorku.ca/volume22/pdfs/05_lewchuk_et_al_press.pdf.

– 2015. *The Precarity Penalty*. Poverty and Employment Precarity in Southern Ontario. http://www.unitedwaytoronto.com/document.doc?id=307.

Ligeti, Arik. "Hey, J-schools: Do Your Students a Favour and Teach Them Entrepreneurial Skills." *J-source.ca*, 13 February. http://j-source.ca/article/hey-j-schools-do-your-students-favour-and-teach-them-entrepreneurial-skills.

Linder, Marc. 1992. *Farewell to the Self-Employed: Deconstructing a Socioeconomic and Legal Solipsism*. New York: Greenwood Press.

Lorey, Isabell. 2009. "Governmentality and Self-Precarization: On the Normalization of Cultural Producers." In *Art and Contemporary Critical Practice: Reinventing Institutional Critique*, edited by Gerald Raunig and Gene Ray, translated by Lisa Rosenblatt and Dagmar Fink, 187–202. London: MayFly Books.

Lorimer, Rowland, Mike Gasher, and David Skinner. 2008. *Mass Communication in Canada*. 7th ed. Toronto: Oxford University Press.

Lorinc, John. 2005. *Creators and Copyright in Canada: The Working Conditions of Creators in Quebec and Canada*. Report prepared for Creators' Copyright Coalition and Droit D'auteur/Multimédia-Internet/Copyright.

Lucianovic, Stephanie. 2013. "Why I Write for Free." *Wire*, 6 March. http://www.thewire.com/business/2013/03/why-i-write-free/62808/.

Lui, Chang-de. 2006. "De-skilling Effects on Journalists: ICTs and the

Labour Process of Taiwanese Newspaper Reporters." *Canadian Journal of Communication* 31 (3): 695–714.

Macharia, Sarah. 2015. *Who Makes the News? Global Media Monitoring Project 2015*. Toronto: World Association of Christian Communication. http://cdn.agilitycms.com/who-makes-the-ews/Imported/reports_2015 /global/gmmp_global_report_en.pdf.

Machlup, Fritz. 1962. *The Production and Distribution of Knowledge in the United States*. Princeton: Princeton University Press.

MacPhee, Josh. 2012. "Who's the Shop Steward on Your Kickstarter?" *Baffler* 21. http://www.thebaffler.com/salvos/whos-the-shop-steward-on-your-kickstarter.

MacPherson, Elizabeth. 1999. "Collective Bargaining for Independent Contractors: Is the *Status of the Artist Act* a Model for Other Industrial Sectors?" *Canadian Labour & Employment Law Journal* 7: 355–88.

Macpherson, James. 2012. "And Now, a Penny for My Thoughts." Journtent, 21 August. http://journtent.blogspot.ca/2012/08/and-now-penny-for-my-thoughts.html.

Madison, Lucy. 2012. "How 25 National Magazine Award Nominations Went to 25 Male Writers." *Awl*, 12 April. http://www.theawl.com/2012 /04/how-25-national-magazine-award-nominations-went-to-25-male-writers.

Magary, Drew. 2014. "Freelancing Sucks." *Concourse*, 7 August. http://theconcourse.deadspin.com/freelancing-sucks-1617518517.

Magazines Canada. 2008. *Industry Facts: Magazines Canada Members and Industry Profile*. http://www.magazinescanada.ca/industry_facts.

– 2010a. *Magazine Trends*. Toronto: Magazines Canada. http://www .magazinescanada.ca/uploads/File/AdServices/Research/IndustryTrends /MagTrends2010Fall.ppt.

– 2010b. *Magazines: A Comparison of Canada and the US*. Toronto: Magazines Canada.

– 2011. *Consumer Magazines Factbook 2011*. http://www.magazinescanada.ca/uploads/File/AdServices/FactBooks/2011/ConsumerEN.pdf.

Mandel, Ernest. 1972. *Late Capitalism*. London: Verso.

Mangalindan, J.P. 2013. "So Who's Making Money Publishing on the Web?" *Fortune*, 10 May. http://fortune.com/2013/05/10/so-whos-making-money-publishing-on-the-web.

Marjoribanks, Timothy. 2003. "Strategising Technological Innovation: The Case of News Corporation." In Cottle, *Media Organization and Production*, 59–75.

Massing, Michael. 2015. "Digital Journalism: How Good Is It?" *New York Review of Books*, 4 June. http://www.nybooks.com/articles/archives/2015/jun/04/digital-journalism-how-good-is-it/.

Marx, Karl. 1978a. "Economic and Philosophic Manuscripts of 1884." In Tucker, *The Marx-Engels Reader*, 594–617.

– 1978b. "The Eighteenth Brumaire of Louis Bonaparte." In Tucker, *The Marx-Engels Reader*, 66–135.

– (1867) 1990. *Capital: A Critique of Political Economy*, vol. 1. London: Penguin Books.

Mason, Paul. 2015. *Postcapitalism: A Guide to Our Future*. London: Allen Lane.

Massey, Brian L., and Cindy J. Elmore. 2011. "Happier Working for Themselves? Job Satisfaction and Women Freelance Journalists." *Journalism Practice* 5 (6): 672–86.

Maxwell, Richard, ed. 2015. *The Routledge Companion to Labor and Media*. New York: Routledge.

May, Christopher. 2002a. *The Information Society: A Sceptical View*. Cambridge, UK: Polity.

– 2002b. "The Political Economy of Proximity: Intellectual Property and the Global Division of Information Labour." *New Political Economy* 7 (3): 317–42.

Mayer, Vicki, Miranda J. Banks, and John T. Caldwell, eds. 2009. *Production Studies: Cultural Studies of Media Industries*. New York: Routledge.

McChesney, Robert W. 2008. *The Political Economy of Media: Enduring Issues, Emerging Dilemmas*. New York: Monthly Review Press.

— 2013. *Digital Disconnect: How Capitalism Is Turning the Internet against Democracy*. New York: The New Press.

McChesney, Robert W., and John Nichols. 2010. *The Death and Life of American Journalism: The Media Revolution That Will Begin the World Again*. New York: Nation Books.

McKercher, Catherine. 2001. "Commerce versus Culture: The Print Media in Canada and Mexico." In *Continental Order? Integrating North America for Cyber Capitalism*, edited by Vincent Mosco and Dan Schiller, 189–206. Lanham, MD: Rowman & Littlefield.

– 2002. *Newsworkers Unite: Labor, Convergence, and North American Newspapers*. Lanham, MD: Rowman & Littlefield.

– 2009. "Writing on the Margins: Precarity and the Freelance Journalist." *Feminist Media Studies* 9 (3): 370–74.

– 2014. "Precarious Times, Precarious Work: A Feminist Political Economy of Freelance Journalists in Canada and the United States." In *Critique, Social Media and the Information Society*, edited by Christian Fuchs and Marisol Sandoval, 219–30. New York: Routledge.

McKercher, Catherine, and Vincent Mosco, eds. 2007. *Knowledge Workers in the Information Society*. Lanham, MD: Lexington.

McLeod, Kembrew. 2001. *Owning Culture: Authorship, Ownership and Intellectual Property Law*. New York: Peter Lang.

McRobbie, Angela. 2000. "The Return to Cultural Production Case Study, Fashion Journalism." In Curran and Gurevitch, *Mass Media and Society*, 255–67.

– 2002a. "From Holloway to Hollywood: Happiness at Work in the New Cultural Economy?" In *Cultural Economy: Cultural Analysis and Commercial Life*, edited by Paul du Gay and Michael Pryke, 97–114. London: Sage.

– 2002b. "Clubs to Companies: Notes on the Decline of Political Culture in Speeded up Creative Worlds." *Cultural Studies* 64 (4): 516–31.

– 2004. "'Everyone Is Creative': Artists as Pioneers of the New Economy?" In *Contemporary Culture and Everyday Life*, edited by Elizabeth B. Silva and Tony Bennett, 186–202. Durham, UK: Sociologypress.

– 2007. "The Los Angelisation of London: Three Short-Waves of Young People's Micro-economies of Culture and Creativity in the UK." eipcp, January. http://eipcp.net/transversal/0207/mcrobbie/en.

– 2011. "Re-thinking Creative Economy as Radical Social Enterprise." *Variant* (41): 32–3.

Menger, Pierre-Michel. 1999. "Artistic Labor Markets and Careers." *Annual Review of Sociology* 25: 541–74.

Mercer. 2009. *2008 Canadian Magazine Industry Market Compensation Survey*. Cultural Human Resources Council. http://www.culturalhrc.ca/research/CHRC_Magazine-Compensation-Study-en.pdf.

Meyer, Michael. 2015. "Survival Strategies of an Online Freelancer." *Columbia Journalism Review*, March/April. http://www.cjr.org/the_profile/survival_strategies_of_an_online_freelancer.php.

Miège, Bernard. 1989. *The Capitalization of Cultural Production*. New York: International General.

Miller, John. 2006. "Who's Telling the News? Racial Representation among News Gatherers in Canada's Daily Newsrooms." *International Journal of Diversity in Organisations, Communities & Nations* 5 (4): 133–42.

Mills, C. Wright. 1956. *White Collar: The American Middle Classes*. New York: Oxford University Press.

Mills, Jennifer. 2013. "Pay the Writers." Overland, 6 March. https://overland
.org.au/2013/03/pay-the-writers.

Miner, Michael. 2012. "Tribune Company Does Deal with Journatic."
Bleader, 24 April. http://www.chicagoreader.com/chicago/blogs/Post
?id=Bleader&year=2012&month=04&day=24&basename=tribune-
company-does-deal-with-journatic.

Miner, Valerie. 1985. "Rumours from the Cauldron: Competition among
Feminist Writers." Women's Studies International Forum 8 (1): 45–50.

Moody, Kim. 1997. Workers in a Lean World: Unions in the International
Economy. London: Verso.

Moore, Christopher. 2007. "History." The Writers' Union of Canada.
http://www.writersunion.ca/au_history.asp.

Morini, Cristina. 2007. "The Feminization of Labour in Cognitive Capitalism." Feminist Review 87: 40–59.

Mosco, Vincent. 2009. The Political Economy of Communication. 2nd ed.
London: Sage.

Mosco, Vincent, and Catherine McKercher. 2006. "Editorial: The Labour-
ing of Communication." Canadian Journal of Communication 31 (3):
493–7.

– 2008. The Laboring of Communication: Will Knowledge Workers of the
World Unite? Lanham, MD: Lexington Books.

Moses, Lucia. 2014. "Entertainment Weekly Goes the Platform Route."
Digiday, 27 March. http://digiday.com/publishers/entertainment-week-
ly-taking-page-huffington-post.

Mott, Frank Luther. 1957a. A History of American Magazines 1741–1850.
Vol. 1. Cambridge, MA: Harvard University Press.

— 1957b. A History of American Magazines 1865–1885. Vol. 3. Cambridge,
MA: Harvard University Press.

Munk, Nina. 2000. "The Price of Freedom." New York Times Magazine, 5
March. http://www.nytimes.com/2000/03/05/magazine/the-price-of-
freedom.html.

Murdock, Graham. 2003. "Back to Work: Cultural Labor in Altered
Times." In Beck, Cultural Work, 15–36.

Murdock, Graham, and Peter Golding. 2005. "Culture, Communications
and Political Economy." In Curran and Gurevitch, Mass Media and Society, 4th ed., 60–83.

Murphy, David. 1991. "Journalists and the Labour Process: White-Collar
Production Workers." In Smith, Knights, and Willmott, White-Collar
Work, 139–61.

Murray, Jill. 1999. "Social Justice for Women? The ILO's Convention on

Part-Time Work." *International Journal of Comparative Labour Law & Industrial Relations* 15 (1): 3–19.

Murray, Laura J., and Samuel E. Trosow. 2007. *Canadian Copyright: A Citizen's Guide*. Toronto: Between the Lines.

n+1. 2014. "The Free and the Antifree: On Payment for Writers." *n+1* 20 (Fall). https://nplusonemag.com/issue-20/the-intellectual-situation /the-free-and-the-antifree/.

Nathan, George Jean. 1911. "The Magazine in the Making." *The Bookman: A Review of Books and Life* 34 (4): 414–16.

National Union of Journalists. 2004. *Battling for Copyright: Freelance Journalists versus the Media Conglomerates*. London: National Union of Journalists.

National Writers Union. 2011. "What's Up with the Boycott of the Huffington Post?" 20 October. http://www.nwu.org/what's-boycott-huffington-post.

Neff, Gina. 2007. "The Lure of Risk: Surviving and Welcoming Uncertainty in the New Economy." In *Surviving the New Economy*, edited by John Amman, Tris Carpenter, and Gina Neff, 33–46. Boulder, CO: Paradigm Publishers.

Neff, Gina, Elizabeth Wissinger, and Sharon Zukin. 2005. "Entrepreneurial Labor among Cultural Producers: 'Cool' Jobs in 'Hot' Industries." *Social Semiotics* 15 (3): 307–34.

Neil, Garry. 2010. *Status of the Artist in Canada: An Update on the 20th Anniversary of the UNESCO Recommendation Concerning the Status of the Artist*. Ottawa: Canada Conference of the Arts. http://www.capprt-tcrpap.gc.ca/eic/site/capprt-tcrpap.nsf/vwapj/CCA_SAA_eng.pdf /$file/CCA_SAA_eng.pdf.

Neilson, Brett, and Mark Coté. 2014. "Introduction: Are We All Cultural Workers Now?" *Journal of Cultural Economy* 7 (1): 2–11.

Neilson, Brett, and Ned Rossiter. 2005. "From Precarity to Precariousness and Back Again: Labour, Life and Unstable Networks." *The Fibreculture Journal* 5. http://five.fibreculturejournal.org/fcj-022-from-precarity-to-precariousness-and-back-again-labour-life-and-unstable-networks.

Neilson, Tai. 2012. "Journalists Strike Online: Visibility, Field, and the *Huffington Post*." *Global Media Journal* 12 (20): 1–10.

The New Inquiry. 2012. *The New Inquiry*. 1 February. http://thenewinquiry .com/wp-content/uploads/2012/02/Precarity-Vol-1_TNI-Magazine.pdf.

Nies, Gerd, and Roberto. Pedersini. 2003. *Freelance Journalists in the European Media Industry*. European Federation of Journalists. http://www.ifj-europe.org/pdfs/FinalReportFreelance.pdf.

Nolan, Hamilton. 2015. "Why We've Decided to Organize." *Gawker*, 16 April. http://gawker.com/why-weve-decided-to-organize-1698246231.

Nova Scotia. 2012. "Province Supports Nova Scotia Artists with New Legislation." Communities, Culture and Heritage. http://gov.ns.ca/news /details.asp?id=20120330002.

Oakley, Kate. 2013. "Absentee Workers: Representation and Participation in the Cultural Industries." In Banks, Gill, and Taylor, *Theorizing Cultural Work*, 56–68.

– 2014. "Good Work? Rethinking Cultural Entrepreneurship." In *Handbook of Management and Creativity*, edited by Chris Bilton and Stephen Cummings, 145–59. Cheltenham, UK: Edward Elger.

Oakley, Kate, and Justin O'Connor, eds. 2015. *The Routledge Companion to the Cultural Industries*. New York: Routledge.

OFL [Ontario Federation of Labour]. n.d. The Ontario Federation of Labour's Cultural Industries Working Group. http://ofl.ca/index.php /html/index_in/submission_to_the_ministers_advisory_council_for _arts_and_culture/P1/.

Ohmann, Richard. 1996. *Selling Culture: Magazines, Markets, and Class at the Turn of the Century*. London: Verso.

O'Leary, Michael Gratton. 1961. *Report, Royal Commission on Publications*. Ottawa: Queen's Printer.

Olmstead, Kenneth, and Kristine Lu. 2015. "Digital News – Revenue: Fact Sheet." Pew Research Center, 29 April. http://www.journalism.org /2015/04/29/digital-news-revenue-fact-sheet.

Ong, Aihwa. 2006. *Neoliberalism as Exception: Mutations in Citizenship and Sovereignty*. Durham: Duke University Press.

Ontario. 2007. Status of Ontario's Artists Act, S.O. c. 7. http://www.e- http://www.ontario.ca/laws/statute/07s07.

Ontario Media Development Corporation (OMDC). 2009a. Industry Profile: Magazine Publishing. Ontario Media Development Corporation. http://www.omdc.on.ca/AssetFactory.aspx?did=6565.

– 2009b. *Annual Report 2008–09*. Toronto: Ministry of Culture. http://www.omdc.on.ca/AssetFactory.aspx?did=7115.

Ontario New Democratic Party. 2012. "Tabuns Bill to Bring Fairness to Film, Television, Radio, and New Media Workplaces." Andrea Horwath, 3 October. http://ontariondp.com/en/tabuns-bill-to-bring-fairness-to-film-television-radio-and-new-media-workplaces.

OReilly, Michael. 1996. "Highway Robbery on the Internet." *Media* 3 (1): 8.

– 2011. "CFU Concerned about LFP's Move to Encourage 'Free' Content."

21 April. http://www.cfunion.ca/services/CFU_LFP_letter_of_concern .html.

Örnebring, Henrick. 2009. *The Two Professionalisms of Journalism: Journalism and the Changing Context of Work*. University of Oxford: Reuters Institute for the Study of Journalism.

– 2010. "Technology and Journalism-as-Labor: Historical Perspectives." *Journalism* 11 (1): 58–74.

Osnowitz, Debra. 2010. *Freelancing Expertise: Contract Professionals in the New Economy*. Ithaca: ILR/Cornell.

Owen, Lynette. 2006. *Selling Rights*. 5th ed. London: Routledge.

Panel on Fair Access to the Professions. 2009. *Unleashing Aspirations: Final Report of the Panel on Fair Access to the Professions*. London: Cabinet Office.

Paré, J. 1976. Letter to PWAC. PWAC archives, folder 1-2, Periodical Writers Association of Canada (Beginnings), 1976, 1978. Box R 11523, #1.

Paris, Erna. 1978. Confidential Letter to all Members of PWAC, 30 October. PWAC archives, folder 5-3, executive minutes, 1977–1978. Box R 11523, #5.

Paul, Ari. 2014. "A Union of One." *Jacobin*, 28 October. https://www .jacobinmag.com/2014/10/freelancers-union/.

Payne, Darwin. 1989. "The Age of Mass Magazines, 1900–Present." In Sloan and Stovall, *The Media in America*, 348–64.

Peck, Jamie. 1996. *Work-Place: The Social Regulation of Labor Markets.* New York: The Guilford Press.

Perlin, Ross. 2012. "The Graduate with a Precarious Future." *New Left Project*, 22 March. http://www.newleftproject.org/index.php/site/article _comments/the_graduate_with_a_precarious_future.

Peter, Tom A. 2014. "The Media Must Find a Way to Support Freelancers Who Risk Their Lives." *New Republic*, 4 September. http://www. newrepublic.com/article/119313/steven-sotloff-james-foley-beheadings-expose-failed-freelancer-model.

Peters, Jeremy W. 2010. "In Online Journalism, Burnout Starts Younger." *New York Times*, 18 July, B1.

Peterson, Theodore. 1964. *Magazines in the Twentieth Century*. Urbana: University of Illinois Press.

Peterson, Tim. 2015. "The Huffington Post Opens Citizen Journalism Video Network with BroadbandTV." *Advertising Age*, 9 June. http://adage.com/article/digital/huffington-post-broadbandtv-citizen-journalism-video/298929.

Petre, Caitlin. 2015. *The Traffic Factories: Metrics at Chartbeat, Gawker Media, and the New York Times.* Tow Center for Digital Journalism. New York: Columbia Journalism School. http://towcenter.org/research /traffic-factories.

Pickard, Victor. 2011. "Can Government Support the Press? Historicizing and Internationalizing a Policy Approach to the Journalism Crisis." *Communication Review* 14 (2): 73–95.

Pilkington, Ed. 2012. "Huffington Bloggers Lose Legal Fight for AOL Millions." *Guardian,* 1 April. http://www.guardian.co.uk/media/2012/apr /01/huffington-post-bloggers-aol-millions.

Pink, Daniel H. 2001. *Free Agent Nation: How America's New Independent Workers Are Transforming the Way We Live.* New York: Warner.

Platman, Kerry. 2004. "'Portfolio Careers' and the Search for Flexibility in Later Life." *Work, Employment & Society* 18 (3): 573–99.

Pollert, Anna. 1988. "Dismantling Flexibility." *Capital & Class* 34: 42–75.

Pritchard, David, and Florian Sauvageau. 1998. "The Journalists and Journalisms of Canada." In *The Global Journalist: News People around the World,* edited by David Weaver, 373–93. Cresskill, NJ: Hampton Press.

Project for Excellence in Journalism. 2008. *The Changing Newsroom.* http://www.journalism.org/node/11961.

Project Word. 2015. *Untold Stories: A Survey of Freelance Investigative Reporters.* Great Barrington, MA: Project Word. http://projectword.org /sites/default/files/PW_Freelancer_Survey_Feb2015.pdf.

Pugh Yi, Robin H., and Craig T. Dearfield. 2012. *The Status of Women in the U.S. Media 2012.* Women's Media Centre. http://action .womensmediacenter.com/page/-/WMC%20Status%20of%20Women %20in%20US%20Media%202012.pdf.

Pupo, Norene, and Mark Thomas. 2010. "Work in the New Economy: Critical Reflections." In *Interrogating the New Economy: Restructuring Work in the 21st Century,* edited by Norene J. Pupo and Mark P. Thomas, ix–xxii. Toronto: University of Toronto Press.

PWAC. n.d. PWAC archives, folder 7-18. Box R 11523-7.

– 1976a. PWAC archives, folder 1-2, Periodical Writers Association of Canada (Beginnings), 1976, 1978. Box R 11523, #1.

– 1976b. Founding Writers' Meeting. PWAC archives, folder 1-1. Box R 11523.

– 1976c. Minutes of the Writers' Meeting. May 1. PWAC archives, folder 5-1, executive minutes, 1976–1977. Box R 11523, #5.

– 1977. Minutes of the Executive Meeting. August 8. PWAC archives, folder 5-1, executive minutes, 1976–1977. Box R 11523, #5.

– 1978. Press release, April 27. PWAC archives, folder 1-2, Periodical Writers Association of Canada (Beginnings), 1976, 1978. Box R 11523, #1.

– 1990. AGM, Victoria, 24–27 May. PWAC archives, folder 4-3, AGM Victoria. Box R 11523, #4.

– 1991. Reassessing PWAC Workshop, AGM, Charlottetown, 7–9 June. PWAC archives, folder 4-6. Box R 11523, #4.

– 2006. *Canadian Professional Writers Survey: A Profile of the Freelance Writing Sector in Canada*. Toronto, May. http://pwac.ca/wp-content/uploads /2014/03/PWACsurvey.pdf.

– 2009. *Annual Report*. http://www.pwac.ca/about/pwacadvocacy.

– 2015. "PWAC's Mandate." pwac.ca/index.php/en/page/about-us.

Raymond, Joad. 1996. *The Invention of the Newspaper: English Newsbooks 1641–1649*. Oxford: Clarendon Press.

Reid, C. 1993. "NWU Seeks 'Cultural Workers' Group." *Publishers Weekly* 240 (46): 25.

Ritea, Steve. 2003. "Byline Strikes: The Protest That Knows No Name." *American Journalism Review* 25 (2): 12–13.

Rivers, William L., and Alison R. Work. 1986. *Free-lancer and Staff Writer*. 4th ed. Belmont, CA: Wadsworth Publishing.

Roderick, Kevin. 2010. "Pasadena Now Goes to the Outsource Card Again." *LA Observed*, 26 September. http://www.laobserved.com/archive /2010/09/pasadena_now_goes_to_the.php.

Rodgers, William M. III. 2010. *The Threat of Nonpayment: Unpaid Wages and New York's Self-Employed*. Heldrich Center for Workforce Development Bloustein School of Planning and Public Policy Rutgers, the State University of New Jersey. http://www.fu-res.org/pdfs/advocacy /2010-unpaid-wages-report.pdf.

Rogers, Charles E. 1931. *Journalistic Vocations*. New York: D. Appleton and Company.

Rogers Communications Inc. 2010. *Seamless Connections: 2010 Annual Report*. http://ca.zinio.com/reader.jsp?issue=416195853&o=ext.

– 2015. *One Rogers: 2014 Annual Report*. https://www.rogers.com/cms /investors/pdf/annual-reports/Rogers-2014-Annual-Report.pdf.

Ross, Andrew. 2000. "The Mental Labor Problem." *Social Text* 18 (2): 1–31.

– 2001. "No-Collar Labour in America's 'New Economy.'" *Socialist Register*: 77–87.

– 2003. *No Collar: The Human Workplace and Its Hidden Costs*. Philadelphia: Temple University Press.

– 2009a. *Nice Work If You Can Get It: Life and Labor in Precarious Times*. New York: New York University Press.

– 2009b. "The Political Economy of Amateurism." *Television & New Media* 10 (1): 136–7.

– 2013. "In Search of the Lost Paycheck." In *Digital Labor: The Internet as Playground and Factory*, edited by Trebor Scholz, 13–32. New York: Routledge.

Ross, Karen. 2002. "Selling Women (Down the River): Gendered Relations and the Political Economy of Broadcast News." In *Sex & Money: Feminism and Political Economy in the Media*, edited by Eileen R. Meehan and Ellen Riordan, 112–29. Minneapolis: University of Minnesota Press.

Ross, Stephanie. 2008. "Social Unionism and Membership Participation: What Role for Union Democracy?" *Studies in Political Economy* 81: 129–57.

Rossiter, Ned. 2006. *Organized Networks: Media Theory, Creative Labour, New Institutions*. Rotterdam: NAi Publishers.

Roth, Daniel. 2009. "The Answer Factory: Demand Media and the Fast, Disposable, and Profitable as Hell Media Model." *Wired*, 19 October. http://www.wired.com/magazine/2009/10/ff_demandmedia.

Rowe, Dan. 2015. "What Jonathan Kay Has Wrong about Diversity in Journalism." *J-source.ca*, 2 April. http://j-source.ca/article/what-jonathan-kay-has-wrong-about-diversity-journalism.

Ruscitti, Joe. 2011. "Make Your Voice Heard in the Paper." *London Free Press*, 15 April. http://www.lfpress.com/comment/columnists/editors_desk/2011/04/15/18011841.html.

Rutherford, Paul. 1982. *A Victorian Authority: The Daily Press in Late Nineteenth-Century Canada*. Toronto: University of Toronto Press.

Ryan, Bill. 1992. *Making Capital from Culture: The Corporate Form of Capitalist Cultural Production*. Berlin: Walter de Gruyter.

Ryan, Kathleen M. 2009. "The Performative Journalist: Job Satisfaction, Temporary Workers and American Television News." *Journalism* 10 (5): 647–64.

Sabbagh, Dan. 2011. "Bloggers Take Legal Action over Huffington Post Sale." *Guardian*, 12 April. http://www.guardian.co.uk/media/2011/apr/12/arianna-huffington-post-sale.

Salamon, Errol. 2016. "E-lancer Resistance: Precarious Freelance Journalists Use Digital Communications to Refuse Rights-Grabbing Contracts." *Digital Journalism*. http://www.tandfonline.com/doi/abs/10.1080/21670811.2015.1116953.

Salario, Alizah. 2014. "In Journalism, Temporary Is the New Full-Time."

Medium, 29 May. https://medium.com/@Alirosa/in-journalism-temporary-is-the-new-full-time-756115c592f9.

Salcetti, Marianne. 1995. "The Emergence of the Reporter: Mechanization and the Devaluation of Editorial Workers." In Hardt and Brennen, *Newsworkers*, 48–74. Minneapolis: University of Minnesota Press.

Salmon, Felix. 2015. "To All the Young Journalists Asking for Advice." *Genius*, 9 February. http://genius.it/fusion.net/story/45832/to-all-the-young-journalists-asking-for-advice.

Sanders, Rachel. 2013. "2013: The Year of the Angry Freelancer." Story Board, 19 December. http://www.thestoryboard.ca/the-year-of-the-angry-freelancer.

– 2014. "Desmond Cole on Crowdfunding to Get to Ferguson." Story Board, 4 December. http://www.thestoryboard.ca/desmond-cole-crowdfunding-get-ferguson/.

– 2015a. "Writer Scott Carney Launches WordRates & PitchLab Kickstarter." *J-Source.ca*, 7 May. http://j-source.ca/article/writer-scott-carney-launches-wordrates-pitchlab-kickstarter.

– 2015b. "How Do Freelancers Take Vacations?" Story Board, 5 July. http://www.thestoryboard.ca/how-do-freelancers-take-vacations.

Sayers, Sean. 2005. "Why Work? Marx and Human Nature." *Science & Society* 69 (4): 606–16.

Schiller, Dan. 1996. *Theorizing Communication: A History*. Oxford: Oxford University Press.

Schudson, Michael. 1978. *Discovering the News: A Social History of American Newspapers*. New York: Basic Books.

Scott, D.B. 2009. *Respect and Remuneration: Attitudes about Editorial Working Conditions in the Canadian Magazine Industry*. Toronto: Professional Writers Association of Canada. http://www.pwac.ca/files/PDF/Respect&Renumeration.May09.pdf.

– 2010. "Rogers Syndication Practices Called into Question by Canadian Writers Group." *Canadian Magazines*, 2 October. http://canadianmags.blogspot.com/2010/10/rogers-syndiction-practices-called-into.html.

Semuels, Alana. 2008. "Book Publisher Finds Teen Lit Adapts Well in Hollywood." *Los Angeles Times*, 2 August. http://articles.latimes.com/2008/aug/02/business/fi-alloy2.

Shafrir, Doree. 2008. "Freelance Fizzle! The Decline and Fall of the Writer." *New York Observer*, 1 April. http://www.observer.com/2008/mag-hell-o.

Shaver, Davis. 2010. "Your Guide to Next Generation 'Content Farms.'"

MediaShift, 19 July. http://www.pbs.org/mediashift/2010/07/your-guide-to-next-generation-content-farms200.html.

Sheffield, Hazel. 2012. "Pasadena Publisher Launches a System for Outsourcing Local News." *Columbia Journalism Review*, 7 August. http://www.cjr.org/behind_the_news/pasadena_publisher_launches_a.php.

Shelley, Allison. 2014. "The Dangerous World of Freelance Journalism." *Los Angeles Times*, 6 September. http://www.latimes.com/opinion/op-ed/la-oe-shelley-freelance-journalists-foley-sotloff-20140907-story.html.

Shukaitis, Stevphen. 2014. "Learning Not to Labor." *Rethinking Marxism* 26 (2): 193–205.

Sibley, Robert. 2015. "Artists Approve Historic Labour Deal with National Gallery of Canada." *Ottawa Citizen*, 25 February. http://ottawacitizen.com/news/local-news/artists-approve-historic-labour-deal-national-gallery-of-canada.

Sicha, Choire, et al. 2013. "How Much Should a Writer Be Paid, If Anything." *Awl*, 6 March. http://www.theawl.com/2013/03/how-much-should-a-writer-get-paid-a-conversation.

Siegelbaum, Sasu, and Ryan J. Thomas. 2015. "Putting the Work (Back) into Newswork." *Journalism Practice*: 1–18. Online.

Silcoff, Mireille. 2015. "On the Declining Prospects of the Young Journalist (Or: To the Writers of the Future: Good Luck with That)." *National Post*, 9 January. http://news.nationalpost.com/arts/weekend-post/on-the-declining-prospects-of-the-young-journalist-or-to-the-writers-of-the-future-good-luck-with-that.

Sillesen, Lene Bech. 2015. "A New Website Wants to Disrupt How Freelancers Do Business." *Columbia Journalism Review*, 20 May. http://www.cjr.org/business_of_news/wordrates_freelancers.php.

Singer, Jane B. 2011. "Journalism in a Network." In Deuze, *Managing Media Work*, 103–9.

Skinner, David, James R. Compton, and Mike Gasher. 2005. *Converging Media, Diverging Politics: A Political Economy of News Media in the United States and Canada*. Lanham, MD: Lexington.

Sloan, William David, and James G. Stovall. 1989. *The Media in America: A History*. Worthington, OH: Publishing Horizons.

Smith, Chris, and Alan McKinlay, eds. 2009a. *Creative Labour: Working in the Creative Industries*. London: Palgrave Macmillan.

– 2009b. "Creative Labour: Content, Contract, and Control." In McKinlay and Smith, *Creative Labour*, 29–50.

– 2009c. "Creative Industries and Labour Process Analysis." In McKinlay and Smith, *Creative Labour*, 2–28.

Smith, Chris, David Knights, and Hugh Willmott, eds. 1991. *White-Collar Work: The Non-manual Labour Process*. London: Macmillan.

Smith, Rachel. 2013. "Rachel's List Show Me the Money Survey 2013 Infographic." Rachel's List, 26 July. http://www.rachelslist.com.au/?p=988.

Smith, Ryan. 2012. "Journatic: Newspaper Executives Are Responsible for This Faustian Deal." *Guardian*, 16 July. http://www.theguardian.com /commentisfree/2012/jul/16/journatic-newspaper-executives-responsible-faustian.

Smythe, Ted Curtis. 1980. "The Reporter, 1880–1900: Working Conditions and Their Influence on the News." *Journalism History* 7 (1): 1–10.

Solomon, William S. 1995. "The Site of Newsroom Labor: The Division of Editorial Practices." In Hardt and Brennen, *Newsworkers*, 110–34.

Soroka, Chelcie. 2011. "Sarah Dennis: Herald Heiress." *King's Journalism Review*. http://kjr.kingsjournalism.com/?p=6832.

Sotiron, Minko. 1997. *From Politics to Profit: The Commercialization of Canadian Daily Newspapers, 1890–1920*. Montreal: McGill-Queen's University Press.

Spangler, Nicholas. 2010. "In Demand: A Week inside the Future of Journalism." *Columbia Journalism Review* (December). http://www.cjr.org/feature/in_demand.php.

Spilsbury, Mark. 2013. *Journalists at Work: Their Views on Training, Recruitment, and Conditions*. National Council for the Training of Journalists. http://www.nctj.com/downloadlibrary/jaw_final_higher_2.pdf.

Stahl, Matt. 2010. "Cultural Labor's 'Democratic Deficits': Employment, Autonomy and Alienation in US Film Animation." *Journal for Cultural Research* 14 (3): 271–93.

– 2013a. *Unfree Masters: Recording Artists and the Politics of Work*. Durham, NC: Duke University Press.

– 2013b. "Specificity, Ambivalence and the Commodity Form in Creative Work." In Banks, Gill, and Taylor, *Theorizing Cultural Work*, 71–84.

Standing, Guy. 2011. The Precariat: *The New Dangerous Class*. London: Bloomsbury.

– 2014. *A Precariat Charter: From Denizens to Citizens*. London: Bloomsbury.

Stanworth, Celia, and John Stanworth. 1995. "The Self-Employed without Employees—Autonomous or Atypical?" *Industrial Relations Journal* 26 (3): 221–29.

Statistics Canada. 2011a. *Periodical Publishing*. Statistics Canada.
  http://www.statcan.gc.ca/cgi-bin/af-fdr.cgi?l=eng&loc=http://www
  .statcan.gc.ca/pub/87f0005x/87f0005x2011001-eng.pdf&t=Periodical
  %20Publishing.

– 2011b. *Newspaper Publishers 2010*. Catalogue no. 63-241-X. http://www
  .statcan.gc.ca/pub/63-241-x/63-241-x2012001-eng.htm?WT.mc
  _id=twtB1742.

– 2011c. National Household Survey, Statistics Canada Catalogue no.
  99-012-X2011033.

– 2012. Occupations in Art, Culture, Recreation and Sport. National
  Occupational Classification 2011. http://www.statcan.gc.ca/cgi-
  bin/imdb/p3VD.pl?Function=getVDDetail&db=imdb&dis=2
  &adm=8&TVD=122372&CVD=122373&CPV=5&CST=01012011
  &MLV=4&CLV=1&CHVD=122374.

– 2013. Table 361-0010 – Periodical Publishers, Summary Statistics, by
  North American Industry Classification System (NAICS). CANSIM.
  http://www5.statcan.gc.ca/cansim/a26?lang=eng&retrLang=eng
  &id=3610010&paSer=&pattern=&stByVal=1&p1=1&p2=37
  &tabMode=dataTable&csid=.

– 2014. "Journalists." http://www.servicecanada.gc.ca/eng/qc/job_futures
  /statistics/5123.shtml#outlook.

– 2016. "Newspaper publishers, 2014." 31 March. http://www.statcan.gc.ca
  /daily-quotidien/160331/dq160331e-eng.htm.

Stone, Katherine V.W. 2004. *From Widgets to Digits: Employment Regulation
  for the Changing Workplace*. Cambridge, UK: Cambridge University Press.

Story Board. 2010. "Rogers Refuses to Remove Writer's Work from
  Yahoo." Story Board, 30 November. http://www.thestoryboard.ca/?p=142.

– 2011a. "New Star Freelance Contracts Raising Eyebrows." Story Board,
  30 June. http://www.thestoryboard.ca/?p=1385#comment-2189.

– 2011b. "PWAC Toronto's 2011/2012 Professional Development Series."
  Story Board, 27 September. http://www.thestoryboard.ca/?p=1916.

– 2011c. "Canadian Magazine Freelancers Survey: The Results." Story
  Board, 10 June. http://www.thestoryboard.ca/canadian-magazine-free-
  lancers-survey-the-results/.

– 2011d. "CWG/CMG Representing *Toronto Star* and *The Grid* Freelancers
  in Talks with Senior Management." Story Board, 5 October.
  http://www.thestoryboard.ca/?p=1949.

– 2012a. "Settlement Reached between Writer Patricia Pearson and
  Rogers Publishing." Story Board, 22 March. http://www.thestory-

board.ca/settlement-reached-between-writer-patricia-pearson-and-rogers-publishing.

– 2012b. "cwg Negotiates New Deal with Reader's Digest." Story Board, 3 January. http://www.thestoryboard.ca/cwg-negotiates-new-deal-with-readers-digest-on-behalf-of-freelancers.

– 2012c. "Defamation Clause in New Canada Wide Media Contract Remains Unchanged." Story Board, 7 November. http://www.thestoryboard.ca/libel-clause-in-new-canada-wide-media-contract-remains-unchanged/.

– 2013. "Transcontinental Media Agreement Expands Copyright Demands." Story Board, 8 February. http://www.thestoryboard.ca/new-transcontinental-media-contract-contains-expanded-copyright-demands.

Sumner, David E. 2010. *The Magazine Century: American Magazine since 1900*. New York: Peter Lang.

Sutherland, Fraser. 1989. *The Monthly Epic: A History of Canadian Magazines, 1789–1989*. Markham: Fitzhenry & Whiteside.

Sutherland, James. 1986. *The Restoration Newspaper and Its Development*. Cambridge, UK: Cambridge University Press.

Svendsen, Lars. 2008. *Work*. Stocksfield, UK: Acumen.

Swarns, Rachel. 2014. "Freelancers in the 'Gig' Economy Find a Mix of Freedom and Uncertainty." *New York Times*, 9 February. http://www.nytimes.com/2014/02/10/nyregion/for-freelancers-in-the-gig-economy-a-mix-of-freedom-and-uncertainty.html.

Szemen, Imre. 2015. "Entrepreneurship as the New Common Sense." *South Atlantic Quarterly* 114 (3): 471–90.

Tasini, Jonathan. 2012. "Other Professionals Don't Work for Free. So Why Are Writers Expected To?" *Guardian*, 23 April. http://www.guardian.co.uk/commentisfree/2012/apr/23/professionals-work-free-writers-expected.

Taylor, Astra. 2014. *The People's Platform: Taking Back Power and Culture in the Digital Age*. New York: Metropolitan Books.

tci Management Consultants. 2008. *A Strategic Study of the Magazine Industry in Ontario*. Toronto: Ontario Media Development Corporation. http://www.omdc.on.ca/AssetFactory.aspx?did=6366.

tc Transcontinental. 2014. *Annual Report 2014*. http://tctranscontinental.com/documents/10180/37760/2014_Annual_Report_12895.pdf.

Tebbel, John. 1969. *The American Magazine: A Compact History*. New York: Hawthorn Books.

Tebbel, John, and Mary Ellen Zuckerman. 1991. *The Magazine in America, 1741–1990*. Oxford: Oxford University Press.

Teicher, Jordan. 2014. "This Site Should Terrify Publishers Who Don't Pay Up." *Contently*, 25 March. http://contently.com/strategist/2014/03/25/this-site-should-terrify-publishers-who-dont-pay-up/.

– 2015. "Contently Study: The State of Freelancing in 2015." *Contently*, 22 June. http://contently.net/2015/06/22/resources/contently-study-state-freelancing-2015/.

Teitel, Jay. 2013. "An Open Letter to Transcontinental." Story Board, 4 March. http://www.thestoryboard.ca/an-open-letter-to-transcontinental-by-jay-teitel/.

Thompson, Paul. 1990. "Crawling from the Wreckage: The Labour Process and the Politics of Production." In *Labour Process Theory*, edited by David Knights and Hugh Willmott, 95–124. London: Macmillan.

Thompson, Paul, Michael Jones, and Chris Warhurst. 2009. "From Conception to Consumption: Creativity and the Missing Managerial Link." In McKinlay and Smith, *Creative Labour*, 51–71.

Thompson, Paul, and Chris Smith. 2010. "Debating Labour Process Theory and the Sociology of Work." In *Working Life: Renewing Labour Process Analysis*, edited by Paul Thompson and Chris Smith, 11–28. New York: Palgrave Macmillan.

Thomsen, Michael. 2015. "Will Unionizing Gawker and Vice Help Freelance Writers Earn a Living Wage?" *Forbes*, 24 August. http://www.forbes.com/sites/michaelthomsen/2015/08/24/will-unionizing-gawker-and-vice-help-freelance-writers-earn-a-living-wage/.

Tokumitsu, Miya. 2014. "In the Name of Love." *Jacobin* 13. https://www.jacobinmag.com/2014/01/in-the-name-of-love/.

Toronto Star. 2008. "The Atkinson Principles." http://www.thestar.com/atkinsonseries/article/542441.

Toughill, Kelly. 2014. "The Globe and Mail's Bonus Plan Could Backfire." *J-Source.ca*, 9 January. http://j-source.ca/article/globe-and-mail%E2%80%99s-bonus-plan-could-backfire.

Towse, Ruth. 2003. "Copyright Policy, Cultural Policy and Support for Artists." In *The Economics of Copyright*, edited by W.J. Gordon and R. Watt, 66–80. Cheltenham, UK: Edward Elgar.

Tucker, Robert C., ed. 1978. *The Marx-Engels Reader*. 2nd ed. New York: Norton.

Tucker, Sean, and Alex Mucalov. 2012. "Industrial Voluntarism in Canada." *Relations industrielles/Industrial Relations* 65 (2): 215–35.

Tunstall, Jeremy. 1996. *Newspaper Power: The New National Press in Britain*. Oxford: Oxford University Press.

Turow, Joseph. 2012. "Buying Digital Advertising: A Brief Overview." *Pew Research Center*, 13 February. http://www.journalism.org/2012/02/13/buying-digital-advertising-brief-overview.

TWUC [The Writers' Union of Canada]. 2010. "Why Writers Need a Strong Status of the Artist Legislation in Ontario." http://www.writersunion.ca/av_campaignstatusartist.asp.

UNESCO. 1980. *Recommendation Concerning the Status of the Artist*. http://portal.unesco.org/en/ev.php-URL_ID=13138&URL_DO=DO_TOPIC&URL_SECTION=201.html.

Ungerleider, Charles S. 1991. "Media, Minorities and Misconceptions: The Portrayal by and Representation of Minorities in Canadian News Media." *Canadian Ethnic Studies/Etudes ethniques au Canada* 23 (3): 158–64.

Unifor. 2015. "Community Chapters." http://www.unifor.org/en/about-unifor/community-chapters.

United States. 1935. National Labor Relations Act, 29 U.S.C., 151–69. http://www.nlrb.gov/resources/national-labor-relations-act.

Ursell, Gillian. 2000. "Television Production: Issues of Exploitation, Commodification and Subjectivity in UK Television Labour Markets." *Media, Culture & Society* 22 (6): 805–25.

Uzelman, Scott. 2012. "Autonomous Media: Reconceptualizing Alternative Media Practices." In Kozolanka, Mazepa, and Skinner, *Alternative Media in Canada*, 65–84.

van Parijs, Philippe. 1992. "Competing Justification of Basic Income." In *Arguing for Basic Income: Ethical Foundations for a Radical Reform*, edited by Philippe van Parijs, 3–43. London: Verso.

VIDA. 2012. "The 2011 Count." *VIDA Women in Literary Arts*, 27 February. http://www.vidaweb.org/the-2011-count.

Vosko, Leah F. 2000. *Temporary Work: The Gendered Rise of a Precarious Employment Relationship*. Toronto: University of Toronto Press.

– 2005. "The Precarious Status of the Artist: Freelance Editors' Struggle for Collective Bargaining Rights." In Cranford, Fudge, Tucker, and Vosko, *Self-Employed Workers Organize*, 136–70.

– ed. 2006a. *Precarious Employment: Understanding Labour Market Insecurity in Canada*. Montreal: McGill-Queen's University Press.

– 2006b. "Precarious Employment: Towards an Improved Understanding of Labour Market Insecurity." In Vosko, *Precarious Employment*, 3–39.

– 2010. *Managing the Margins: Gender, Citizenship, and the International Regulation of Precarious Employment*. New York: Oxford University Press.

Vosko, Leah F., and Nancy Zukewich. 2006. "Precarious by Choice? Gender and Self-Employment." In Vosko, *Precarious Employment*, 67–89.

Vosko, Leah F., and Lisa F. Clark. 2009. "Gendered Precariousness and Social Reproduction." In Vosko, MacDonald, and Campbell, *Gender and the Contours of Precarious Employment*, 26–42.

Vosko, Leah F., Martha MacDonald, and Iain Campbell, eds. 2009a. *Gender and the Contours of Precarious Employment*. London: Routledge.

– 2009b. "Gender and the Concept of Precarious Employment." In Vosko, MacDonald, and Campbell, *Gender and the Contours of Precarious Employment*, 1–25.

Wager, Whitney. 2010. "Editors in Distress." *Ryerson Review of Journalism*. http://rrj.ca/editors-in-distress-2/.

Wallenstein, Andrew, and Todd Spangler. 2013. "Epic Fail: The Rise and Fall of Demand Media." *Variety*, 30 December. http://variety.com/2013/biz/news/epic-fail-the-rise-and-fall-of-demand-media-1200914646/.

Walters, Emma, Christopher Warren, and Mike Dobbie. 2006. *The Changing Nature of Work: A Global Survey and Case Study of Atypical Work in the Media Industry*. Switzerland: International Federation of Journalists. http://www.ifj.org/pdfs/ILOReport070606.pdf.

Waring, Marilyn. 1999. *Counting for Nothing: What Men Value and What Women Are Worth*. 2nd ed. Toronto: University of Toronto Press.

Warren, James. 2015. "A Q-and-A with Hamilton Nolan on Gawker Media's Union Vote." Poynter.org, 8 June. http://www.poynter.org/news/mediawire/349685/a-q-and-a-with-hamilton-nolan-on-gawker-medias-union-vote/.

Wasserman, Edward. 2012. "Assembly Line News for a Digital Age." *Sun Chronicle*, 17 July. http://www.thesunchronicle.com/opinion/columns/edward-wasserman-assembly-line-news-for-a-digital-age/article_94bcfeec-d046-11e1-8f1f-0019bb2963f4.html.

Watson, H.G. 2015. "Freelancers Fighting Full Copyright Claim by Nonprofit Media Company." *rabble.ca*, 3 February. http://rabble.ca/news/2015/02/freelancers-fighting-full-copyright-claim-non-profit-media-company.

Wayne, Mike. 2003. *Marxism and Media Studies: Key Concepts and Contemporary Trends*. London: Pluto Press.

Weaver, David H., Randal A. Beam, Bonnie J. Brownlee, Paul S. Voakes, and G. Cleveland Wilhoit. 2007. *The American Journalist in the 21st Century*. Mahwah, NJ: Lawrence Erlbaum.

Weeks, Kathi. 2011. *The Problem with Work: Feminism, Marxism, Antiwork Politics and Postwork Imaginaries*. Durham, NC: Duke University Press.

Weingarten, Gene. 2011. "How Branding Is Ruining Journalism." *Washington Post*, 23 June. http://www.washingtonpost.com/lifestyle /magazine/gene-weingarten-how-branding-is-ruining-journalism/2011 /06/07/AGBegthH_story.html.

West, James L.W. 1988. *American Authors and the Literary Marketplace since 1900*. Philadelphia: University of Pennsylvania Press.

Who Organizes Writers? 2014. A panel discussion hosted by the National Writers Union, New York City, 14 November.

Williams, Alex T. 2015. "Why Aren't There More Minority Journalists?" *Columbia Journalism Review*, 22 July. http://www.cjr.org/analysis/in_the _span_of_two.php.

Williams, Raymond. 1989. *Resources of Hope: Culture, Democracy, Socialism*, edited by Robin Gale. London: Verso.

Willis, Ellen. 1998. "The Writer's Voice: Intellectual Work in the Culture of Austerity." In *Post-Work: The Wages of Cybernation*, edited by Stanley Aronowitz and J. Cutler, 257–74. Routledge: New York.

Willnat, Lars, and David H Weaver. 2014. *The American Journalist in the Digital Age: Key Findings*. Bloomington, IN: School of Journalism, Indiana University.

Wilson, Christopher P. 1985. *The Labor of Words: Literary Professionalism in the Progressive Era*. Athens, GA: University of Georgia Press.

Wilson, Melissa. 2010. "Battle Ready." *Ryerson Review of Journalism*. http://rrj.ca/battle-ready-2/.

Winseck, Dwayne. 2010. "Financialization and the 'Crisis of the Media': The Rise and Fall of (Some) Media Conglomerates in Canada." *Canadian Journal of Communication* 35 (3): 365–93.

– 2011. "The Political Economies of Media and the Transformation of the Global Media Industries." In *The Political Economies of Media: The Transformation of the Global Media Industries*, edited by Dwayne Winseck and Dal Yong Jin, 3–48. London: Bloomsbury.

Women's Media Center. 2014. *The Status of Women in the U.S. Media 2014*. http://wmc.3cdn.net/6dd3de8ca65852dbd4_fjm6yck90.pdf.

Wong, Julia Carrie. 2014. "Writing, Prestige, and Other Things That Don't Pay the Rent." *Nation*, 7 April. http://www.thenation.com/blog /179170/writing-prestige-and-other-things-dont-pay-rent.

Woodmansee, Martha. 1984. "The Genius and the Copyright: Economic and Legal Conditions of the Emergence of the 'Author.'" *Eighteenth Century Studies* 17 (4): 425–48.

Woods Gordon. 1984. *A Study of the Canadian Periodical Publishing Industry: A Report Prepared by Woods Gordon for the Department of Communication*. Toronto: Department of Communications.

Wright, Erik Olin. 1978. "Intellectuals and the Class Structure of Capitalist Society." In *Between Labor and Capital*, edited by Pat Walker, 191–211. Montreal: Black Rose Books.

– 1997. *Class Counts: Comparative Studies in Class Analysis*. New York: Cambridge University Press.

– 2010. *Envisioning Real Utopias*. London: Verso.

Writers' Guild of Great Britain. 2015. "Free Is Not an Option." 3 March.

Writers' Union of Canada. 2015. *Devaluing Creators, Endangering Creativity*. Toronto: The Writers' Union of Canada. http://www.writersunion.ca/sites/all/files/DevaluingCreatorsEndangeringCreativity_0.pdf#overlay-context=news/canadian-writers-working-harder-while-earning-less.

Yates, Michael D. 2009. *Why Unions Matter*. 2nd ed. New York: Monthly Review Press.

Index